Advances in Information Security

Sushil Jajodia
Consulting Editor
Center for Secure Information Systems
George Mason University
Fairfax, VA 22030-4444
email: jajodia@gmu.edu

The goals of the Springer International Series on ADVANCES IN INFORMATION SECURITY are, one, to establish the state of the art of, and set the course for future research in information security and, two, to serve as a central reference source for advanced and timely topics in information security research and development. The scope of this series includes all aspects of computer and network security and related areas such as fault tolerance and software assurance.

ADVANCES IN INFORMATION SECURITY aims to publish thorough and cohesive overviews of specific topics in information security, as well as works that are larger in scope or that contain more detailed background information than can be accommodated in shorter survey articles. The series also serves as a forum for topics that may not have reached a level of maturity to warrant a comprehensive textbook treatment.

Researchers, as well as developers, are encouraged to contact Professor Sushil Jajodia with ideas for books under this series.

More information about this series at http://www.springer.com/series/5576

Angelo Genovese • Vincenzo Piuri • Fabio Scotti

Touchless Palmprint Recognition Systems

 Springer

Angelo Genovese
Department of Computer Science
Università degli Studi di Milano
Crema, Italy

Vincenzo Piuri
Department of Computer Science
Università degli Studi di Milano
Crema, Italy

Fabio Scotti
Department of Computer Science
Università degli Studi di Milano
Crema, Italy

ISSN 1568-2633
ISBN 978-3-319-38398-9   ISBN 978-3-319-10365-5 (eBook)
DOI 10.1007/978-3-319-10365-5
Springer Cham Heidelberg New York Dordrecht London

Printed on acid-free paper

Springer is part of Springer Science+Business Media (www.springer.com)

Preface

Biometric systems consist of devices, algorithms, and procedures used to recognize individuals or classes of individuals based on their physical or behavioral characteristics, called biometric traits. These systems are particularly relevant to security (such as access control and government applications) and are increasingly a part of daily life.

However, the procedures typically used for collecting biometric traits require user cooperation, controlled environments, contact between the surveyed body part and the sensor, or illumination perceived as unpleasant, too strong, or harmful. These constraints limit the usability and social acceptance of biometric technologies in daily life. Techniques for touchless and less-constrained biometric recognition have been studied to address these issues, increase the use of biometric systems, and expand the application of biometric technologies to other fields.

In this context, the palmprint is a hand-based biometric trait that permits sufficiently accurate recognition and whose acquisition is generally well accepted by users because it is not perceived as too intrusive or privacy-sensitive. Moreover, palmprints can be captured using low-cost devices and, unlike fingerprints, are sufficiently redundant to be used even when the palm's surface is partially damaged, such as in elderly people or manual workers. Unfortunately, traditional palmprint-based systems use touch-based acquisitions with pegs that constrain the position of the hand to facilitate biometric trait acquisition, limiting its ease of use.

The aim of this book is to make palmprint biometrics easier to use in practical, daily-life applications. Innovative, original methods for touchless and less-constrained palmprint recognition are presented that overcome the typical constraints and limits described above.

Our innovative multiple-view acquisition systems, which are based on CCD cameras and LED illumination, are designed to capture high-quality palmprint images. Original image processing algorithms have been devised to analyze palmprints. Three-dimensional reconstruction techniques are also applied to reconstruct the hand's shape and surface, invariant to position and orientation, and pattern recognition methods are introduced to extract and match the palmprint's distinctive features. Our novel methods permit individual recognition via the acquisition of biometric traits in a single time instant and without requiring their hands to touch any surface or adopt a specific position. Accurate biometric recognition is achieved, in many cases superior to the most recent approaches described in the literature, while simultaneously enhancing usability and social acceptance. Moreover, our innovative setups and methods have a lower cost and capture images in a more efficient way.

Therefore, this book will be of interest to researchers and professionals in the field of biometric technologies and applications, as well as students and those interested in understanding the emerging technological area of touchless and less-constrained palmprint recognition, because it provides a comprehensive view of the field and an in-depth presentation of innovative, effective approaches well suited for daily-life applications.

Crema, Italy   Angelo Genovese
                                                                Vincenzo Piuri
                                                                  Fabio Scotti

Acknowledgments

The research reported here has been partially supported by the European Union Seventh Framework Programme within the integrated project "ABC gates for Europe (ABC4EU)," under grant agreement FP7-SEC-2012-312797, and by the Italian Ministry of Research within the PRIN project "GenData 2020," contract 2010RTFWBH.

Contents

Chapter 1
Introduction

The use of biometric systems, which recognize individuals based on their physical characteristics rather than their knowledge (e.g., a password) or objects (e.g., a smartcard), is expanding and is increasingly a component of daily life for many people.

In many cases, the effective and efficient acquisition of biometric data requires the cooperation of the user in a controlled environment or is achieved by means of complex, expensive or intrusive procedures. These constraints limit the usability and social acceptance of biometric technologies in daily life and, consequently, the expansion of their application.

In this context, biometric systems based on palmprints are generally well accepted by users because they are not perceived as too intrusive or privacy-sensitive. In addition, palmprints can be captured using low-cost devices, thus making them viable for many daily-life applications with low-cost requirements. Palmprints are also sufficiently redundant to enable the accurate recognition of even a partially damaged palm surface. Unfortunately, traditional systems for palmprint recognition rely on touch-based acquisitions with pegs that constrain the position of the hand, reducing their ease of use.

This book aims at making palmprint recognition easier to use and more accepted in daily-life applications. Innovative, original methods for touchless and less-constrained palmprint recognition are presented that overcome the typical constraints and limits described above.

To provide context for the described technologies, this chapter presents the basic concepts of biometrics and biometric recognition, touchless and less-constrained biometric systems, and palmprint recognition. These aspects will then be analyzed in greater detail in subsequent chapters to provide a concise state-of-the art, which will provide a foundation for evaluating and appreciating our innovative solutions. The core part of this book is dedicated to our innovative methods for touchless and less-constrained palmprint recognition. The proposed approaches will be carefully analyzed and compared with the literature to describe their advantages and limits for effective use in daily-life applications.

© Springer International Publishing Switzerland 2014
A. Genovese et al., *Touchless Palmprint Recognition Systems*,
Advances in Information Security 60, DOI 10.1007/978-3-319-10365-5_1

1.1 Basic Concepts of Biometrics

The discipline of biometrics concerns the measurement of bodily features typical of human beings for identity recognition or body-condition detection. Specifically, the term biometrics is defined by the International Organization for Standardization (ISO) as "*the automated recognition of individuals based on their behavioral and biological characteristics*" [164].

Currently, the main applications of biometrics are in the security and medical fields. In the medical field, biometrics can be used to support diagnosis. In the security field, biometric measurements are typically used for government applications (e.g., border control, ID cards, criminal identification), regulating physical access to restricted areas (e.g., airports, stadiums, banks, military zones), controlling access to logical resources and services (e.g., home banking, ATMs, e-commerce, personal devices), and forensic analysis (e.g., the identification of suspects, kinship analysis). In this book, we focus our attention on the use of biometrics for security applications, specifically, for identity recognition.

Biometric systems consist of devices, algorithms, and procedures used to recognize individuals or classes of individuals based on their physical or behavioral characteristics, called biometric traits, rather than their knowledge (e.g., a password) or objects (e.g., a smartcard). Biometric features are (a) distinct for each individual and (b) cannot be forgotten (like passwords) or stolen (like smartcards).

A biometric trait is a characteristic of a person that can be used for recognition [171]. Biometric traits can be physiological (biological) or behavioral. In the first case, recognition is based on physical traits related to the body of the person, such as their fingerprint, iris, face, hand shape, or palmprint. Behavioral traits are related to the actions performed by a person and include, for example, gait, voice, and signature.

Biometric systems for security applications employ two modalities: authentication and identification. In the authentication mode, the individual states his identity and provides his biometric trait. The biometric system then compares the biometric trait with one previously stored to determine if the traits match; if so, the person is positively recognized. Biometric systems that work in authentication mode include those that regulate access to restricted areas.

In identification mode, the individual does not state his identity, and the system compares the biometric trait of the individual with all the traits stored in its database to determine the person's identity. Examples of biometric systems working in identification mode include surveillance systems used to monitor a critical area and detect possible suspects and forensics systems used to analyze latent fingerprints found at a crime scene and identify criminals.

1.2 Touchless and Less-Constrained Biometrics

Traditionally, biometric systems require the user to be cooperative and willing to present his biometric trait to the sensor. In many cases, biometric acquisitions require controlled procedures or contact between the biometric trait and the sensor. For example, the user must assume a certain pose, place his biometric trait in a particular place, and remain still for the duration of the biometric acquisition.

Biometric traits that typically require constrained acquisition procedures include the face, iris, fingerprint, and palmprint. For face acquisition, the user must stand in a specified position and remain still with a neutral expression. In most cases, the illumination conditions are controlled.

Iris acquisitions are performed by placing the eye, properly opened, in a specific position. Infrared illumination, often perceived as unpleasant or harmful, is used.

Fingerprints are captured by touching a small sensor with the proper pressure. Because hands can be dirty or sweaty, the sensor can easily become dirty, which has consequences for both acquisition quality and user acceptability. People may dislike using a sensor that has been touched by many people, particularly in areas where hygiene might be important.

Palmprint characteristics are measured by placing the hand on a surface on which pegs are used to constrain the hand in a specific pose. Similarly to fingerprint sensors, palmprint acquisition surfaces can be dirty. Moreover, the presence of pegs can be a problem for the elderly or those with muscular or joint problems (e.g., arthritis).

To reduce or eliminate these constraints, techniques for less-constrained biometric recognition have been studied. Less-constrained recognition methods typically have shorter acquisition times, improved usability, and greater social acceptance, potentially facilitating the expansion of the use of accurate biometric traits to new applications and scenarios. For example, less-constrained iris recognition enables superior recognition accuracy in surveillance applications, mobile phones, and biometric gates. Similar applications could be realized with touchless biometric systems based on fingerprint or palmprint recognition.

In this book, the term "touch-based" is used to refer to biometric acquisition procedures that require contact of the biometric trait with the sensor, whereas "touchless" refers to procedures that do not require contact with the sensor. The equivalent terms "contact-based" and "contactless" are sometimes used in the literature.

1.3 Palmprint Recognition

Palmprint recognition has been increasingly investigated over the past 15 years. Many aspects of this biometric trait are similar to those of fingerprints, facilitating progress in palmprint recognition research. In addition, palmprints present many distinctive features that can be exploited for highly accurate recognition. However, in contrast to fingerprints, palmprint recognition systems can use low-cost acquisition devices and can achieve good results even with a partially damaged palm surface (for example, in elderly people or manual laborers), due to the higher number of features that can be extracted at different levels of detail.

Palmprint recognition can be achieved using touch-based and touchless methods, depending on the type of contact with the sensor needed to perform the acquisition. Moreover, these approaches can be further partitioned into methods based on two-dimensional and three-dimensional samples.

Currently, the majority of approaches presented in the literature perform recognition using touch-based two-dimensional acquisitions with flatbed scanners or CCD-based devices. Flatbed scanners are particularly useful for low-cost systems, while CCD-based devices offer good-quality samples and short acquisition times. Touch-based three-dimensional acquisition devices based on CCD cameras and projectors have been proposed to increase recognition accuracy, despite requiring a complex, more expensive setup.

The major drawbacks of touch-based methods are distortion, dirt, and user acceptability. Distortions are caused by non-uniform pressure of the hand on the sensor. Dirt accumulates after repeated acquisitions and can reduce the quality of the acquisitions. User acceptability can be problematic if people dislike touching surfaces that have been touched by other people because of hygienic reasons.

To overcome the above drawbacks, touchless acquisition devices have been studied. However, touchless methods can be affected by disadvantages, including lower contrast, a more complex background, and non-uniform acquisition distances. In addition, touchless approaches are sensitive to lighting conditions. To address these problems, three-dimensional touchless methods have recently been studied. These methods are more robust and can account for different acquisition distances, lighting conditions, backgrounds, noise, and spoofing attacks. However, they require more complex and more expensive setups than two-dimensional touchless methods.

1.4 Innovative Methods for Touchless and Less-Constrained Palmprint Recognition

The aim of this book is to describe innovative methods for touchless and less-constrained biometric recognition of palmprint characteristics. Original methods are presented that achieve recognition without requiring contact of the palm with the sensor surface of placement of the hand in a specific position and that collect the palmprint in a single acquisition time.

Specifically, the methods involve the use of three-dimensional reconstruction techniques to compute a metric representation of the palm that is invariant with respect to the position, distance, and orientation of the hand at the moment of acquisition.

Using these techniques, accurate biometric recognition can be performed. The usability and social acceptance of the biometric recognition system can also be improved. To ensure usability in many daily-life applications, the cost of the setup has also been carefully considered during the design of the system.

The approaches described in this book have two main advantages compared to previously reported touch-based methods: (a) they avoid problems resulting from palm contact with the sensor (such as distortion, dirt, sweat, or latent impressions), and (b) they do not require fixed placement surfaces, guides or pegs to place the hand in the correct position for acquisition. These characteristics increase the usability and acceptability of the system. Compared to methods in the literature that use only two-dimensional samples, the methods described in this book are innovative because they use three-dimensional information to produce a measurable (metric) and more accurate representation of the palm that is invariant with respect to the position, orientation, and distance of the acquisition. In this way, a less-constrained acquisition can be performed with a relaxed and non-fixed position of the hand.

Compared to the touchless three-dimensional palmprint acquisition methods described in the literature, the novelty of the approaches described in this book is the use of an innovative hardware acquisition setup that enables reduced cost and rapid image acquisition.

In the following chapters, a touchless palmprint recognition method based on two-view acquisitions performed at a fixed distance is first analyzed. This technique achieves good recognition accuracy, comparable to those of the most recently reported methods, without the distortions of touch-based acquisitions and without requiring contact between the palm and surface. Although the back of the hand must be placed against a fixed surface to ensure proper focusing of the acquisition, contact with the back of the hand is usually considered more hygienic than contact with the palm.

The results obtained with this first system enabled the design and implementation of an innovative, fully touchless, less-constrained palmprint acquisition technique that does not require contact of the palm with any surface or a fixed hand position. This method uses three-dimensional reconstruction techniques to achieve a metric representation of the hand, invariant to the pose and orientation. This method achieves good recognition accuracy (in many cases superior to the most recent approaches described in the literature) and is robust to changes in hand orientation as well as differences in environmental illumination.

Other biometric aspects are considered to evaluate the feasibility of these innovative methods for large-scale biometric recognition applications. In particular, good results were obtained with respect to the usability and social acceptance of the described methods. Computational speed, cost, interoperability, security, and privacy are also considered and discussed.

1.5   Structure of the Book

This book is structured as follows:

- *Chapter 2* is a brief introduction to biometric recognition and the general structure of biometric systems. A survey of major biometric traits is presented, and the methodologies used to evaluate biometric systems are described. Research trends in biometric recognition are also summarized.
- *Chapter 3* presents an introduction to less-constrained biometric systems and surveys the research on touchless and less-constrained recognition. First, methods are presented for the touchless recognition of biometric traits that are traditionally captured using touch-based sensors. Then, less-constrained techniques for biometric recognition using traits captured by touchless acquisition are described.
- *Chapter 4* provides an overview of the state-of-the-art in the field of palmprint recognition. First, an introduction to palmprint recognition is presented, including its key characteristics and applications. Then, touch-based and touchless palmprint recognition systems are reviewed. Both categories are partitioned into methods based on two-dimensional and three-dimensional samples. A review of the methods used to estimate the quality of the samples and classify palmprints is also presented.
- *Chapter 5* presents our innovative methods for palmprint recognition. First, touchless palmprint recognition based on acquisitions performed at a fixed distance with the back of the hand placed against a fixed surface is analyzed. Then, the design and implementation of an innovative fully touchless, less-constrained method based on acquisition at an uncontrolled distance is described.
- *Chapter 6* discusses the application of the described methods and their experimental evaluation. The datasets collected and the evaluation metrics used are described. The accuracy and robustness of the methods are evaluated, as well as other aspects related to computational speed, cost, interoperability, usability, social acceptance, security, and privacy.
- *Chapter 7* summarizes the research performed, the results obtained using the innovative methods, and the originality of the contributions. Future developments are also proposed.

Chapter 2
Biometric Systems

This chapter presents an overview of biometric systems, with the goal of providing context for the technology described in the presented work. The principles of biometric recognition, their general structure and basic functioning methods are introduced, and the most commonly used biometric traits are described. Then, the methods used for evaluating biometric systems are detailed. To conclude the chapter, current research trends in the field of biometric recognition are discussed.

2.1 Introduction to Biometric Recognition

The discipline of biometrics involves the measurement of bodily features typical of human beings. As defined by the International Organization for Standardization, biometrics is *"the automated recognition of individuals based on their behavioral and biological characteristics"* [164].

The use of biometric systems is expanding, and the costs of deployment are decreasing. In fact, the market for biometric technologies is increasing in size [303]. The value of the biometrics market reached 5 billion dollars in 2011, and forecasts indicate that it will reach 12 billion dollars in 2015 [163].

The main applications for biometrics are in the medical and security fields. In the medical field, biometrics can aid diagnoses when used in conjunction with other techniques for medical analysis. In the security field, biometric measurements are used to regulate access to restricted areas (e.g., military zones, airports, stadiums, banks), for government applications (e.g., border control, ID cards, suspect identification), for controlling access to logical resources (e.g., home banking, ATMs, e-commerce, personal devices), and for forensic analysis (e.g., suspect identification, kinship analysis) [171].

Biometric systems used in security applications consist of a combination of devices, procedures, and algorithms used to recognize individuals based on their

© Springer International Publishing Switzerland 2014
A. Genovese et al., *Touchless Palmprint Recognition Systems*,
Advances in Information Security 60, DOI 10.1007/978-3-319-10365-5_2

bodily features rather than their knowledge (e.g., a password) or objects (e.g., a smartcard). For example, instead of requiring a password to be entered (e.g., for accessing a video terminal) or a magnetic card to be scanned (e.g., for withdrawing money from an ATM), the details of a fingerprint, a face, or the shape of a hand can be used to determine the identity of a person and regulate their access to restricted services. The advantages of biometric features are that they cannot be forgotten or stolen and are unique to each individual. In this way, biometric measurements provide increased confidence of the identification of the recognized individual.

In this context, a biometric trait is the particular characteristic that is measured to perform the recognition. Biometric traits can be physiological or behavioral. For the former, recognition is based on physical traits related to the body of the person, such as his fingerprint, iris, face, or hand shape. By contrast, behavioral traits are related to the actions performed by a person, such as his gait, voice, and signature.

A multitude of biometric systems have been implemented for a variety of different applications. Different traits and technologies are selected based on factors such as accuracy, speed, cost, usability, and privacy risks. These different factors must be considered in the selection of a biometric system for a specific operational scenario. For example, in an environment where high security is required (e.g., a military structure), the recognition performance of the system must be as high as possible, whereas speed and privacy can be sacrificed if necessary. By contrast, for biometric systems installed in low-security environments (e.g., an amusement park), high speed, low invasiveness, and low privacy risk are emphasized.

2.2   Structure of Biometric Systems

Biometric recognition consists of the procedures used by biometric systems to compare the biometric traits of individuals, compute their similarity, and determine whether or not they belong to the same person. The recognition process can be divided into five modules:

1. *Acquisition*: Based on the biometric trait used, a specific sensor is used to capture the trait belonging to the user. The captured trait can be an image, an audio sample, or a frame sequence. The trait captured by the sensor is called the "sample".
2. *Segmentation*: The region of the sample containing the biometric information is isolated. For example, in the case of an image from an iris acquisition, the eyelashes and eyelids are eliminated so that only the iris region is considered.
3. *Feature Extraction*: The distinctive features are extracted from the segmented sample, and an abstract representation of the biometric trait (the "template") is computed. This template is better suited for storage in a database and analysis by an automated information processing system. Templates can be strings of bits, coordinates of particular points in the image, images, signals, or algebraic functions.

4. *Identity Matching*: The template is compared with one or more templates present in the database. The database can be centralized or stored on a device possessed by the user. The result of the identity matching step is a "match score", which is a measure of the similarity between the two compared templates.
5. *Decision*: The match score is used to produce the final decision of the biometric system. In most cases, a threshold for the match score value is used to transform the match score into a Boolean decision, which determines if the compared templates belong to the same individual.

Biometric systems can work in two modalities: authentication and identification. In authentication mode, the individual states his identity (for example, by showing an ID card) and presents his biometric trait to the biometric system that regulates access (for example, by placing his fingerprint on the sensor), which captures the corresponding sample. Then, a template is computed from the captured sample, and an identity-matching algorithm is used to compare the template with the template previously stored in the database for the presented identity. The system evaluates a 1:1 match between the stated and presented identities and grants access based on a thresholding operation on the resulting match score. A biometric system working in authentication mode can be included in any system that regulates access to a sensitive resource, such as an ATM, a personal device, or a restricted area.

In identification mode, the individual does not state his identity, and the system performs a 1:N matching by comparing the template computed from the biometric trait presented by (or extracted from) the individual with all the templates stored in the database. Then, the identity of the individual corresponding to the most similar template, based on the resulting match scores, is selected. The identification modality is typical of biometric systems in law-enforcement installments, such as the Automated Fingerprint Identification System (AFIS). In AFIS, a fingerprint extracted from a crime scene must be compared with every fingerprint present in the database to determine the identity of the associated individual.

In most cases, the general term "recognition" is used to refer to the process of biometric matching when there is not a need to make a distinction between the authentication and identification modalities.

Biometric systems functioning in the authentication and identification modalities require an enrollment step, similar to a registration procedure, in which a template is computed from the biometric trait of the user and stored in the database of the system, along with the associated identity. An illustration of the enrollment step is shown in Fig. 2.1. A biometric system functioning in authentication mode is shown in Fig. 2.2, while a system functioning in identification mode is shown in Fig. 2.3.

2.3 Biometric Traits

In this section, the types of biometric traits and their characteristics are described. An overview of the main biometric traits is then presented.

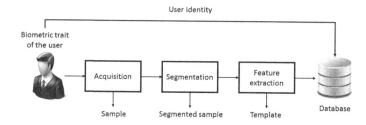

Fig. 2.1 Schematic of the enrollment step in a biometric system

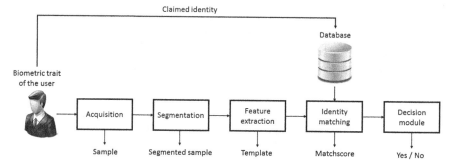

Fig. 2.2 Schematic of a biometric system functioning in authentication mode

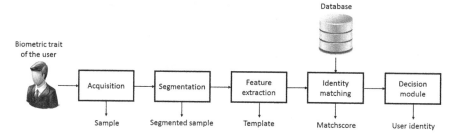

Fig. 2.3 Schematic of a biometric system functioning in identification mode

As noted in Sect. 2.1, biometric traits can be classified as physiological or behavioral. Physiological traits are the features physically possessed by the body of the person to be recognized, such as a fingerprint [102, 238], palmprint [196], iris [74, 86], face [217], hand geometry [329], vein pattern of the hand (or palm vein [49], ear shape [154], DNA [147], or electrocardiogram ECG [272] (Fig. 2.4). Behavioral traits are related to actions performed by the person for recognition. Examples include voice [131], gait [41], signature [155], and keystroke [324] (Fig. 2.5). Physiological traits are usually more accurate than behavioral traits. Moreover, while physiological traits are always present in an individual, in the case

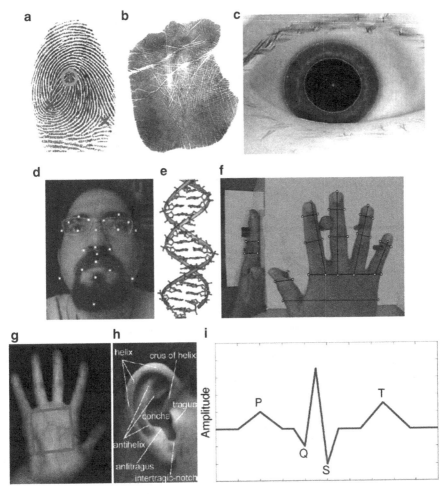

Fig. 2.4 Examples of physiological biometric traits: (**a**) fingerprint [84] (reproduced by permission of IEEE); (**b**) palmprint [170] (reproduced by permission of IEEE); (**c**) iris [74] (reproduced by permission of Springer); (**d**) face [315] (reproduced by permission of Springer); (**e**) DNA [1] (reproduced by permission of IEEE); (**f**) hand geometry [329] (reproduced by permission of Springer); (**g**) vein pattern of the hand [252] (reproduced by permission of IEEE); (**h**) shape of the ear [154] (reproduced by permission of Springer); (**i**) ECG [100] (reproduced by permission of IEEE)

of behavioral traits, individuals can refuse to perform the required action if they do not want to be recognized. For example, a user can refuse to speak or alter his voice.

Every characteristic of the body can potentially be used as a biometric trait. In fact, despite the numerous biometric traits used in recognition systems, innovative biometric features are continually evaluated to improve performance, speed, cost, or

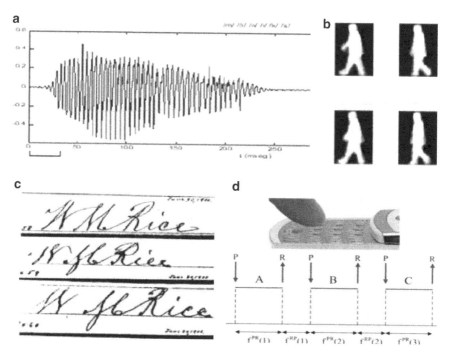

Fig. 2.5 Examples of behavioral biometric traits: (**a**) voice [131] (reproduced by permission of Springer); (**b**) gait [314] (reproduced by permission of Springer); (**c**) signature [120] (reproduced by permission of Springer); (**d**) keystroke [37] (reproduced by permission of IEEE)

reduce privacy risks. However, to be used for recognition purposes, a biometric trait must possess the following characteristics [173]:

- *Universality*: the biometric trait should be possessed by everyone;
- *Distinctiveness*: the biometric trait should distinguish individuals;
- *Permanence*: the biometric trait should not change over time;
- *Collectability*: the biometric trait must be quantitatively measurable.

Other important characteristics of the biometric trait must also be considered:

- *Performance*: the accuracy and speed that can be obtained using the biometric trait;
- *Acceptability*: how willing individuals are to provide their biometric traits for recognition;
- *Circumvention*: the difficulty of hacking the biometric system to gain unautho-rized access.

Biometric traits can also be divided into hard and soft. Hard traits include the aforementioned physiological and behavioral traits, which are characterized by high distinctiveness and permanence. By contrast, soft biometric traits have low distinctiveness or low permanence. These traits cannot be used to recognize

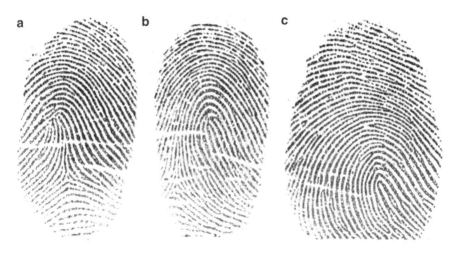

Fig. 2.6 Examples of three different fingerprints: (**a**) index finger; (**b**) middle finger; (**c**) thumb

individuals with sufficient confidence over a period of time but can be used for low-security environments or contexts in which an individual must only be recognized over a short period of time. Soft traits usually have low invasiveness and can be combined to increase the performance of a biometric system [305].

Soft biometric traits can be either continuous or discrete [168]. Continuous soft biometric traits include height [76], weight [91,350], and the size of body parts [77]. Discrete biometric traits include gender [75], race [75], eye color [72], and clothing color [77].

Biometric systems based on fingerprint recognition (Fig. 2.6) are currently the most widespread. These systems are low cost (fingerprint sensors can even be placed on laptops or on USB pen drives) and have good performance. Moreover, they are not considered too invasive by the majority of individuals. Because of their good accuracy and speed, biometric systems based on fingerprints can be used for both authentication and identification purposes. Biometric systems based on fingerprints are typically used for access control, border control, and forensic applications, and centralized fingerprint databases are employed in many countries for the large-scale identification of fingerprints [193]. The analysis of fingerprint features can be performed on three levels, depending on the resolution of the imaging device. Level 1 analysis extracts features related to ridge flow, orientation, frequency, and position of the singular points. Level 2 analysis [130] is the most widely used and is based on the extraction and matching of the positions of specific points called minutiae. Level 3 analysis considers the position of the pores of the skin and the incipient ridges [238].

Biometric systems based on the iris are increasingly used, particularly in situations in which high recognition accuracy and high speed are required, such as border control stations and airports. In fact, iris-based systems have the highest accuracy among biometric traits (except DNA), and the identification procedure is

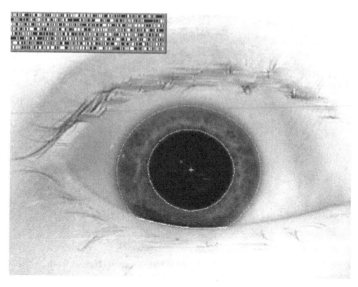

Fig. 2.7 Example of a segmented iris image and the corresponding IrisCode [74] (reproduced by permission of Springer)

very fast, permitting real-time identification over a large-scale database. However, iris-based biometric systems are costly and can be perceived as invasive. The acquisition procedure requires the user to place his open eye near IR illumination. One of the most widely used iris recognition algorithms is based on IrisCode [74], a bit string representation of the random pattern typical of the iris (Fig. 2.7).

Face recognition systems (Fig. 2.8) are a widely studied type of biometric system. These systems offer low invasiveness because people naturally recognize others by viewing faces. Moreover, the acquisition of face samples is performed in a touchless manner using cameras. For these reasons, face recognition systems can be used in many situations, ranging from access control for mobile devices to border control scenarios. Moreover, face recognition can be used in surveillance applications to recognize people at a distance and in unconstrained scenarios. However, biometric systems based on the face do not possess the same accuracy as systems based on fingerprint or iris recognition because of the substantial influence of differences in pose, illumination, facial expressions, occlusions (e.g., hat, glasses, etc.) and changes in physical attributes over time (e.g., beard, hair, aging). The majority of the algorithms used for face recognition are based on transformations or on the definition of attributes [217].

Systems based on hand geometry (Fig. 2.9) are characterized by low accuracy but have very low invasiveness and high acceptability by users. Moreover, a biometric system based on hand geometry can be produced with low hardware costs [329]. For these reasons, these systems can be used positively in situations where high recognition accuracy is not needed. For example, in some methods, recognition is based on the finger shape [190, 237, 375, 428] or finger knuckle [45, 204].

Fig. 2.8 Examples of face recognition systems: (**a**) face recognition of a collaborative subject [315] (reproduced by permission of Springer); (**b**) face recognition in surveillance applications [10] (reproduced by permission of Springer)

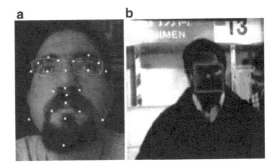

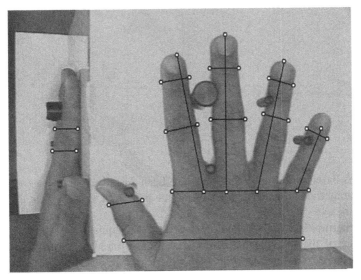

Fig. 2.9 Example of a biometric system based on hand geometry [329] (reproduced by permission of Springer)

Other biometric recognition systems based on the features of the hand, such as the palmprint [196] or the vein pattern of the hand [49], also possess low invasiveness and high user acceptability. Biometric systems based on palmprint recognition can use optical sensors or low-cost devices such as flatbed scanners or CCD-based devices, while systems based on vein pattern recognition usually use an infrared or near-infrared camera. These systems are typically more accurate than systems based only on hand geometry.

Biometric systems based on DNA [147] are the most accurate means of recognizing an individual. However, DNA-based procedures are extremely expensive and time consuming and cannot be used to distinguish identical twins.

Some reports have also described the use of ear shape to perform biometric recognition [154] (Fig. 2.10). An important advantage of this biometric trait is that the shape of the ear can be acquired in a touchless manner and even at long distances.

Fig. 2.10 Examples of features used for the recognition based on ear shape [304] (reproduced by permission of IEEE)

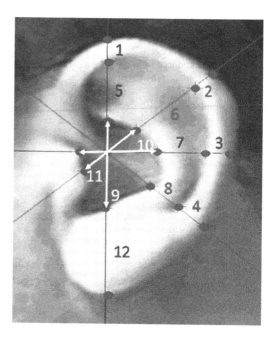

Systems based on retinal scans have also been described [309]. These systems perform biometric recognition by acquiring the pattern of veins present in the rear region of the eye.

Facial thermography is a technology based on the acquisition of the vein pattern on the face of the individual. In most cases, an infrared camera is used. Most aspects of the recognition algorithms are similar to those used in face recognition systems [48].

Behavioral traits such as a person's voice [131], gait [41], signature [155], and keystroke [324] are usually well accepted by users, in part because they can be partially altered to prevent recognition (e.g., a person can change the way he walks or talks) or even hidden (e.g., a person can refuse to speak or sign). However, these traits are associated with lower recognition accuracy.

Similarly, soft biometric traits do not permit the unequivocal recognition of an individual [168]. However, they can be used when the number of users is limited. Soft traits can also be used to perform preliminary screening of a large database to save time by reducing the number of hard biometric comparisons required. Moreover, soft biometric traits can be used for unobtrusive, continuous authentication [271] (e.g., recognizing the user in front of a terminal by simply checking his clothes).

To increase biometric recognition accuracy, multimodal or multibiometric systems can be created by combining information from multiple biometric traits, multiple samples, or different recognition algorithms [13, 14, 57, 128, 129, 305]. Multibiometric systems can combine multiple hard biometric traits (e.g., iris and face) in situations where very high security is critical. Multiple low-accuracy traits

Table 2.1 Characteristics of the main biometric traits [173] (reproduced by permission of IEEE)

Trait	Univ.	Uniq.	Perm.	Coll.	Perf.	Acc.	Circ.
Face	H	L	M	H	L	H	L
Fingerprint	M	H	H	M	H	M	H
Hand geometry	M	M	M	H	M	M	M
Keystrokes	L	L	L	M	L	M	M
Hand vein	M	M	M	M	M	M	H
Iris	H	H	H	M	H	L	H
Retinal scan	H	H	M	L	H	L	H
Signature	L	L	L	H	L	H	L
Voice	M	L	L	M	L	H	L
Face thermograms	H	H	L	H	M	H	H
Odor	H	H	H	L	L	M	L
DNA	H	H	H	L	H	L	L
Gait	M	L	L	H	L	H	M
Ear	M	M	H	M	M	H	M

Notes: *Univ.* universality, *Uniq.*, uniqueness, *Perm.* permanence, *Coll.* collectability, *Perf.* performance, *Acc.* acceptability, *Circ.* circumvention, *H* high, *M* medium, *L* low

(e.g., height and weight) can also be combined to obtain a low-invasiveness system with increased accuracy.

A summary of the characteristics of the main biometric traits is presented in Table 2.1.

2.4 Evaluation of Biometric Systems

Several aspects must be considered in the evaluation of biometric systems, such as accuracy, speed, usability, cost, privacy, social acceptance, scalability, interoperability, and security (Fig. 2.11). Moreover, the methods used for evaluating the different aspects belong to numerous different fields, ranging from engineering and computer science, to social sciences and economics.

In this section, the different factors considered during the evaluation of biometric systems are described, and the different strategies used are discussed.

2.4.1 Evaluation Aspects

Accuracy metrics are usually the most important means of evaluating biometric systems and are used to evaluate every biometric method. However, an efficient

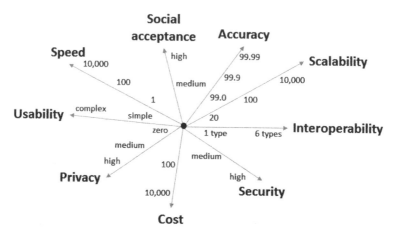

Fig. 2.11 The different aspects that must be considered when evaluating biometric systems

balance of accuracy with several other aspects is necessary to create a successful biometric technology. In particular, nine different aspects must be considered:

- *Accuracy* is a measure of the ability of the biometric system to discriminate between individuals based on the biometric trait used. Accuracy metrics are described in greater detail in Sect. 2.4.3.
- *Speed* is the amount of time needed to perform the enrollment and authentication or identification processes. Speed is particularly important for biometric systems functioning in the identification modality. Moreover, the time needed for the different steps of the biometric system must be considered separately. For example, a long acquisition time could result in a less usable system.
- *Usability* describes how easy the system is to use as well as how easily people can learn to use it. Usability is measured using the acquisition time and the number of incorrectly captured samples. However, because social and personal factors can influence the usability of a system, surveys are often used for a superior evaluation [342].
- *Cost* is a measure of the cost of the design, the development of the hardware system, and the implementation of the recognition algorithms. Expensive biometric systems usually have superior accuracy and speed compared to cheaper systems, but lower cost can favor widespread adoption of a system.
- *Privacy* is the possibility that a biometric trait can be stolen or misused by the biometric system. Because biometric traits cannot be changed, a biometric system must have effective ways of protecting personal data. Privacy considerations related to biometric systems are described in greater detail in Sect. 2.4.4.
- *Social acceptance* refers to how the system is perceived by users. This measure can be related to public knowledge about the performance of the system, the perceived privacy risks, its invasiveness, and its usability. Personal factors can also play an important role in determining the social acceptance of a biometric system (e.g., some people do not like to touch biometric sensors) [111].

- *Scalability* describes the ability of the system to function efficiently when the load increases, for example, a greater number of enrolled users or an increase in the number of queries to the central biometric database. This aspect can be related to the hardware architecture chosen (e.g., CPU frequency, hard drive speed, network bandwidth) or the efficiency of the software implementation of the biometric recognition algorithms.
- *Interoperability* refers to the compatibility of different biometric systems based on the same biometric trait. This factor can be influenced by the type and quality of the biometric sample (e.g., a low-cost device will produce a different sample than a high-end device), the data format used for storing the templates, the measure of similarity used as the output of the matching process, etc. To partially address cross-compatibility issues, biometric standards are used [308].
- *Security* is the robustness of the system against attack. In particular, security against fake biometric traits must be investigated to design an efficient biometric system. Moreover, the robustness of the computer architecture and the network infrastructure to attacks and the processing software to malicious software must be considered.

2.4.2 Evaluation Strategies

Different evaluation strategies can be used to assess the performance and usability of biometric systems at different stages of their design and implementation. Evaluation strategies can be divided into (a) technology evaluations, (b) scenario evaluations, and (c) operational evaluations, which are respectively characterized by an increasing number of uncontrolled variables.

- *Technology Evaluations.* These procedures are used to evaluate the accuracy performance of the biometric system. Technology evaluations are usually performed on standard databases of biometric samples, which are made public to provide a common ground for the comparison of the performances of different recognition algorithms. An example of technology evaluation is the ICB Competition on Iris Recognition [7].
- *Scenario Evaluations.* These procedures consider the application of the biometric technology in a specific context by testing different technologies. For example, in a scenario evaluation, biometric systems based on iris or fingerprint recognition might be tested to develop a fast, accurate system to control access to critical areas. Scenario evaluations are performed using different biometric traits from the same individuals, and a large number of samples are usually collected to ensure statistically significant results. However, scenario evaluations can be difficult to repeat completely. An example of a scenario evaluation is the UK Biometric Product Testing [240].
- *Operational Evaluations.* These evaluations are performed using the chosen biometric system operating in the desired scenario, and the real users (every

user or a subset) that will be using the biometric system are considered. Operational evaluations are not used to measure the performance of the biometric system. Rather, they are used to analyze the impact on the workflow caused by the introduction of the biometric system and the possible advantages and disadvantages. Operational evaluations are often difficult or impossible to repeat.

The three different evaluation strategies should be performed in sequence to successfully pass from the design phase to the installation of the biometric system. First, the technology evaluation should be performed to ensure that the biometric system performs sufficiently. Then, a scenario evaluation must be used to determine the best biometric technology for a particular situation. Finally, an operational evaluation should be performed to analyze the economic impact and generate the business reports necessary for potential installations.

2.4.3 Accuracy Evaluation

In the literature, common figures of merit are used in the form of standard indices [173] to measure the accuracy of a biometric system. These indices can be used to describe the performance of a biometric system in a synthetic way and to compare the results obtained by different methods. Standard databases of biometric samples are often used for accuracy evaluation, and the use of standard indices facilitates the comparison of the results with other results obtained using the same database [121].

In this section, the term B_{ij} describes the j-th biometric sample pertaining to the i-th individual, T_{ij} indicates the corresponding biometric template, n_i describes the number of templates available for individual i, N indicates the number of enrolled identities, and $M(\cdot)$ represents the biometric matching function.

Matching functions can be symmetrical or asymmetrical. For symmetrical matching functions, the following equation is used:

$$M(T_{ij}, T_{kl}) = M(T_{kl}, T_{ij}) \qquad (ij) \neq (kl), \qquad (2.1)$$

where $M(\cdot)$ represents the matching function. For asymmetrical matching functions, the following equation is used:

$$M(T_{ij}, T_{kl}) \neq M(T_{kl}, T_{ij}) \qquad (ij) \neq (kl). \qquad (2.2)$$

Some accuracy measures are valid only for symmetrical matching functions [167]. However, the procedures for accuracy evaluation described here can be used for both symmetrical and asymmetrical matching functions [126, 127, 369].

Accuracy evaluation procedures are usually used to characterize the performance of biometric systems by considering the results of the enrollment step, the identity-matching step, and the decision module.

2.4.3.1 Enrollment Step

In this step, the index REJ_{ENROLL} is used to describe the number of errors that prevent the creation and storage of a biometric template T_{ij}, using the sample B_{ij}. Errors can potentially be caused by failures in the acquisition process, timeouts (the algorithms exceeds the maximum allowed time), and crashes.

In particular, the Failure to Accept Rate (FTAR) is used to describe the expected proportion of enrollment tries for which it is not possible to generate a sample of sufficient quality. In addition, the Failure to Enroll Rate (FER) is used to describe the expected percentage of the population for which it is not possible to generate a repeatable template [238].

2.4.3.2 Identity Matching Step

The procedure used to evaluate the biometric system in the identity matching step, considering symmetrical matching functions, is based on matching each template T_{ij} with the templates T_{ik}, with $j < k \leq n_i$. The resulting match scores are stored in a genuine match score matrix gms_{ijk}, where the term "genuine" is used to refer to matching scores obtained by matching identities pertaining to the same individual i. Thus, a genuine match score matrix is computed for each individual i (Fig. 2.12a). The matrix is square, and because it is symmetrical, only the upper triangular matrix is computed.

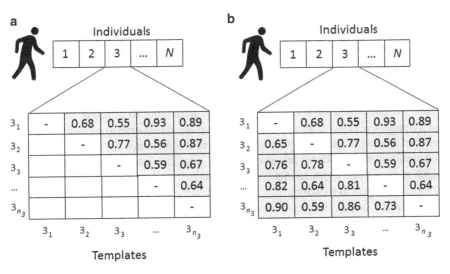

Fig. 2.12 Matrices of genuine matching scores gms_{ijk} for symmetrical and asymmetrical matching functions: (**a**) gms_{ijk} for symmetrical matching functions; (**b**) gms_{ijk} for asymmetrical matching functions

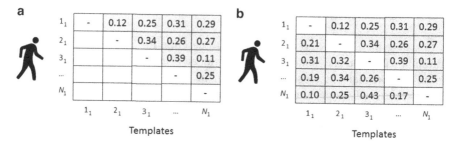

Fig. 2.13 Matrices of impostor matching scores ims_{ik} using symmetrical and asymmetrical matching functions: (**a**) ims_{ik} for symmetrical matching functions; (**b**) ims_{ik} for asymmetrical matching functions

For asymmetrical matching functions, match scores are computed by matching each template T_{ij} with the templates T_{ik}, with $k \neq j$. The matrix gms_{ijk} is computed for each individual. The resulting matrices are square but not symmetrical (Fig. 2.12b).

For symmetrical matching functions, the Number of Genuine Recognition Attempts (NGRA) can be defined as follows:

$$NGRA_{symmetric} = \frac{1}{2}\sum_{i=1}^{N} n_i(n_i - 1), \tag{2.3}$$

assuming $REJ_{ENROLL} = 0$.

For the case of asymmetrical matching functions and $REJ_{ENROLL} = 0$, the NGRA is defined as follows:

$$NGRA_{asymmetric} = \sum_{i=1}^{N} n_i(n_i - 1). \tag{2.4}$$

The match scores must also be considered relative to impostor comparisons, which are performed by comparing templates pertaining to different individuals. For symmetrical matching functions, each template T_{i1} relative to an individual i is matched against the first template of the different individuals T_{k1}, with $i < k \leq N$. The resulting match scores are stored in the impostor match score matrix ims_{ik}, which is square and upper triangular (Fig. 2.13a).

For asymmetrical matching functions, each template T_{i1} is matched against the first template of the different individuals T_{k1}, with $i \neq k$. The resulting match scores are stored in the impostor match score matrix ims_{ik}, which is square but not triangular (Fig. 2.13b).

For symmetrical matching functions, the Number of Impostor Recognition Attempts (NIRA) assuming $REJ_{ENROLL} = 0$, is then defined as follows:

$$NIRA_{symmetric} = \frac{1}{2}N(N - 1). \tag{2.5}$$

For asymmetrical matching functions, and assuming $REJ_{ENROLL} = 0$, the NIRA is defined as follows:

$$NIRA_{asymmetric} = N(N-1). \tag{2.6}$$

During the identity matching step, errors due to failures (the biometric sample cannot be processed), timeouts (the algorithms exceed the maximum allowed time), and crashes (the algorithm crashes) can occur. These events result in missing values in the matrices gms_{ijk} and ims_{ik}, which are respectively accumulated in the variables REJ_{NGRA} and REJ_{NIRA}.

2.4.3.3 Decision Module

The values computed from both the genuine and impostor identity comparisons can be used to determine the aggregate indices that describe the accuracy of the biometric system. The accuracy indices are computed by considering biometric systems that have multiple templates or permit multiple recognition attempts, and each match score is considered as comparison between a template computed from a single submitted sample and a single enrolled template.

The most important indices are the False Match Rate (FMR(t)) and the False Non-Match Rate (FNMR(t). These indices are functions of the threshold value t, which is used in the decision module to classify each match score as the result of a comparison of identities pertaining to either the same person or different individuals. In particular, the FMR describes the expected probability that a template will be incorrectly determined to match a template from a different individual (false positive), while the FNMR describes the expected probability that a template will be incorrectly declared not to match a template corresponding to the same individual (false negative).

The FMR and FNMR values are computed by classifying each match score in ims_{ik} and gms_{ijk} with the values of the threshold, which ranges from 0 to 1, where 0 corresponds to the minimum possible similarity between the template and the sample and 1 corresponds to the maximum possible similarity between the template and the sample.

The formulas for FMR and FNMR are defined as follows [238]:

$$FMR(t) = \frac{card\{ims_{ik}|ims_{ik} \geq t\}}{NIRA}$$

$$FNMR(t) = \frac{card\{gms_{ijk}|gms_{ijk} < t\}}{NGRA} + REJ_{NGRA}, \tag{2.7}$$

where card($\cdot$) represents the cardinality of the set. To summarize the FMR and FNMR values, the EER value, which corresponds to the threshold value t for which FMR(t) = FNMR(t), is often used.

The FMR and FNMR values are usually visualized using two error plots, the Receiver Operating Characteristic (ROC) and the Detection Error Tradeoff (DET). Linear or logarithmic axes can be used for visualization purposes.

The ROC curve shows the percentage of false negatives as a function of the percentage of false positives, according to the threshold value t. ROC curves are used in binary classification systems, of which biometric systems are a particular case, and are computed by plotting the FMR values on the x axis and the $(1 - \text{FNMR})$ values on the y axis (Fig. 2.14a).

The DET plot is computed by plotting the FMR values on the x axis and the FNMR values on the y axis (Fig. 2.14b).

The advantage of ROC curves is that they facilitate easy comparisons of the accuracies of different biometric systems because the most accurate system is visualized as the curve that remains above all other curves for all values of the threshold t. In the case of the DET plot, the curve corresponding to the most accurate system remains below all other curves for all values of the threshold. However, in most cases, a system has better accuracy only in a certain region of the ROC curve, corresponding to a particular range of threshold values.

Moreover, to evaluate the distribution of genuine and impostor matching scores, it is often useful to plot a graph that separately describes the frequency of the genuine and impostor comparisons, as contained in the matrices gms_{ijk} and ims_{ik}, for each possible matching score value. If the two distributions are completely separated, a threshold value t exists that can classify the matching scores with $FMR = FNMR = EER = 0$. An example of two genuine and impostor distributions is shown in Fig. 2.15.

Other indices used in the literature include the False Accept Rate (FAR) and the False Reject Rate (FRR). The FAR indicates the number of times a non-authorized person is accepted as authorized, whereas the FRR describes the number of times an authorized person is rejected as non-authorized. These indices differ from the FMR and FNMR because they also consider errors in the acquisition step.

2.4.3.4 Confidence Estimation

Because the accuracy of biometric systems must be evaluated using rather limited databases rather than the entire human population, techniques to estimate the confidence of the performed accuracy measurements are required [239].

Two rules have been proposed for estimating the necessary size of the testing database: the Rule of 3 [181, 228] and the Rule of 30 [80].

The Rule of 3 is used to compute the lowest error rate that can be statistically determined using N biometric comparisons. This error rate p is the error value for which the probability of 0 errors in N trials is equal to a fixed value (usually 5 %). This rule can be expressed as the following:

$$p \approx \frac{3}{N} \quad \text{with } 95\% \text{ confidence.} \tag{2.8}$$

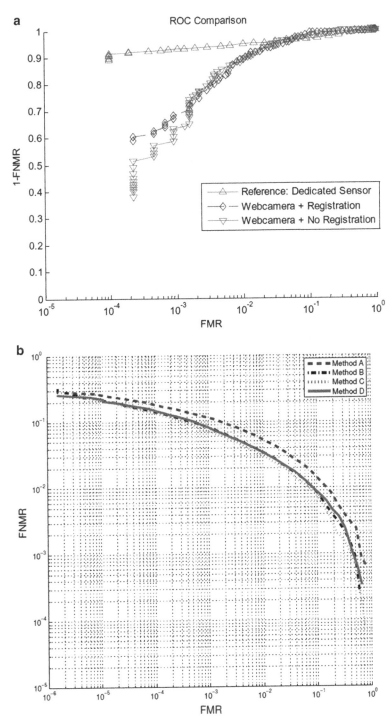

Fig. 2.14 Examples of ROC and DET curves: (**a**) examples of ROC curves [287] (reproduced by permission of IEEE); (**b**) examples of DET curves [93] (reproduced by permission of IEEE)

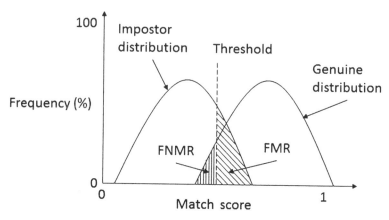

Fig. 2.15 Example score distributions for genuine and impostor matching scores

For example, if a test on 300 samples yields no errors, the computed error rate of the biometric system would be $\leq 1\%$ with 95 % confidence.

The Rule of 30 states that, for 90 % confidence that the true error rate of the biometric system differs no more than $\pm 30\%$ from the computed error rate, at least 30 errors must be present. For example, if there are 30 false non-match errors in 3,000 genuine comparisons, there is 90 % confidence that the true error is between 0.7 and 1.3 %.

Moreover, if the number of samples is sufficiently large, it is possible to evaluate the confidence of the measured accuracy using the central limit theorem [331], which states that the error rate should follow a normal distribution. In this case, $100(1 - \alpha)\%$ confidence boundaries can be estimated using the equation:

$$\hat{p} \pm z \left(1 - \frac{\alpha}{2}\right) \sqrt{\hat{V}(\hat{p})}, \tag{2.9}$$

where $\hat{p}$ is the observed error rate, $\hat{V}(\hat{p})$ is the estimated variance of the observed error rate [239], and $z(\cdot)$ is the inverse of the standard normal cumulative distribution. For example, for 95 % confidence limits, the value $z(0.975)$ is equal to 1.96.

Non-parametric methods based on the bootstrap technique have also been proposed for the estimation of the confidence of accuracy measurements [28, 289]. These techniques do not require assumptions about the distribution of the error rate or the dependencies among the different attempts. In fact, the distributions and dependencies are computed by observing a subset of the used samples obtained by sampling the original samples with replacement. Then, the extracted samples are used for the bootstrap technique to estimate the distribution of the accuracy indices and the confidence interval values. Several studies have evaluated the robustness of bootstrap techniques [215, 216].

Using bootstrap methods, it is possible to directly compute the $100(1 - \alpha)\%$ confidence limits, which include a lower limit L and an upper limit U that are defined such that only $\alpha/2$ bootstrap values are lower than L and $\alpha/2$ bootstrap values higher than U. In the method used in [331], at least 1,000 samples were recommended for 95 % limits and at least 5,000 samples for 99 % limits.

A bootstrap technique that also considers a statistical correlation between the templates computed from the same biometric trait is described in [29]. This approach uses a sampling with replacement technique that extracts only certain subsets of the original data to construct templates pertaining to a single biometric trait or individual.

The confidence of the accuracy of biometric systems has been estimated using a variety of techniques. In [73] a semi-parametric technique based on the multivariate copula model was proposed to account for correlated biometric acquisitions. In addition, the method described a technique for computing the minimum number of samples necessary to obtain appropriate confidence intervals for obtaining an ROC curve of the desired width. Another reported method [290] specifically addressed confidence estimation in multibiometric systems.

2.4.4 Privacy and Security Evaluation

As stated in Sect. 2.1, biometric systems recognize individuals with greater accuracy than that obtained by traditional methods. Moreover, the accuracy of biometric systems is well known and often assumed by the public to be equal to 100 %. While public knowledge of the superior accuracy of biometric systems increases confidence in these systems among users because recognition errors are considered impossible, some individuals may believe that the assessed biometric trait could be used to track their activities and pose a risk to their privacy.

While biometric recognition systems are more accurate and secure than traditional recognition methods, the biometric traits used are strictly associated with each person and cannot be repudiated or altered if a person no longer wishes to be recognized. Moreover, if biometric data are stolen, the thief can impersonate the victim for a long period of time. By contrast, an advantage of passwords and smartcards is that they can be easily changed or discarded in the event of theft or misuse of personal data.

Therefore, the accurate design of biometric systems requires a consideration of the privacy and security risks involved in the handling of personal data, particularly for those systems that use hard biometric traits (e.g., fingerprint, iris, or face). Different aspects must be considered for privacy protection, including the real and perceived risks for the users, the specificity of the application, the use of correct policies, and the methods used for the protection of sensitive data [21, 22, 26, 58–64]. Both real and perceived risks must be considered because, while a system might enforce techniques for privacy protection, users could still perceive violations of their privacy.

To design a privacy-compliant biometric system, three different perspectives must be considered: (a) the risks perceived by the user; (b) the application context; and (c) the biometric trait used.

- *Risks Perceived by the User.* This perspective considers the way that the biometric system is perceived, particularly with respect to privacy risks. The risks perceived by users directly influence the acceptability of a system. Because biometric systems can be perceived differently by different people, this aspect can be difficult to evaluate. Moreover, the evaluation can also fall outside the technical aspects of the biometric system. For example, most people believe that biometric systems have 100 % accuracy or that biometric traits can always be captured from a great distance and used to identify them in every situation, track their activities, operate proscription lists, or be used for malicious purposes. In some cases, biometric systems can be perceived as dangerous. For example, the infrared illuminators used in iris scanners can be erroneously regarded as a danger to the eyes.
- *Application Context.* The context in which the biometric system operates directly influences privacy risks, both real and perceived. A series of application contexts and the corresponding possible privacy risks has been published by the International Biometrics Group [162] and is shown in Table 2.2. Privacy risks can be lower or higher depending on how the system is used (e.g., identification or verification, optional or mandatory, etc.), how the data are stored, who owns the information, and which traits are used.
- *The Biometric Trait Used.* Different aspects of biometric traits can influence privacy risks. For example, greater risks are present if the biometric trait can be used for identification or in covert systems and if the template databases are compatible. For example, biometric traits that can be used in identification systems might present increased privacy risks because the users can be recognized without stating their identity and against their will (e.g., by extracting a latent fingerprint). For similar reasons, covert biometric systems can pose threats to privacy because individuals can be recognized without their knowledge (e.g., from surveillance videos).

  Physiological traits, which cannot be altered and are more permanent, are more privacy invasive than behavioral traits.

  Finally, compatibility between biometric databases can increase privacy risk because the biometric templates can be used in applications other than the one for which the user enrolled his/her trait.

To ensure security, techniques for data verification, integrity, confidentiality, and non-repudiation must be incorporated. These techniques must consider the points at which a biometric system can be attacked to gain access to unauthorized information (Fig. 2.16). There are eight possible points at which an attack can occur [115]:

- *I*: using a fake biometric trait at the acquisition module;
- *II*: resubmitting an old acquisition to the system without capturing a fresh sample;
- *III*: bypassing the feature extraction module;

Table 2.2 Application contexts and privacy risks [99] (reproduced by permission of Springer)

Lower risk	Question	Higher risk
Overt	Is the system deployed overtly or covertly?	Covert
Optional	Is the system optional or mandatory?	Mandatory
Verification	Is the system used for Identification or Verification?	Identification
Fixed period	Is the system deployed for a fixed period of time?	Indefinite
Private sector	Is the system deployed in the private or public sector?	Public sector
Individual/customer	In what role is the user interacting with the system?	Employee/citizen
Enrollee	Who owns the biometric information?	Institution
Personal storage	Where is the biometric data stored?	Database storage
Behavioral	What type of biometric trait is being used?	Physiological
Templates	Does the system use templates, samples or both?	Sample/images

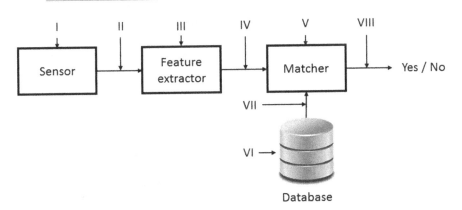

Fig. 2.16 The eight possible points of attack in biometric systems

- *IV*: tampering with the extracted features;
- *V*: bypassing the biometric matching module;
- *VI*: tampering with the templates stored in the database;
- *VII*: performing a channel attack between the stored templates and the matcher module;
- *VIII*: bypassing the decision module.

Different techniques can be used to protect a biometric system from possible attacks, including methods for detecting the liveness of biometric traits, physical and cryptographic methods for the protection of communication channels, methods for secure code execution, and methods for the protection of templates [172].

2.5   Research Trends in Biometric Recognition

Many research groups are working toward the design and implementation of
enhanced biometric systems. The following topics have been studied extensively:

*   *Improvement of Accuracy.* Numerous studies have sought to improve the recog-
    nition accuracy of biometric systems via improved sensors [83, 85, 108, 184, 186,
    219, 237, 360] and recognition algorithms [39, 40, 223, 328].
*   *Use of Multimodal and Multibiometric Systems.* The combined use of multiple
    biometric traits or multiple recognition algorithms improves the accuracy and
    robustness of biometric systems. Thus, improved techniques for the efficient
    fusion of biometric information are being studied [14, 57, 305].
*   *Reduction of Costs.* Reducing the cost of the acquisition module is important for
    increasing the distribution of biometric systems. For example, biometric systems
    based on iris recognition use infrared illuminators and cameras, which can be
    very expensive [74]. For this reason, methods for iris recognition using visible
    light illumination are of interest [32, 95, 96, 101].
*   *Use of Less-Cooperative Acquisition Techniques.* Many biometric techniques
    require a cooperative subject who is willing to provide his biometric trait (e.g.,
    his fingerprint or iris). Methods for less-cooperative biometric acquisition are
    being studied to increase the speed and usability of biometric systems and for the
    use of biometric traits in surveillance applications [182].
*   *Increasing the Distance Between the Trait and the Sensor.* Increasing the distance
    at which biometric traits can be accurately acquired might reduce the perceived
    invasiveness of the acquisition, increase the acquisition speed, and enable the
    use of biometric systems in new applications. For example, many studies have
    focused on the design of iris recognition systems that can function at greater
    distances [245].
*   *Improvement of Usability and Acceptance.* The design of biometric systems with
    increased usability and greater acceptance among the general population could
    result in greater confidence in biometric recognition and lead to the broader
    adoption of biometric technologies [111, 342]. For example, the use of acquisition
    techniques that require less cooperation from the user and increase the distance
    between the trait and sensor might help improve usability and acceptance.
*   *Use of Three-Dimensional Samples.* Three-dimensional samples do not present
    distortions or perspective deformations caused by the mapping of the biometric
    trait onto a two-dimensional plane. Moreover, three-dimensional models describe
    a wider area of the trait that cannot be captured using a single image and use depth
    information to increase recognition accuracy. For example, three-dimensional
    models can be used in biometric recognition applications [403] for the face
    [108, 316], ear [154], fingerprint [83, 360], and palmprint [186, 219].
*   *Improvement of Security and Privacy.* As stated in Sect. 2.4.4, better techniques
    for the protection of the users' privacy and security could permit greater
    distribution of biometric systems by preventing the misuse of biometric data,
    thereby increasing user confidence. However, because increased security can

reduce system speed, more efficient methods for the improvement of security [9] and the protection of privacy [99] are being studied.

- *Use of New Biometric Traits*. The use of new biometric traits for recognition could permit the use of biometric systems in different applications. For example, ECG [100, 272, 288] and photoplethysmogram (PPG) [30] have recently been studied for biometric recognition.

This book focuses on the study of innovative, less-constrained methods for palmprint recognition. In particular, to achieve less-constrained recognition, touchless and less-cooperative acquisition techniques and improved system usability are required.

2.6 Summary

Biometric systems enable the recognition of individuals based on their characteristics rather than objects or knowledge. Biometric traits cannot be lost or forgotten, and the risk of impersonation by a different individual is highly reduced. For this reason, biometric systems are increasingly used in several applications, particularly to permit access to sensitive areas or resources.

Biometric systems can function either in authentication mode to confirm the identity stated by an individual or in identification mode to establish an unknown identity based on evaluation of a biometric trait. The general structure of biometric systems is based on five steps: acquisition, segmentation, feature extraction, identity matching, and decision.

Biometric traits can be divided into physiological, behavioral, and soft biometric traits. Physiological traits are related to the characteristics of a person's body (e.g., fingerprint, iris, face), whereas behavioral traits are related to actions and gestures (e.g., voice, signature, keystroke). Soft biometric traits include features related to the body that have low distinctiveness and permanence (e.g., height, weight, age, gender).

The fingerprint is currently the most used biometric trait because it offers a good compromise between accuracy, speed, and cost. Biometric systems based on the iris have the greatest accuracy and speed but have high costs and can be perceived as invasive. Face recognition systems are considered less invasive, but they have low accuracy and are affected by differences in the acquisition conditions. Systems based on hand geometry are very well accepted and low cost but also have limited accuracy. Systems based on palmprint or vein pattern recognition have greater accuracy. Other biometric traits that have been used include ear shape, retinal pattern, facial thermography, and behavioral traits such as gait, voice, signature, and keystroke. Soft biometric traits are also used to perform continuous authentications or can be combined to improve accuracy using a multibiometric system.

To select the best trait for a particular situation, different aspects must be evaluated. Specifically, the accuracy, speed, usability, social acceptance, cost, privacy, security, scalability, and interoperability of the system must be analyzed. Techniques that evaluate accuracy with confidence values are the most important and most used metrics. However, methods for evaluating privacy risks are also important for ensuring widespread adoption of biometric systems.

Current research is focusing on improving several aspects of biometric systems, including their accuracy, speed, fusion of information in multibiometric systems, usability, acceptance, and techniques for the protection of security and privacy. Many methods have investigated the use of three-dimensional models to increase accuracy. In addition, several methods are being studied to reduce the level of cooperation needed and the costs and to increase the distance required between the trait and the sensor. The use of new biometric traits is also being investigated.

Chapter 3
Touchless and Less-Constrained Biometric Systems

Less-constrained biometric systems are of interest for the implementation of biometric systems that can overcome the limitations of usability, acceptance, and speed of current systems. More specifically, the goals of less-constrained systems are to perform biometric recognition with touchless acquisitions and less cooperation from the users and at greater distances.

In this chapter, an overview of less-constrained biometric systems is presented. First, less-constrained biometric recognition is introduced. Then, the techniques for performing touchless and less-constrained recognition are reviewed by first describing methods based on traits that are traditionally acquired using contact with a sensor (e.g., fingerprint, palmprint). Then, innovative methods for the less-constrained recognition of traits usually captured using a touchless acquisition (e.g., face, iris) are presented.

3.1 Introduction to Less-Constrained Biometric Recognition

Most biometric traits require a cooperative user who is willing to provide his trait to the sensor. In addition, some biometric acquisitions require controlled procedures or contact of the trait with the sensor. For example, the user must assume a certain pose, place his trait on a particular place, and remain still for the duration of the biometric acquisition. This general procedure limits the usability, acceptance, and speed of biometric systems.

To reduce or eliminate these constraints, techniques for less-constrained biometric recognition are being studied. Advances in this area could also lead to the use of biometric traits in a greater number of situations. For example, less-constrained iris recognition would permit high recognition accuracy in surveillance applications, on mobile phones, or at gates [343].

© Springer International Publishing Switzerland 2014
A. Genovese et al., *Touchless Palmprint Recognition Systems*,
Advances in Information Security 60, DOI 10.1007/978-3-319-10365-5_3

Research on less-constrained biometric recognition has had three main focuses:

- *Increasing the Distance Between the Trait and the Sensor.* Increasing the distance at which biometric traits can be accurately acquired might increase the usability, acceptance, and speed of the system. In the case of biometric traits traditionally captured using touch-based systems (e.g., fingerprint), increasing the distance would enable the use of touchless acquisition techniques (e.g., CCD cameras instead of capacitive sensors). For traits traditionally captured using touchless procedures (e.g., face, iris), increasing the distance could enable biometric acquisition without requiring the user to come close to the sensor.
- *Reducing the Requirement for User Cooperation.* Less-cooperative systems require less time to learn how to produce a correct acquisition and only minor effort. Thus, improvements in this area would result in higher acceptability and acquisition speed. For example, a less-cooperative acquisition system could eliminate the need for the user to stand still during the acquisition and capture his traits as he walks.
- *Use of Uncontrolled Light Conditions.* The use of uncontrolled, natural light illumination could enable the use of biometric recognition in a greater number of situations. It could also reduce the level of cooperation needed. If the system can function in uncontrolled light conditions, the user might not need to stand in a particular place.

Innovative methods for capturing and processing biometric data have also been studied:

- *Adaptive Acquisition Systems.* To reduce the level of user cooperation required, the acquisition procedure should adapt to different situations to generate a biometric sample of sufficient quality. In this way, the system can function in a greater number of situations without the intervention of an operator.
- *Adaptive Preprocessing Methods.* If adaptive acquisition procedures are used, methods must be designed that can process biometric samples in a variety of situations. Differences in the acquisition distance and light conditions can create considerable variation between samples.
- *Innovative Feature Extraction and Matching Methods.* In most cases, less-constrained systems produce samples that are different from traditional samples. Thus, new methods must be implemented for feature extraction and matching.
- *Compatibility of Less-Constrained Systems with Traditional Systems.* It is not always possible to replace existing databases with templates computed using less-constrained systems. Thus, the compatibility of new templates with existing ones must be verified.

Less-constrained biometric systems typically use CCD cameras to acquire the biometric trait. In fact, cameras are the most common means of performing touchless acquisition with natural light illumination [343]. Multiple cameras can be combined to create a multi-view acquisition system to increase the captured area or create three-dimensional models of the biometric trait. Capturing a larger area or

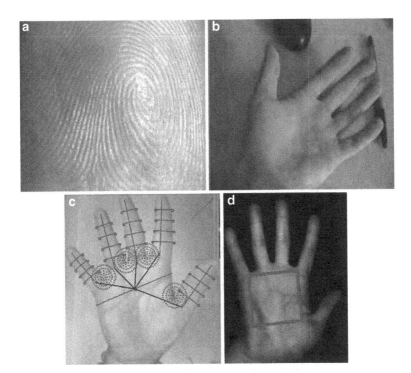

Fig. 3.1 Examples of touch-based traits, captured using less-constrained touchless acquisitions: (**a**) fingerprint [140] (reproduced by permission of IEEE) ; (**b**) palmprint [106] (reproduced by permission of IEEE); (**c**) hand geometry [251] (reproduced by permission of IEEE); (**d**) palm vein [252] (reproduced by permission of IEEE)

using a three-dimensional model of the biometric trait can increase the accuracy and robustness of the recognition.

However, the design of less-constrained systems is a difficult task, and the elimination of constraints leads to a reduction in the recognition accuracy in most cases. Different challenges must be considered for reducing constraints, depending on whether the biometric trait is traditionally captured using a touch-based or touchless acquisition.

For biometric traits traditionally captured using touch-based acquisitions, the main goals are to design acquisition procedures capable of capturing the trait in a touchless manner using a CCD camera and to implement preprocessing methods capable of extracting the distinctive features from the obtained image, particularly for varying light conditions. User cooperation is still required for less-constrained biometric systems that use traits traditionally captured using touch-based sensors, and the light conditions are still partially controlled. For example, in the case of fingerprints, the distinctive pattern is much less visible in images captured using a CCD camera, and special algorithms must be used for its extraction. Moreover, touchless fingerprint recognition is not possible if the user is not cooperative or if the light conditions are completely uncontrolled. Some examples of touch-based traits captured using touchless acquisitions are shown in Fig. 3.1.

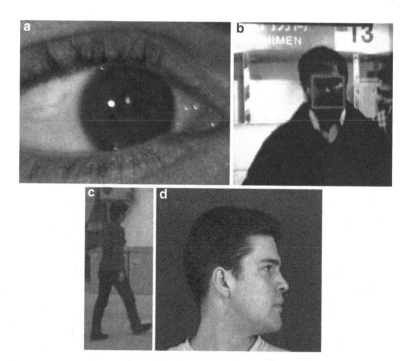

Fig. 3.2 Examples of touchless traits, captured using less-constrained acquisitions: (**a**) iris [101] (reproduced by permission of IEEE); (**b**) face [10] (reproduced by permission of Springer); (**c**) gait [320] (reproduced by permission of Springer); (**d**) ear shape [35] (reproduced by permission of IEEE)

In the case of biometric traits traditionally captured using touchless acquisitions, research is oriented toward designing and implementing biometric systems capable of working at greater distances, with a moving or non-cooperative subject, and with uncontrolled light conditions. However, the problems caused by non-frontal poses, adverse illumination, and excessive distances are still being studied. For example, in the case of the iris, off-axis poses and reflections can seriously reduce the recognition accuracy. Moreover, if the user is too distant from the camera, the iris pattern can be unusable. Some examples of touchless traits captured using less-constrained acquisitions are shown in Fig. 3.2.

Currently, there is no complete unconstrained biometric system with an accuracy comparable to the corresponding traditional system [294]. However, promising results have been obtained for fingerprint [83, 283], palmprint [261], palm vein [125, 256], hand geometry [313], iris [244], face [10], gait [320], and ear shape [35] recognition. Unconstrained recognition using soft biometric traits has also been studied [77].

3.2 Touchless Recognition of Touch-Based Biometric Traits

This section presents the methods reported in the literature for the touchless recognition of biometric traits traditionally captured using touch-based acquisitions. The most widely used touch-based biometric systems are based on the features of the hand, including the fingerprint, palmprint, palm vein, and hand geometry. Palmprint recognition systems are described in greater detail in Chap. 4.

3.2.1 Touchless Fingerprint Recognition

Several methods for touchless fingerprint recognition have been described. Traditional touch-based methods are complicated by the distortions and elastic deformation caused by the contact of the finger with the sensor and by the different pressures exerted on the sensor. Different conditions of the skin can also cause problems (e.g., dry/wet skin, worn-out ridges, sweat, etc.). In addition, dirt and latent fingerprints are left by the contact of the finger after each acquisition, reducing accuracy and increasing security problems [94, 283].

Biometric systems based on fingerprints captured using touchless sensors are designed to overcome these problems and increase user acceptability. Some people are unwilling to touch dirty sensors for cultural reasons or fears about the transmission of diseases. A touchless sensor could also reduce the level of cooperation needed and the speed of the acquisition. Touchless fingerprint systems are typically based on CCD cameras. However, the images captured by a CCD camera present lower contrast, a more complex background, and problems related to perspective effects (Fig. 3.3).

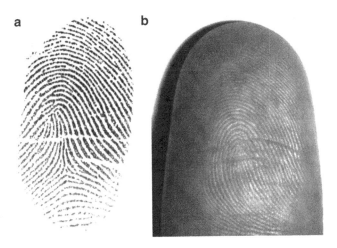

Fig. 3.3 Comparison of touch-based and touchless fingerprints: (**a**) touch-based fingerprint; (**b**) touchless fingerprint

Touchless fingerprint systems can be divided into systems based on two-dimensional samples and systems based on three-dimensional models. In the former, recognition is performed using a single sample captured by a CCD camera. These systems have the aforementioned advantages of touchless acquisition but suffer from perspective effects and a smaller area usable for biometric recognition compared to touch-based systems [78, 84, 93, 97, 98, 140, 149–151, 209, 287, 332]. However, methods based on mosaicking [50] or the use of ring mirrors [355] have been proposed to solve these problems.

By contrast, systems based on three-dimensional models provide a larger area for use in the recognition and can use a metric representation of the captured area. In particular, multiple-view setups [83, 85, 89, 273, 283, 284], photometric techniques [281], and structured light techniques [192, 360, 361] can be used to reconstruct a three-dimensional model. However, to ensure compatibility with existing databases, specific procedures must be used to map the three-dimensional model onto a two-dimensional image [140, 321, 361, 362, 416]. In the majority of cases, guided fingerprint placement and controlled light conditions are needed for correct recognition. Examples of systems used for the three-dimensional reconstruction of fingerprints are shown in Fig. 3.4. Methods for the generation of synthetic three-dimensional fingerprints have also been proposed [90, 92].

Generally, fingerprint images captured using a touchless acquisition system are not compatible with current recognition algorithms, which use high-contrast grayscale images [286] (Fig. 3.3a). Thus, many methods in the literature focus on image enhancement to compute a contact-equivalent acquisition [148–150, 210, 287], that can be processed by current recognition algorithms.

Methods for measuring the quality of touchless fingerprint images have also been proposed [88, 97].

3.2.2   Touchless Palm Vein Recognition

Current palm vein biometric recognition systems use either a CCD camera or a NIR camera to acquire the vascular pattern of the hand. However, the majority of these systems require the user to place his hand on a glass support. In some cases, pegs are also used to guide the user's hand into the correct position [256].

Similarly to the problems associated with touch-based fingerprint acquisitions discussed in Sect. 3.2.1, contact of the hand with a support can cause problems due to different pressures, dirt, skin conditions, or latent impressions.

To overcome the problems of touch-based systems, touchless palm vein acquisition systems have been proposed [125, 143, 252, 256, 425, 426]. The main challenge of these touchless acquisition devices is the need for fast image capture to avoid motion blur effects. Moreover, the acquisition setup must have sufficient depth of focus and controlled, uniform illumination [256]. However, the position of the hand must still be partially controlled because it must be open and oriented frontally toward the sensor. An example of a touchless palm vein setup is shown in Fig. 3.5.

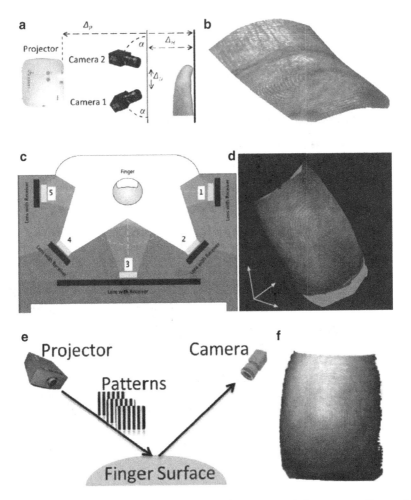

Fig. 3.4 Examples of three-dimensional reconstruction setups and the corresponding models: (**a**) two-view setup [83, 85] (reproduced by permission of IEEE); (**c**) multiple-view setup [284] (reproduced by permission of IEEE); (**e**) structured light illumination setup [361] (reproduced by permission of IEEE); (**b, d, f**) corresponding models for (**a**) [83, 85], (**c**) [284], and (**e**) [361], respectively (reproduced by permission of IEEE)

3.2.3 Touchless Hand Geometry Recognition

Biometric systems employing touch-based analysis of hand geometry can be divided into two categories [185, 329]: touch-based systems that use pegs to correctly place the hand on the sensor [174, 311] and touch-based systems that do not use pegs [381]. The majority of the commercial systems fall into the first category.

While systems based on hand geometry are among the most well accepted by users, several problems limit the use of traditional touch-based systems with pegs.

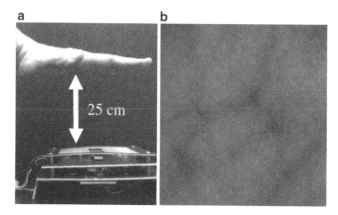

Fig. 3.5 Example of a touchless palm vein acquisition setup [252]: (**a**) acquisition setup; (**b**) corresponding sample (reproduced by permission of IEEE)

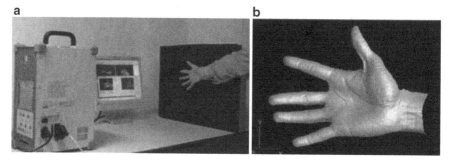

Fig. 3.6 Example of a laser scanner for the touchless acquisition of three-dimensional hand geometry [184–186]: (**a**) the laser scanner used in; (**b**) the corresponding model (reproduced by permission of IEEE)

It can be difficult for the elderly or those with impaired movements to place their hand according to the position of the pegs. There are also the typical problems associated with touch-based sensors, caused by dirt, sweat, or the application of different pressures on the sensor.

Several methods for performing touchless recognition based on hand geometry have been proposed. These methods can be divided into those that use two-dimensional samples and those that use three-dimensional models. The techniques that use two-dimensional samples are based on CCD cameras [33,104,184,251,259, 380], mobile phone cameras [313], or NIR cameras [119,258].

Techniques that use three-dimensional models are based on three-dimensional laser scanners [184–186] or structured light illumination [237,345]. An example of a laser scanner for the touchless acquisition of three-dimensional hand geometry is shown in Fig. 3.6.

3.3   Less-Constrained Recognition of Touchless Biometric Traits

This section describes the methods in the literature for performing less-constrained recognition of biometric traits traditionally captured via touchless acquisition. Specifically, techniques for less-constrained face and iris recognition are described. Methods based on gait, ear shape, and soft biometric traits are also presented.

3.3.1   Less-Constrained Face Recognition

Face recognition systems are highly accepted by users because the face is naturally used to recognize others. However, traditional face recognition systems require controlled acquisitions and a high level of cooperation because the user must stand still with a neutral expression at a certain distance and without covering parts of his face. In some cases, a uniform background is used. For these reasons, face recognition system are usually used for access control to borders, airports, or buildings, and in most cases, a trained user performs the recognition.

Uncontrolled situations pose challenging problems for biometric systems based on face recognition because these systems are extremely sensitive to illumination, pose, aging, and distance [10, 217, 423]. Uncooperative subjects also present difficulties in the recognition process. To address these challenges, many methods have been proposed for less-constrained face recognition systems. Different methods have been described to specifically solve (or mitigate) the problems caused by (a) illumination, (b) pose, and (c) aging:

- *Illumination.* Variations in illumination conditions are one of the most important challenges in the design of less-constrained face recognition systems. Several different techniques have been proposed to achieve illumination invariance. These techniques can be divided into subspace methods, reflectance model methods, and methods based on three-dimensional models. Subspace methods are based on capturing the generic face space and recognizing previously unanalyzed samples. Modified subspace methods have been proposed to achieve greater robustness with respect to illumination variations [346]. Methods based on a reflectance model use a Lambertian description of the reflections by considering a varying albedo field [23]. Methods based on three-dimensional models can use the depth information to increase robustness to local illumination variations, but more complex setups and algorithms are required [11, 27].
- *Pose.* Differences in the pose can be problematic for face recognition algorithms, and methods to compensate for pose variations have been described. Usually, these methods must compute the location of the same points in multiple acquisitions and then estimate the positions of the common points in three-dimensional space. As a result, methods based on three-dimensional models are better suited to compensate for pose variations [316, 414, 423].

- *Aging*. The aging of subjects can be a problem over both short (e.g., changes in beard or hair length) and long time intervals (e.g., matching the face of a child with the face of an adult). Long time intervals can be an issue in investigative or forensic applications. For this reason, methods have been proposed to compensate for aging by simulating older facial features [282] or extracting features that are invariant with respect to age differences [225].

The achievement of a less-constrained face recognition system could greatly increase the range of applications for biometric systems based on face traits. For example, less-constrained face recognition could be useful for applications in (a) surveillance, (b) authentication on mobile devices, or (c) advanced human–computer interfaces.

- *Surveillance Applications*. The ability to perform face recognition in unconstrained (or less-constrained) situations could be used to recognize individuals from surveillance footage, in an automatic way and without the subjects' knowledge. Currently, the analysis of surveillance footage is performed off-line and only in the case of a specific event (e.g., a search for a wanted person). However, face recognition from surveillance videos requires the design of algorithms compatible with subjects captured at a large distance, with considerable variations in pose, and with uncontrolled light conditions (e.g., dark images, reflections). Moreover, the subjects may be partially covering their face (e.g., hats, scarves). Some studies have reported improvements in using face recognition systems for surveillance applications [182, 422] and at distances greater than 15 m [371]. Automatic face indexing systems have also been proposed [51].
- *Authentication on Mobile Devices*. Face recognition systems can be integrated into mobile phones for user authentication. However, these systems must function with low-quality, noisy acquisitions under highly variable light conditions. Moreover, the algorithms must be fast to function correctly with low computational resources [42].
- *Advanced Human–Computer Interfaces*. Less-constrained face recognition systems could be used for the design of advanced human–computer interfaces, such as adaptive home environments, hands-free control of electronic devices (e.g., personal computers, consoles, home entertainment centers), and indoor monitoring of human activities [211, 285].

Some examples of the applications of less-constrained face recognition techniques are shown in Fig. 3.7.

3.3.2   Less-Constrained Iris Recognition

Conventional iris recognition techniques use very controlled acquisition procedures, require a cooperative subject, and are based on complex, expensive equipment. Moreover, the procedure is often considered invasive, and the infrared illumination

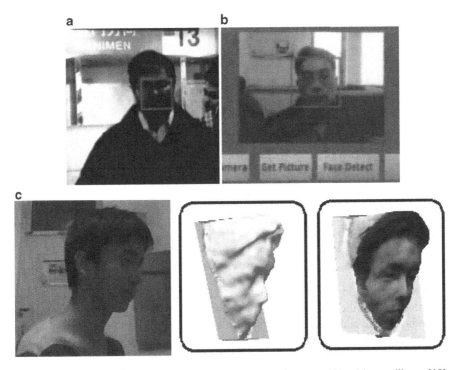

Fig. 3.7 Examples of the application of less-constrained face recognition: (**a**) surveillance [10] (reproduced by permission of IEEE); (**b**) mobile devices [42] (reproduced by permission of IEEE); (**c**) videogames [335] (reproduced by permission of IEEE)

is occasionally perceived (erroneously) as a health risk. For these reasons, biometric systems based on iris recognition are not widespread and are only used when high accuracy and speed are crucial (e.g., airports, borders, military installations).

Less-constrained iris recognition techniques that increase the distance between the eye and the sensor, decrease the level of cooperation needed, and decrease the need for controlled illumination techniques are being studied. Many techniques have been studied for performing iris recognition at a distance, on the move, or with natural illumination.

However, less-constrained iris recognition faces several challenges. The iris region of the eye is relatively small, wet, in continual motion, frequently reflective, and occluded by the eyelids and eyelashes. Even with traditional iris sensors, several trials are sometimes necessary to acquire an accurate sample from a non-expert user.

Current research is focused on improving the different steps involved in iris recognition. In particular, innovative methods for (a) segmentation, (b) gaze assessment, and (c) recognition algorithms are being studied.

- *Segmentation.* The purpose of the segmentation step is to locate the iris region of the eye in the captured images. This task is particularly critical in less-constrained systems because the iris region can be small and partially occluded and have an

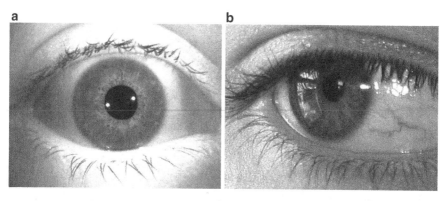

Fig. 3.8 Comparison of irises captured using a traditional acquisition and a less-constrained acquisition [86]: (**a**) traditional acquisition with infrared light; (**b**) less-constrained acquisition captured with natural illumination. The image in (**b**) presents problems related to off-axis orientation, reflections, and occlusions (reproduced by permission of Springer)

off-axis orientation [86] (Fig. 3.8). Moreover, correct segmentation is crucial and directly affects the accuracy of iris recognition systems. For these reasons, several methods have addressed the problem of segmenting the iris in less-constrained acquisitions using computational intelligence [293], active contours [322], or incremental approaches [101]. Methods based on statistical approaches [86] or more complex techniques [318, 319] are used for the segmentation of reflections and occlusions.

- *Gaze Assessment.* In less-constrained iris recognition systems, acquisitions captured using a non-frontal point of view can be challenging. Because these acquisitions can reduce the accuracy of the biometric recognition, methods to estimate the gaze must be designed [317]. Alternatively, multiple cameras can be used to compensate for the effect [55].
- *Recognition.* Images acquired under less-constrained conditions present a less visible iris pattern than images captured using a traditional constrained setup with infrared illumination. Thus, dedicated methods for the enhancement, feature extraction, and matching of iris images captured under less-constrained situations must be designed. A method for the enhancement of iris images captured using a biometric portal is described in [268]. A comparison of the matching performances of different methods operating under different less-constrained situations is described in [32].

Iris recognition systems can be classified based on the techniques used to locate the iris in the captured image, the distance between the user and the sensor, and the level of cooperation required [336]. Based on the combination of these features, the following seven types of iris recognition systems can be defined (Fig. 3.9):

Fig. 3.9 The classification of the different less-constrained iris recognition systems proposed in [336]

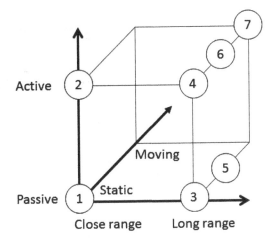

1. *Close Range Iris Recognition.* This method is the most diffuse type of iris recognition and requires the eye to be placed a small distance from the sensor. In addition, the user must stand still during the acquisition.
2. *Active Iris Recognition.* In these systems, the iris is captured at a small distance, but the user does not need to remain still during the acquisition because active cameras automatically locate the iris and adjust their position accordingly. Typically, a wide-angle camera is first used to estimate the position of the iris, and then the camera used for acquiring the iris is moved to the correct position [82].
3. *Iris Recognition at a Distance.* These systems are based on passive cameras that are capable of long-range acquisitions. However, the user must be cooperative and remain still during the acquisition. At large distances, dedicated algorithms must be used to locate and process the iris [113].
4. *Active Iris Recognition at a Distance.* To perform iris recognition at a distance, these systems use active cameras, which autonomously locate the iris and reduce the level of cooperation needed. However, the user must remain still during the acquisition [81].
5. *Passive Iris Recognition on the Move.* In this type of system, the iris is captured as the user moves. However, the walking path must be controlled, and the cooperation of the user is needed. Examples of these systems are iris recognition systems installed on gates. A system composed of multiple passive cameras for iris recognition on the move is described in [245].
6. *Active Iris Recognition on the Move.* In these systems, active cameras are used to automatically locate the irises of people moving in front of a camera. Compared to passive systems used to perform iris recognition on the move, these systems can reduce the level of cooperation needed. However, no example of this type of system has been reported.
7. *Active Iris Recognition for Surveillance.* In surveillance applications, iris recognition must be performed in a completely unconstrained way using a network of active cameras that are capable of locating and extracting the iris pattern of

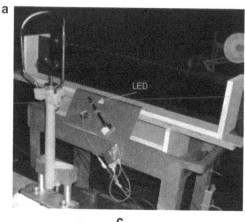

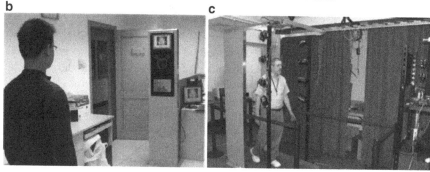

Fig. 3.10 Examples of less-constrained iris recognition systems: (**a**) iris recognition at a distance [113] (reproduced by permission of Springer); (**b**) active iris recognition at a distance [81] (reproduced by permission of IEEE); (**c**) passive iris recognition on the move [245] (reproduced by permission of IEEE)

individuals walking in non-predetermined paths. While this type of system has not yet been designed, its design would expand the range of applications for iris recognition systems.

Some examples of the described categories are shown in Fig. 3.10.

3.3.3 Less-Constrained Gait Recognition

Biometric systems based on gait use frame sequences captured with CCD cameras to perform recognition [41]. Currently, gait recognition methods require little cooperation by users, are non-intrusive, and can work at distances up to tens of meters. However, some studies have proposed the design of gait recognition systems that are even less constrained, for example, by achieving pose invariance [320] or by performing recognition at greater distances [409].

3.3.4 Less-Constrained Ear Shape Recognition

Biometric systems based on ear shape currently represent a non-intrusive means of recognition that is capable of working at great distances and with low-quality images [154]. However, completely unconstrained ear shape recognition [35], even in the case of moving subjects [300], has recently been proposed.

3.3.5 Less-Constrained Soft Biometric Recognition

Soft biometric traits are particularly well-suited for less-constrained recognition. While they cannot be used to perform a strong biometric recognition because of their lack of distinctiveness, they can be captured from uncooperative subjects using unobtrusive methods and at great distances [77, 168, 305]. Soft biometric traits are particularly useful when stronger biometric recognition methods are not possible (e.g., surveillance applications), the number of users to be recognized is sufficiently small, or high accuracy is not necessary (e.g., applications that use continuous authentication).

The method described in [75] is proposed for surveillance applications and uses gender and race information to perform preliminary screening for different biometric recognition methods. The deployment of a multi-camera network is proposed in [76] to recognize individuals based on their color and height information. The method described in [77] uses the color and height of three different parts of the body (head, torso, legs). Gait, height, size, and gender are used in combination in the work described in [299]. A method designed for the unconstrained estimation of the weight of walking individuals is described in [91]. Techniques for weight estimation can be particularly useful in forensic applications because, in many cases, the weight of a person can be inferred from an analysis of a scene. A biometric system for continuous authentication is proposed in [271] and uses information related to the face and clothes.

3.4 Summary

Less-constrained biometric systems can overcome the limitations of traditional biometric systems, which generally require high levels of cooperation, controlled situations, and constraints on user placement. To achieve these goals, advanced techniques must be developed for adaptive acquisitions and the preprocessing of biometric samples. Moreover, innovative biometric features must be defined, and compatibility with existing systems must be ensured.

Less-constrained systems are currently less accurate than traditional biometric systems. Less-constrained systems present different challenges for the acquisition of biometric traits traditionally captured using touch-based acquisitions compared to those traditionally captured using touchless acquisitions. For the former, techniques must be developed for biometric acquisition and processing using images captured by a CCD camera. In this context, less-constrained systems for touchless fingerprint, palmprint, hand geometry, and palm vein recognition have been proposed. For the latter, techniques must be designed to accurately acquire biometric traits at larger distances, with less user cooperation and uncontrolled light conditions. To meet these challenges, less-constrained systems for face, iris, gait, ear shape, and soft biometric traits have been proposed.

Chapter 4
Palmprint Biometrics

The investigation of palmprint recognition as a biometric technology has increased in the last 15 years. Palmprint recognition has many features in common with biometric systems based on fingerprint analysis, and research in the field of palmprint recognition has advanced rapidly due to experience gained in the recognition of fingerprints. Similarly to fingerprints, palmprints possess many distinctive features and can be used for highly accurate biometric recognition. However, compared to fingerprints, palmprints have better user acceptability, can be acquired with low-cost devices, and can be used to extract biometric samples from elderly people or manual workers. Moreover, numerous types of features, at different levels of detail, can be extracted based on the type of acquisition used.

Traditionally, touch-based acquisition systems are used to capture palmprint samples. In some cases, physical constraints are used to guide the placement of the hand. However, such constraints can pose difficulties for elderly people or people with mobility problems. Touch-based systems are also subject to problems related to dirt, sweat, latent impressions, and cultural factors. For these reasons, research is currently focused on the use of touchless and less-constrained acquisition systems.

In this chapter, the state-of-the-art in palmprint recognition systems is described. After introducing palmprint recognition, a survey of the possible applications of palmprint recognition is presented. Then, biometric systems based on the palmprint are discussed. First, touch-based methods are reviewed. Touchless methods for palmprint recognition are then described. For both categories, methods that use two-dimensional samples and methods that use three-dimensional models are considered. The techniques used to estimate the quality of palmprint samples and their classification are reviewed. Finally, the methods used to generate synthetic palmprint samples are introduced.

© Springer International Publishing Switzerland 2014
A. Genovese et al., *Touchless Palmprint Recognition Systems*,
Advances in Information Security 60, DOI 10.1007/978-3-319-10365-5_4

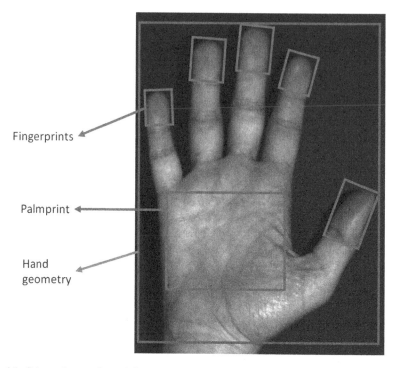

Fingerprints

Palmprint

Hand
geometry

Fig. 4.1 Schematic overview of the palmprint as well as the other biometric traits of the hand, according to the size of the analyzed area

4.1   Introduction to Palmprint Recognition

Palmprint recognition systems are a specific category of hand-based biometric systems that perform recognition by focusing on the area of the hand from the wrist to the base of the fingers. More specifically, palmprint-based systems analyze the skin that covers the inner surface of the hand, which is the same type of skin that covers the fingerprints. A schematic overview of the palmprint and other biometric traits of the hand, according to the size of the analyzed area, is shown in Fig. 4.1.

The palmprint area features three principal lines (or flexion creases), several wrinkles (or secondary creases), and a series of ridges (similar to those that compose fingerprints) that cover the entire palm area. Moreover, the ridges create several features similar to those found in fingerprints, such as singular points and minutiae. The principal lines and major wrinkles are formed between the third and fifth months of prenatal development [38], whereas the other lines do not appear until after birth. Moreover, the three principal lines are dependent on genetic information, while the other lines are not [198]. As in the case of fingerprints, identical twins also possess different palmprint features [198]. Different relationships have been established between palmprint features and genetic diseases [427].

Fig. 4.2 The different
regions of the palm

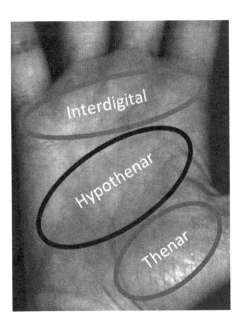

The palm area can be divided into three zones: the thenar, hypothenar, and inter-digital zones [170] (Fig. 4.2). Some studies have proposed biometric recognition of individuals using the thenar area of the palmprint [412, 429, 430].

Depending on the acquisition device used, palmprints can be analyzed at different levels of detail, ranging from a high-detail analysis of the minutiae and ridges to the analysis of texture information captured using low-resolution images. Accurate recognition can be achieved, even with low-cost hardware and at distances greater than those possible for the recognition of fingerprints. Moreover, palmprint recognition methods can be easily integrated into hand-based multibio-metric systems [186].

In this section, the main features of the palmprint are described, and the structure of biometric systems based on palmprint analysis is presented. Then, the approaches used to classify the various methods in the literature are detailed.

4.1.1 Palmprint Features

The features used for palmprint recognition can be divided into the following five categories, according to the level of detail used in analyzing the palmprint images [231, 406]:

- *Geometry Features* are the features related to the geometric shape of the palm, such as its width, length, and area (Fig. 4.3). These features are easy to collect, even with low-resolution devices, but feature low distinctiveness. In some cases,

Fig. 4.3 Geometry features, principal lines, and wrinkles of the hand

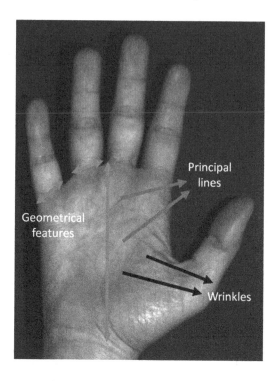

these features are regarded as aspects of hand geometry and are not considered typical of the palmprint itself.

- *Principal line features* include the three principal lines (or flexion creases) present on the palm of every person's hand (Fig. 4.3). These features are important for palmprint recognition because they feature high collectability and permanence and can be captured with low-resolution devices. However, they feature low distinctiveness and can be easily faked. Four different principal palm lines can be defined: the heart line, the head line, the life line, and the fate line (Fig. 4.4).
- *Wrinkle features* can be considered as secondary lines (or secondary creases) and are distinctive because of their high irregularity (Fig. 4.3). These features exhibit good collectability but are less permanent than principal lines and can be faked.
- *Delta point features* are similar to the delta points extracted from fingerprints and correspond to the points where the local ridge orientation is similar to the Greek letter Δ (delta). These features have high permanence but are less distinctive than minutiae features. Moreover, their visualization requires highresolution devices.
- *Minutiae features* are similar to the features typically used for fingerprint recognition and correspond to the points where the ridges of the palmprint merge, bifurcate, end, or start. They are highly distinctive and permanent. However, their acquisition requires the use of high-resolution devices.

Fig. 4.4 The four principal palm lines [5]: (*1*) the heart line; (*2*) the head line; (*3*) the life line; (*4*) the fate line (not always present)

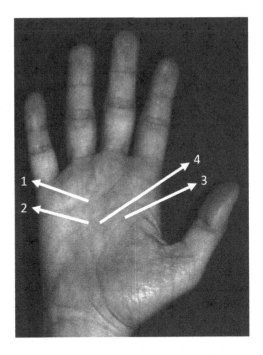

- *Level 3 features* include features such as pores, incipient ridges, or scars. Similarly to minutiae features, level 3 features have high distinctiveness and can be used for the analysis of latent impressions. However, their capture requires devices with very high resolution.

Depending on the desired level of detail, it is possible to use images captured with resolutions ranging from 150 dpi or less and up to 400 dpi or more [196]. In fact, some palmprint recognition systems use high-resolution images to capture the details of the ridges and the minutiae [109, 327]. High-resolution images are often used for forensic applications [3, 66]. However, the majority of research is currently focused on the use of low-resolution images for civil and commercial applications.

Several methods that employ the three-dimensional structure of the palmprint have recently been proposed. The three-dimensional depth of palmprint features is difficult to fake and is more robust to spoofing attacks [406]. However, more complex equipment is required. An example of a three-dimensional model of a palmprint is shown in Fig. 4.5.

4.1.2 Structure of Palmprint Recognition Systems

Based on the definitions of biometric system modalities presented in Sect. 2.2, palmprint recognition systems can be used i n both authentication and identification

Fig. 4.5 Example of a three-dimensional model of a palmprint [219] (reproduced by permission of IEEE)

modes [231]. Methods for optimizing the performance of systems working in the identification modality are presented in [390, 395].

The process of palmprint recognition follows the general structure of biometric systems described in Sect. 2.2 and can be divided into the following steps [231]:

1. *Acquisition.* The techniques used for the acquisition of palmprint samples can be divided into offline or online techniques. Offline acquisition techniques include rolled inked acquisitions and forensic methods for the extraction of latent palmprints. Online acquisition techniques can be based on optical devices, digital scanners, CCD (or CMOS) cameras, or video cameras. CCD-based and video-based techniques can require contact of the palmprint with a surface or use touchless acquisition methods. Structured light illumination systems based on a DLP projector and a CCD camera are also used to capture the three-dimensional model of the palmprint.

2. *Segmentation and Registration.* The methods used for the segmentation and registration of palmprint samples usually binarize the input image to extract the contour of the hand and then detect some keypoints that are used to align the images. Usually, the spaces between the fingers are used as reference points. Then, a reference coordinate system is adjusted using the extracted keypoints, and the central part of the hand (the actual palmprint) is extracted.

3. *Image Enhancement.* Different image enhancement procedures have been proposed, depending on which features are used to perform the recognition. The image enhancement algorithms used for palmprint recognition include edge detectors (e.g., Canny, Sobel, derivative, or ad-hoc edge detectors), the Hough transform, wavelet transforms, the Fourier transform, and Gabor filters.

4. *Feature Extraction.* The features that can be used for palmprint recognition include the edges corresponding to the principal and secondary lines as well as their magnitude and orientation, the coefficients of the transform function used (e.g., Hough, wavelet, Fourier), the magnitude and orientation of the filter response (e.g., magnitude of the Gabor-filtered image), texture descriptors (e.g.,

local binary pattern (LBP)), statistical measures, and the positions of certain points of interest (e.g., delta points, minutiae). Some techniques use feature extraction methods based on Principal Component Analysis (PCA), Linear Discriminant analysis (LDA), or Independent Component Analysis (ICA).
5. *Matching.* Matching functions include the Euclidean distance between the feature vectors, Artificial Neural Networks, Support Vector Machines (SVM), the Root Mean Square distance, and the Hamming distance.

4.1.3   Classification of Palmprint Recognition Approaches

Palmprint recognition methods can be classified based on the techniques used to extract and match the features or the type of acquisition device used.

In the literature, approaches are usually classified based on the techniques used to extract and match the features [196], yielding five categories:

1. *Ridge-based approaches* use the pattern of the ridges, the position of the delta points, and the location of the minutiae to perform recognition. These methods are derived from the methods used for touch-based fingerprint recognition and are traditionally adopted for offline palmprint acquisitions or for palmprints captured using an optical device.
2. *Line-based approaches* focus on the extraction of the principal and secondary lines of the palmprint. They are traditionally based on the use of edge detectors to extract the lines. The extracted lines are matched according to their position or direction or by using edge descriptors.
3. *Subspace-based approaches* use feature extraction methods such as PCA, LDA, or ICA. Feature extraction is performed directly on the input sample or on the image obtained after performing a transformation using wavelets, Fourier transform, kernels, or Gabor filtering. The subspace coefficients are considered as features, and different distance measures can be used to classify the extracted features.
4. *Statistical approaches* can be divided into methods based on local or global statistics. In the former, the image is divided into several subregions, and local statistics (e.g., mean and variance) are computed for each region and considered as features. In the latter, global statistics are computed directly for the entire image. Image transformations (e.g., wavelets, Gabor filters, Fourier transform) can be applied. Several distance measures can be used for classification.
5. *Coding-based approaches* apply a preliminary filter to the image and then encode the result by quantizing the magnitude or phase of the response. The most widely used coding-based methods are based on PalmCode and its derivatives. These methods use a Gabor filtering procedure on the input image and then encode the phase information as a bit string. The Hamming distance is used to compute the similarity between the templates.

Fig. 4.6 Example of an
inked palmprint acquisition
[407] (reproduced by
permission of Springer)

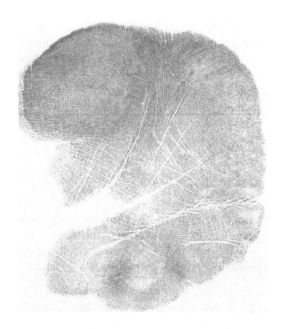

Palmprint recognition approaches can also be classified based on the type of acquisition device used to capture the samples, resulting in the definition of four categories, depending on the type of contact needed (touch-based or touchless) and the type of sample used (two-dimensional or three-dimensional):

1. *Touch-based two-dimensional methods* can be divided into offline and online methods. Offline methods include the scanning of inked palmprints (Fig. 4.6) and the lifting of latent impressions (Fig. 4.7).

   Online methods use an acquisition device that requires the user to place his hand on a fixed support to capture a two-dimensional sample of the palmprint. This category includes methods based on optical devices (Fig. 4.8), digital scanners (Fig. 4.9), and CCD-based devices (Fig. 4.10).

2. *Touch-based three-dimensional methods* use an acquisition device that requires the user to place his hand on a fixed support. Then, structured light illumination techniques are used to reconstruct a three-dimensional model of the palmprint (Fig. 4.11). In most cases, a two-dimensional sample is also captured.

3. *Touchless two-dimensional methods* are based on CCD cameras, smartphone cameras, or video cameras. These methods can be used to design a low-cost, less-constrained palmprint recognition system.

4. *Touchless three-dimensional methods* are based on three-dimensional laser scanners (Fig. 4.12) and enable accurate, less-constrained palmprint recognition. However, the cost of these acquisition devices is high.

A taxonomy of the methods based on the type of the acquisition device used is shown in Fig. 4.13.

Fig. 4.7 Example of a latent
palmprint [170] (reproduced
by permission of IEEE)

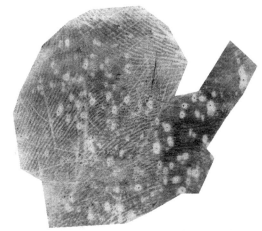

Fig. 4.8 Example of a
two-dimensional palmprint
acquisition captured using an
optical device [70]
(reproduced by permission of
IEEE)

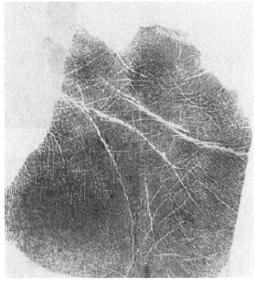

Offline palmprint recognition methods based on two-dimensional samples are usually used for investigative and forensic applications and are not suitable for real-time applications.

Online palmprint recognition methods using touch-based, two-dimensional CCD acquisition devices offer good-quality samples and short acquisition times. Thus, these methods can be used for real-time applications. Moreover, compared to optical devices, they can offer a greater number of details at intermediate resolution. Touch-based CCD acquisition devices usually use pegs to constrain the user's hand in a particular position [407]. However, the presence of pegs can be problematic for the elderly or those with muscular or joint problems (e.g., arthritis). Therefore, some methods use pegless CCD-based acquisition devices [203] or are based on

Fig. 4.9 Example of a
two-dimensional palmprint
acquisition captured using a
digital flatbed scanner [279]
(reproduced by permission of
IEEE)

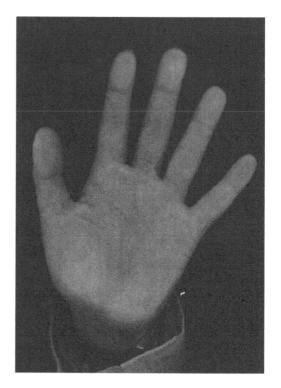

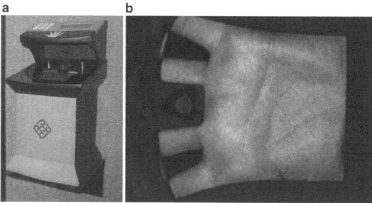

Fig. 4.10 Example of a CCD-based device for touch-based, two-dimensional palmprint acquisition used in [231]: (**a**) the device; (**b**) the corresponding sample (reproduced by permission of Springer)

digital scanners [278]. Palmprint recognition systems based on digital scanners can be produced with low-cost equipment (e.g., off-the-shelf scanners) but require a long scanning time and are thus not as wellsuited for real-time applications.

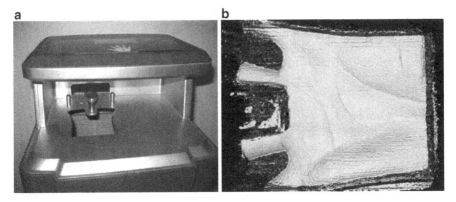

Fig. 4.11 Example of a structured light illumination device for touch-based, three-dimensional palmprint acquisition used in [404]: (a) the device; (b) the corresponding sample (reproduced by permission of IEEE)

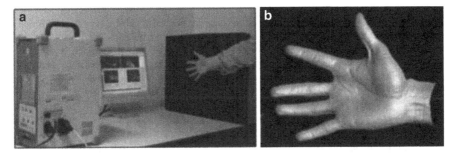

Fig. 4.12 Example of a 3D laser scanner for touchless, three-dimensional palmprint acquisition used in [186]: (a) the device; (b) the corresponding sample (reproduced by permission of IEEE)

Three-dimensional touch-based methods have recently been developed to increase recognition accuracy and robustness to lighting, occlusions, noise, and spoofing attacks [219] compared to two-dimensional CCD acquisition devices.

However, all touch-based methods are subject to distortion, dirt, and sweat as well as potential problems with user acceptability because some people may not want to touch a sensor that has been touched by the hands of other people. Hands are frequently dirty or sweaty. Touchless acquisition devices have been investigated [141], but touchless methods generally have lower contrast, a more complex background, and non-uniform acquisition distances and are sensitive to lighting conditions.

To overcome the problems of touchless acquisitions and achieve a greater accuracy, three-dimensional touchless methods [186] have been proposed. Importantly, three-dimensional touchless systems are more robust to different acquisition distances, lighting conditions, different backgrounds, noise, and spoofing attacks. However, they require more complex, expensive setups.

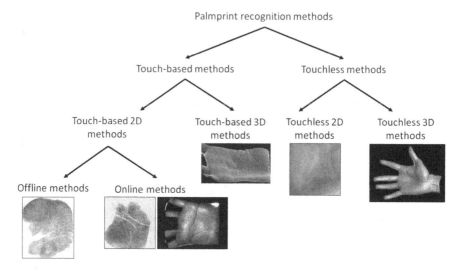

Fig. 4.13 Classification of palmprint recognition approaches based on the type of acquisition device used (the images for touch-based, two-dimensional, offline methods [407], touch-based, two-dimensional, online methods [231] are reproduced by permission of Springer; the images for touch-based, two-dimensional, online methods [70], touch-based, three-dimensional methods [219], touchless, two-dimensional methods [103], and touchless, three-dimensional methods [186] are reproduced by permission of IEEE)

In this chapter, palmprint recognition methods are classified according to the type of acquisition device used. For each category, the different methods used in each step of the recognition process are described, including the techniques used for acquisition, segmentation, image enhancement, feature extraction and matching

In the remainder of the chapter, some applications of palmprint recognition systems are discussed (Sect. 4.2). Touch-based methods for palmprint recognition are also described (Sect. 4.3) and a distinction is made between methods based on two-dimensional images and three-dimensional samples. Touchless methods are described (Sect. 4.4), including methods that use two-dimensional images and three-dimensional samples. Then, the methods used to estimate the quality of palmprint biometric samples (Sect. 4.5) and classify them (Sect. 4.6) are reviewed. To conclude the chapter, methods for the generation of synthetic palmprint samples (Sect. 4.7) are introduced.

4.2   Applications of Palmprint Recognition Systems

Palmprint recognition systems can be used in different contexts. One of the first applications of palmprint recognition was the analysis of latent palmprints in forensic applications [34, 170, 226]. Latent palmprints are frequently found at crime scenes [79] and can provide a greater recognition area than fingerprints. In this context, high-resolution devices for palmprint scanning [66] have been designed, and the Automated Palmprint Identification System (APIS) has been developed [3].

However, the majority of palmprint recognition devices are designed for civil access control applications [231] and use touch-based acquisition systems. Different acquisition techniques can be used to capture the palmprint sample, such as digital scanners, CCD cameras, or video cameras [196]. Multispectral imaging systems are also used [399].

Several approaches have recently been described for personal authentication systems based on webcams [118, 141, 250] and mobile phones [52, 122, 142, 175, 212, 257]. Studies on palmprint recognition in less-constrained environments have also been reported [118, 141, 249].

4.3   Touch-Based Palmprint Recognition

This section contains a description of the methods used for performing palmprint recognition using a touch-based acquisition of the hand. Methods based on two-dimensional images and three-dimensional models are reviewed.

4.3.1   Two-Dimensional Touch-Based Palmprint Recognition

Two-dimensional touch-based palmprint recognition methods require the user to place the palm of his hand on a surface to capture a two-dimensional image, which is used as a biometric sample. Different acquisition devices can be used, including optical devices, digital scanners (with live or inked acquisitions), and CCD-based acquisition devices. In this section, touch-based two-dimensional acquisition methods are reviewed. In particular, the four different steps of acquisition, segmentation and registration, image enhancement, feature extraction and matching are discussed.

4.3.1.1   Acquisition

Two-dimensional touch-based palmprint acquisition techniques can be divided into offline and online techniques. Offline techniques include the scanning of ink-based acquisitions and the lifting of latent prints. Online acquisition devices include optical devices, digital scanners, and CCD-based devices operating in visible light or different wavelengths:

- *Offline Techniques*:

  1. Ink-based acquisition using a digital scanner;
  2. Acquisition of a latent palmprint.

Fig. 4.14 Example of an inked palmprint acquisition [407] (reproduced by permission of Springer)

- *Online Techniques*:

    1. Acquisition using an optical device;
    2. Live acquisition using a digital scanner;
    3. CCD-based acquisition in visible light;
    4. CCD-based multispectral acquisition.

Ink-Based Acquisition Using a Digital Scanner

The use of ink-based offline acquisitions with low resolution (100 dpi) for palmprint recognition has been investigated in preliminary research to evaluate the feasibility of palmprints as a biometric recognition system [327, 405]. Similar methods using high-resolution (500 dpi) images have recently been studied for forensic applications [213, 214, 417, 419].

Ink-based acquisition methods involve inking the palm of the user and pressing it onto a white sheet of paper. Then, the paper is digitized using a flatbed scanner to capture the palmprint (Fig. 4.14). A method involving placement of the hand on a rubber surface that is subsequently used to print the palmprint on a sheet of paper is described in [109]. After printing, the sheet is scanned using a digital scanner.

These methods can only be used for offline recognition and are not suitable for real-time acquisitions. Moreover, the acquisition procedure is highly dependent on

Fig. 4.15 Example of a
latent palmprint [170]
(reproduced by permission of
IEEE)

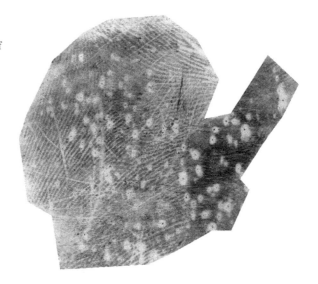

the expertise of the operator because the proper amount of ink must be used. The use
of either too much or too little ink can yield low-quality acquisitions. A document
containing practical guidelines for inked palmprint acquisition has been released by
the FBI [116]. Moreover, a revision of the ANSI NIST ITL-2000 Type 15 standard
for the exchange of palmprint data is currently underway [266].

Acquisition of a Latent Palmprint

Several studies have addressed the offline analysis of latent palmprints
[169, 170, 207, 208, 226, 330, 337, 357, 424]. A resolution of 500 dpi is the standard
in forensic applications [170]. However, specific techniques must be used by an
expert operator to lift latent palmprints [117] (Fig. 4.15). A specific method has
been proposed to identify the left palm given the right palm and vice versa using
latent palmprints [138].

Acquisition Using an Optical Device

Some methods for palmprint recognition use samples captured using an optical
device [66] (Fig. 4.16), similar to those used for touch-based fingerprint recognition.
These methods use high-resolution images (500 dpi) to extract features related to
ridges, singular points, or minutiae, in addition to the features of the principal and
secondary palm lines [39, 70, 71, 153]. Some databases of palmprints captured using
optical devices are publicly available [71].

Fig. 4.16 Example of a
palmprint captured using an
optical device [71]
(reproduced by permission of
IEEE)

Live Acquisition Using a Digital Scanner

Digital scanners are used in several cases for palmprint acquisition because they can be incorporated into low-cost palmprint recognition systems. In addition, it is relatively easy to place the hand in a correct position, and the majority of users are familiar with the device. However, acquisition times can be long, depending on the resolution used and the quality of the scanner hardware. Moreover, distortions due to the pressure of the hand on the surface of the scanner are often present in the thenar and hypothenar regions of the palm (Fig. 4.17).

Several methods using digital scanners to design low-cost palmprint recognition systems have been described [65,123,183,242,265,275–280,297,302,326,356,363–368,385,386]. A variety of different resolutions have been used, ranging from 72 to 300 dpi.

Multibiometric methods based on palmprints captured using digital scanners have also been described. Specifically, palmprint samples obtained by this method have been combined with facial features [301], hand geometry [54, 124, 379], and fingerprints [187].

CCD-Based Acquisition in Visible Light

The majority of devices used for the touch-based acquisition of palmprint images with a CCD camera operate with visible light illumination and have a general structure that includes a camera and a transparent support. To perform the acquisition, the user must place his hand on the transparent surface. The advantages of CCD

Fig. 4.17 Example of a palmprint captured using a digital scanner [279]. Distortions are visible in the thenar and hypothenar regions of the palm (reproduced by permission of IEEE)

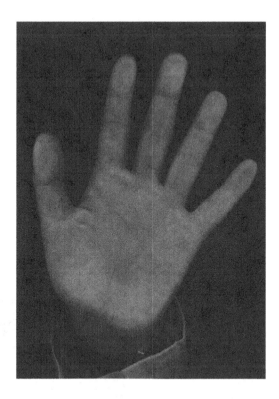

based devices are that the acquisition can be performed in a short period of time (almost instantly). The use of a surface placed at a fixed distance helps to reduce motion blur and to control the focus and acquisition distance. Moreover, the surface enhances the user experience because people naturally tend to place their hand on a surface. However, this type of acquisition method is subject to the typical problems associated with touch-based acquisitions, such as dirt, sweat, and latent impressions.

The majority of the palmprint recognition methods that have been described [16, 110, 135, 152, 176, 177, 195, 197, 218, 220, 233, 241, 264, 269, 270, 292, 323, 358, 359, 374, 377, 390, 395, 396, 402] are based on palmprint samples captured using the CCD-based acquisition device described in [402]. This device requires the user to place his hand on a glass surface and includes a series of pegs used to constrain the hand in a fixed position, which simplifies the subsequent segmentation and alignment processes [402] (Fig. 4.18a). That particular device captures images at 75 dpi (Fig. 4.18b). A database of palmprints captured using this device is publicly available [341].

Several multibiometric systems based on the samples captured using the device described in [402] have been proposed. For example, methods for the fusion of palmprint biometric data with facial features [133, 179, 180, 232, 298, 351, 384, 432] and features obtained from the finger knuckle [410] have been described.

Fig. 4.18 The touch-based
two-dimensional CCD
acquisition device described
in [402]: (**a**) schematic of the
device; (**b**) example of an
acquisition (reproduced by
permission of IEEE)

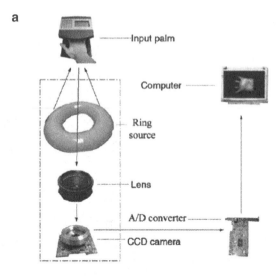

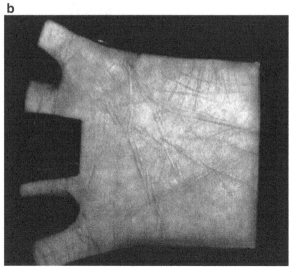

Other touch-based two-dimensional acquisition devices based on digital cameras
have been described [12, 203, 224, 408]. A device comprising a low-cost CMOS
camera, a ring illuminator, and a casing that provides a transparent support for
the palm of the hand is described in [224] (Fig. 4.19a). The device was designed
to be small so that it could be used as a personal identification device for online
applications. The devices captures images with a resolution of 65 dpi (Fig. 4.19b).
A similar device for low-cost recognition is described in [203] (Fig. 4.20)

A real-time recognition device is described in [408]. This device is composed of
a CCD camera, a ring illuminator, and a casing that provides support for the user's

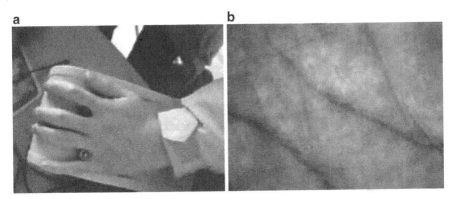

Fig. 4.19 The touch-based two-dimensional CCD acquisition device described in [224]: (**a**) the device; (**b**) example of acquisition (reproduced by permission of IEEE)

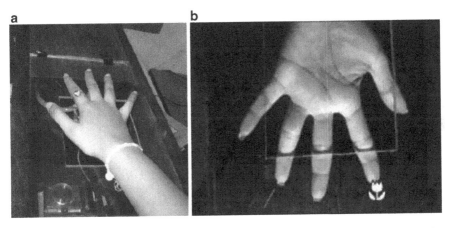

Fig. 4.20 The touch-based two-dimensional CCD acquisition device described in [203]: (**a**) the device; (**b**) example of acquisition (reproduced by permission of IEEE)

hand (Fig. 4.21a). This device captures high-resolution samples to use the pattern of ridges for recognition (Fig. 4.21b).

A low-cost device with reduced acquisition constraints is described in [12]. With this device, the user is free to move his hand across the acquisition surface, and the background is uncontrolled (Fig. 4.22).

CCD-Based Multispectral Acquisition

Several studies have proposed acquisition devices that can capture palmprint samples using different illumination wavelengths. Importantly, different wavelengths penetrate the human skin to different depths, enhancing different details [136]. An evaluation of the best wavelengths for the enhancement of palmprint details

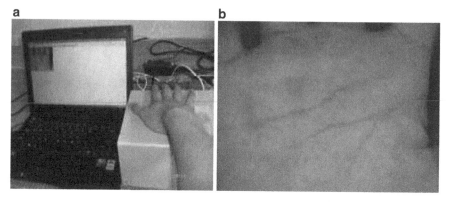

Fig. 4.21 The touch-based two-dimensional CCD acquisition device described in [408]: (**a**) the device; (**b**) example of acquisition (reproduced by permission of IEEE)

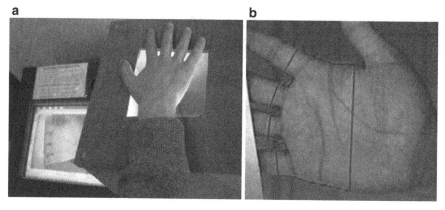

Fig. 4.22 The touch-based two-dimensional CCD acquisition device described in [12]: (**a**) the device; (**b**) example of acquisition (reproduced by permission of Elsevier)

is described in [134]. A combination of 580 nm (yellow spectrum), 760 nm (red spectrum) and 990 nm (NIR spectrum) wavelengths provided the best results. The database used for the experiments is publicly available [339].

The majority of multispectral palmprint recognition methods [68, 134, 139, 188, 199, 230, 248, 325, 348, 382, 399, 413] tested have used samples captured using the device described in [139, 399] (Fig. 4.23). This device uses four different illuminators emitting red, green, blue, and NIR wavelengths of light to enhance the different details of the palmprint. Then, a standard low-cost CCD camera is used to capture the images, which are taken at short time intervals (Fig. 4.23b–e). A database of multispectral palmprint samples captured using this device is publicly available [340].

Several multibiometric systems based on multispectral acquisition devices have been described for the joint recognition of palmprint and palm vein features [36,234,

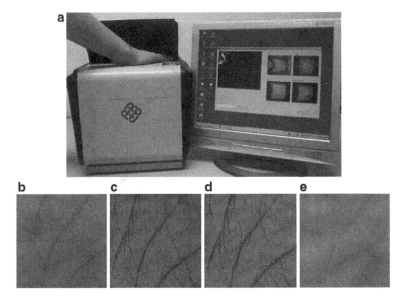

Fig. 4.23 The touch-based two-dimensional CCD multispectral acquisition device described in [399]: (**a**) the device; (**b**) acquisition with the red illuminator; (**c**) acquisition with the green illuminator; (**d**) acquisition with the blue illuminator; (**e**) acquisition with the NIR illuminator (reproduced by permission of IEEE)

353,354,400]. For example, the device described in [234,400] uses two light sources to illuminate the palm, which is placed on a glass surface (Fig. 4.24a). A blue LED is used as the illumination source for capturing the palmprint with visible light, while a NIR illuminator is used to enhance the details of the vein pattern of the hand. A standard low-cost CCD camera is used to capture the two images (Fig. 4.24b, c), with a short time interval between the two acquisitions.

The method described in [36,354] uses an image-level fusion scheme to generate a combined image from two acquisitions, one captured with visible light and one captured using NIR illumination. A similar device is proposed in [353].

4.3.1.2 Segmentation and Registration

The purpose of the segmentation and registration step (or preprocessing step) is to extract and align the region of interest (ROI) of the palmprint image. In the majority of the approaches in the literature, the segmentation and registration step can be divided into four phases:

1. Binarization of the palm image and extraction of the contours of the hand;
2. Detection of the keypoints and establishment of a coordinate system;
3. Extraction of the central part of the palm;
4. Registration.

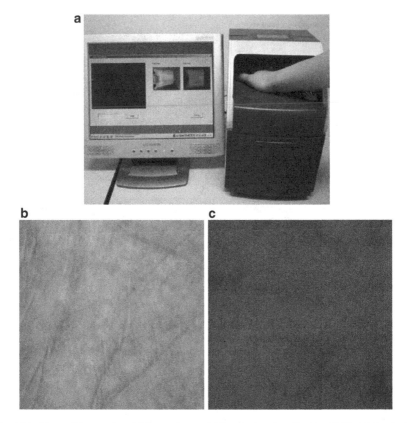

Fig. 4.24 The multispectral multibiometric acquisition device described in [400]: (**a**) the device; (**b**) palmprint acquisition with the blue LED illuminator; (**c**) palm vein acquisition with the NIR illuminator (reproduced by permission of Elsevier)

In this section, the most significant methods for each phase of the segmentation process in palmprint acquisitions are reviewed.

Binarization of the Palm Image and Extraction of the Contours of the Hand

The methods used for binarization of the palm image and extraction of the contours of the hand are different for offline and online acquisitions.

Usually, variance-based approaches are used to binarize offline and optical-based palmprint acquisitions and to extract the contours of the hand. For offline palmprint acquisitions, the binarization step and the extraction of the contours are usually the only steps required for segmentation of the ROI. However, specific approaches are described in [39, 169, 417, 424].

In the approach described in [417], the image is divided into several blocks, and the variance and proportion of white pixels for each block are computed to discriminate palmprint regions from blank regions. In addition, a connected component analysis is used to eliminate the isolated knuckle regions, and a convex component analysis is used to eliminate the connected knuckle regions.

A method for the segmentation of latent palmprint images is described in [424]. This method involves the use of gradient functions in the spatial domain and the use of energy functions in the frequency domain to describe the orientation and periodicity of the palmprint texture. A threshold is used to segment the palmprint regions from the non-palmprint regions.

An Active Contour Model (ACM) is used in [169] for the segmentation of latent palmprint images. This method uses a Gabor filtering step to enhance the details of the palmprint, divides the image into several blocks, and computes the Average Absolute Deviation (AAD) for each block of the image. A spline function is used to enclose the region corresponding to high AAD values.

A binarization method based on thresholding of a gradient intensity map is used in [39] for the segmentation of palmprints captured using an optical device.

Online palmprint acquisition methods often use global thresholding methods to binarize the palm image and extract the contours of the hand, particularly when the acquisition is controlled and the background is uniform. In this case, there is a considerable difference between the foreground and background. However, specific methods have been described [187, 242, 326] to account for uncontrolled backgrounds [12].

A method for the extraction of the central region of the palm using acquisitions made with a digital scanner is described in [326]. This method is based on a thresholding operation, and the region corresponding to the pixels with the most homogeneous intensity, color, texture, and shape is extracted.

A method based on hysteresis thresholding is used in [242].

The method described in [187] uses a Gabor filtering step to enhance the fingerprint and palmprint image. Otsu's thresholding is then used to automatically compute the best threshold for binarizing the image.

Detection of the Keypoints and Establishment of a Reference Coordinate System

Detection of the keypoints enables the definition of a reference coordinate system that can be used to robustly align the palmprint images and extract the central part of the palmprint, which contains the majority of the information. Most reported palmprint recognition methods use the spaces between the fingers as the keypoints.

The method described in [366] uses the position of two gaps between the fingers to compute a reference system (Fig. 4.25).

The approach described in [297] computes the number of connected components in the right and left region of the hand to determine the orientation of the hand (Fig. 4.26). The images are then oriented in a common direction. The positions of the three gaps between the fingers are subsequently extracted, and the centers of

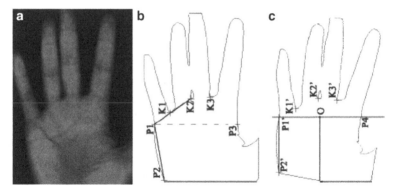

Fig. 4.25 The keypoint extraction method described in [366]: (**a**) the original image; (**b**) the extracted gaps $K1, K2$ and the points $P1, P2$; (**c**) the aligned image and the center O of the reference system as the middle point of the segment $P1'P4$ (reproduced by permission of IEEE)

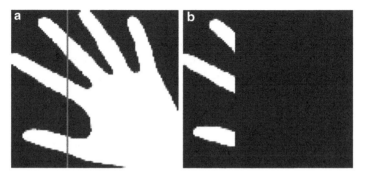

Fig. 4.26 Method for determining the orientation of the hand described in [297]: (**a**) extraction of the left region; (**b**) the number of connected components is ≥ 3, which indicates that the hand is oriented toward the left (reproduced by permission of IEEE)

gravity of each gap are computed (Fig. 4.27a). The outermost centers of gravity are connected to form the baseline of the reference system (Fig. 4.27b).

A similar method based on extracting the centers of the gaps between the fingers is used in [65]. These points are used as the baseline of the reference system (Fig. 4.28). A similar method is also used in [16].

A method based on fitting an ellipse through the binarized shape of the hand is proposed in [242]. In this method, the centers of the two axes of the ellipse are used as the base of the reference system (Fig. 4.29).

The method described in [402] uses a boundary-tracking algorithm to compute two gaps between the fingers. The first gap is between the forefinger and the middle finger, while the second gap is between the ring finger and the little finger (Fig. 4.30b). These two points are used as the coordinates of the reference system (Fig. 4.30c).

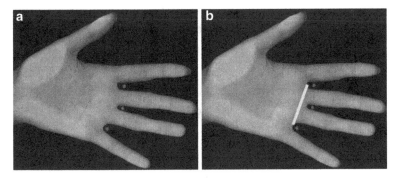

Fig. 4.27 Method for the extraction of keypoints described in [297]: (**a**) the gaps between the fingers and the corresponding centers of gravity; (**b**) the baseline of the reference system (reproduced by permission of IEEE)

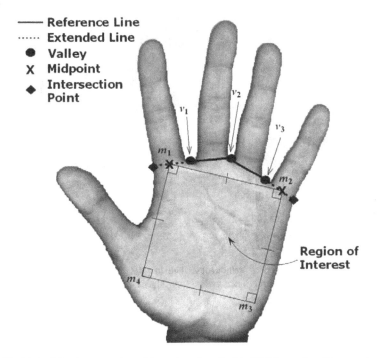

Fig. 4.28 Method for the extraction of keypoints described in [65] (reproduced by permission of Elsevier)

A method based on two points, the root of the middle finger and the center of the wrist, is described in [323]. A linear boundary search algorithm is used to find the points, and the center of the segment connecting them is used as the base of the reference system (Fig. 4.31).

Fig. 4.29 Method for the
extraction of keypoints
described in [242]
(reproduced by permission
of IEEE)

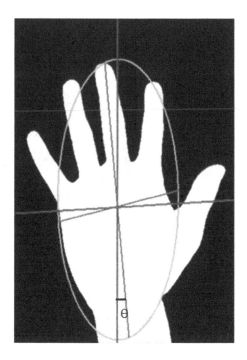

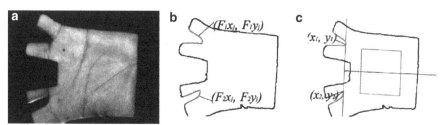

Fig. 4.30 The keypoint extraction method described in [402]: (**a**) the original image; (**b**) the
extracted gaps; (**c**) the extracted reference system (reproduced by permission of IEEE)

A method based on Active Appearance Models (AAMs) is used in [12] for
the segmentation of palmprint images captured with a CCD-based device under
uncontrolled background conditions. An AAM is a statistical method used to match
a previously computed model of shape and texture to unseen samples.

Extraction of the Central Part of the Palm

The majority of methods for segmentation of the palmprint use the computed
reference coordinate system to extract a square region containing the central part
of the palmprint [16, 65, 297, 366, 402].

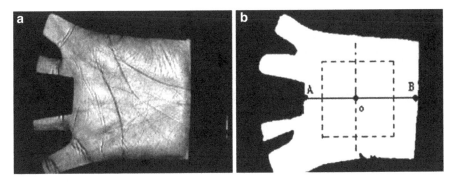

Fig. 4.31 The keypoint extraction method described in [323]: (**a**) the original image; (**b**) the extracted keypoints and the reference system (reproduced by permission of Elsevier)

Registration

For the majority of palmprint recognition methods, if the ROI is extracted according to a computed reference system based on keypoints and has a constant shape and size, the registration of the images is trivial. Moreover, if the acquisition is based on a constrained hand position, a registration step might not be necessary. However, approaches have been proposed to perform a finer registration [218] or for use in cases in which the ROI is not extracted using a reference system [70, 224].

A method based on the alignment of the orientation field is used in [70] for the registration of high-resolution palmprint images captured using an optical device.

The method proposed in [218] first extracts the ROI using the method described in [402], then computes the position of the principal lines of the palm. An Iterative Closest Point (ICP) algorithm is then applied on the binarized images of the principal lines to align the palmprint acquisitions more precisely.

The method described in [224] extracts two blocks from the first image (Fig. 4.32a) with a 45° line connecting them and searches for the best matching blocks in the second image. The angle of the line connecting the blocks in the second image is used to align the image (Fig. 4.32b). A similar procedure is used to find the translation between the two images.

4.3.1.3   Image Enhancement

Image enhancement techniques for palmprint recognition are strongly correlated with the type of features used for recognition. Moreover, enhancement methods differ depending on the device used for sample acquisition. In this section, the most significant methods used to enhance palmprint acquisitions are reviewed.

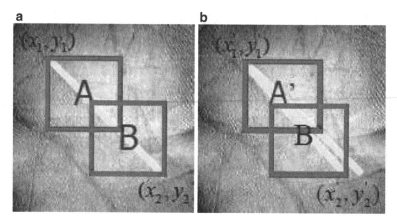

Fig. 4.32 The registration method described in [224]: (**a**) two blocks *A* and *B* are extracted from the first image; (**b**) two matching blocks A' and B' are extracted from the second image and the line connecting them is used to align the image (reproduced by permission of IEEE)

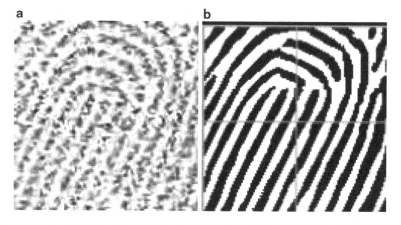

Fig. 4.33 The enhancement method described in [420]: (**a**) a specific region of the original image; (**b**) the enhanced image (reproduced by permission of IEEE)

An enhancement method used for offline palmprint acquisitions is described in [214]. The method is based on computing the orientation field of the palmprint. A series of O'Gorman and Nickerson oriented filters are subsequently used to reduce the noise and enhance the pattern of the ridges. Finally, Otsu's threshold method is used to binarize the image (Fig. 4.33).

The method described in [170] is used to enhance latent palmprints and computes the orientation field and frequency map of the palmprint image. Then, a series of oriented Gabor filters is used to enhance the details of the ridge pattern and the minutiae. A region-growing algorithm is applied to connect broken ridges and avoid the introduction of false minutiae (Fig. 4.34).

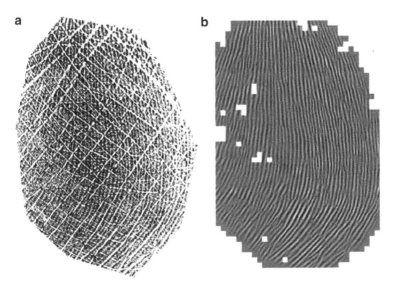

Fig. 4.34 The enhancement method described in [170]: (**a**) the original image; (**b**) the enhanced image (reproduced by permission of IEEE)

A contrast-limited adaptive histogram equalization technique is used in [169] for the enhancement of latent palmprints. The method is based on an improved version of the adaptive histogram equalization technique, which divides the image into several regions and performs histogram equalization on each region separately.

Methods based on computation of the orientation field and frequency map, and subsequent enhancement using Gabor filters, are typically used for online palmprint acquisitions captured using optical devices [39, 71].

Palmprint recognition methods that use a feature extraction step based on the extraction of the principal lines typically use edge detectors to enhance the images. Examples of edge detectors include the Canny edge detector [54, 183, 326], the Sobel operator [377], and derivative-based operators [124]. Steerable filters are used in [365]. Ad-hoc edge detectors are also used [301], including a fuzzy unsharp masking method [363].

Several methods use an enhancement step based on Gabor filtering [110, 124, 135, 195, 233, 278–280, 297, 298, 302, 358, 396, 402], wavelet transforms [65, 124, 265, 292, 359, 367, 368, 379], Fourier transform [220, 330], contourlet transforms [241, 242, 276], Radon transforms [152, 176, 177], Discrete Cosine Transforms (DCT) [180], directional filter bank transforms [264], Riesz transforms [410], or Karhunen–Loève transforms [15]. In most cases, the values of the resulting image after the transformation are directly used as features.

4.3.1.4 Feature Extraction and Matching

As mentioned in Sect. 4.1.3, the methods used for the extraction and matching of features can be divided into the following categories:

1. Ridge-based approaches;
2. Line-based approaches;
3. Subspace-based approaches;
4. Statistical approaches;
5. Coding-based approaches;
6. Other approaches.

In this section, the most relevant methods for feature extraction among each of the described categories are reviewed.

Ridge-Based Approaches

The method proposed in [214] is designed for offline palmprint acquisitions and combines the positions of the minutiae and the local structure of the ridge orientation around each minutia point to perform the recognition. For each minutia, a descriptor is computed using the extracted information and the information of the neighboring minutiae. The Euclidean distance between the descriptors is used as the match score.

A minutiae-based method for latent palmprint matching is proposed in [226]. First, a clustering algorithm is used to group the minutiae points into several clusters, based on local features such as the local orientation and frequency. For each cluster, a reduced number of correspondences between minutiae is computed. A local structure for each minutia, based on the position and type of the surrounding minutiae [170], is used to compute the similarity. Each minutia correspondence is used as the start of a propagation algorithm to search for other matching minutiae. The match score is computed as the longest computed propagation.

A local minutiae descriptor, which combines minutia features with SIFT features, is used in [207] for partial palmprint matching. A Euclidean distance-based matching is used to compare the descriptors and compute the match score.

A minutiae-matching scheme based on triangulation is adopted in [357]. The method compares the radial triangulations computed using restricted sets of minutiae to perform matching of partial latent palmprints. The result of the comparison between triangulations is used to align the image and perform a global minutiae comparison.

A 2D wavelet transform is used in [138] to extract the features of the palmprint to recognize an individual's right hand given his left hand and vice versa. A clustering algorithm is used to classify the features to find the most similar ones.

A method that combines minutiae and SIFT keypoints is used in [169] to match latent palmprint acquisitions. A weighted sum is used to combine the two match scores.

Line-Based Approaches

A method based on the extraction of feature points lying on the principal lines of the palmprint is described in [109]. The feature points are chosen as the points lying on the lines that have maximum intensity in their local block. For each point, the local ridge orientation is computed. The images are then aligned, and the feature sets of the extracted points are matched in the Euclidean space. The number of matching pairs and the average distance are used as match scores. A discriminant analysis is used to reduce the two-dimensional classification problem to a one-dimensional problem.

The positions of the data points corresponding to the endpoints and midpoints of the principal lines are used in [405], along with the direction of the palm lines, which are subdivided into several straight-line segments. The positions of the endpoints of each segment, expressed in the coordinate system defined by the positions of the data points, are used as features. The number of segments with a Euclidean distance below a specified threshold is used as the match score.

The method described in [269] is based on the extraction of feature points corresponding to the intersection of palm lines and creases. The SIFT descriptors for each point are computed and used to match different palmprint acquisitions. In addition, an SVD of the proximity matrix constructed using the positions of the points is used to match the points based on their position.

A Sobel operator is used in [377] to extract the palm images. Then, a series of features related to the magnitude and direction of the lines is computed. A method based on HMMs is used for the classification.

Subspace-Based Approaches

The method proposed in [279] first enhances the image using Gabor filters, then uses a 2D PCA analysis followed by a Locality-Preserving Projection (LPP) to extract the features. The Euclidean distance is used as a measure of the similarity between the palmprint acquisitions.

A combination of palm lines and LPP is used in [177]. First, the palm lines are extracted from the images. Matching is performed by considering the percentage of lines in common [152]. Then, the LPP is applied to the images, and the Euclidean distance is used to compute the similarity of the LPP feature set. A method based on the product rule is used to combine the two measures.

A Gabor filtering step, followed by a 2D PCA analysis, is used in [302] to separately extract features from the R, G, B channels of the image. The Euclidean distance is used to measure the similarity between the feature sets.

A method that compares PCA, Fisher Discriminant Analysis (FDA), and ICA is described in [65]. The use of a preliminary enhancement with a wavelet transform is also proposed. A Probabilistic Neural Network (PNN) is used to classify the features.

A method proposing the use of FDA to extract features is described in [265]. As a preliminary step, a dual-tree complex wavelet transform is used to enhance the images. However, instead of directly using the wavelet coefficients as features, the wavelet response is modeled using Gaussian shape descriptors.

The method described in [275] uses a technique based on Non-negative Matrix Factorization (NMF) to extract the local features of the palmprint image. Then, a PCA is used to extract the image features at a global level. Different fusion rules are tested for combining the local and global features, and a nearest-neighbor classifier is used.

A method that uses 2D PCA and LDA to extract distinctive features is described in [356]. A nearest-neighbor classifier is used for classification. A similar method employing kernel Fisher discriminant analysis (KFDA) is proposed in [364].

The method described in [264] uses an enhancement procedure based on shiftable Complex Directional Filter Banks (CDFB), which produces a representation of the image that is invariant to grayscale values. Then, histograms of the LBPs are computed for each subregion of the image, and a Fisher linear discriminant classifier is used to compare the palmprint samples.

A sparse representation of the palmprint images is computed in [270] by solving a minimization problem to increase the efficiency of the matching process. Then, a comparison of PCA and LDA for the feature extraction step is described.

Statistical Approaches

The method described in [368] uses the texture features of palmprint images by expressing the palm lines as direction fields in the Riemannian geometry. Then, a dual-tree complex wavelet transform is used to enhance the images, and the histograms of the LBPs are extracted and used as the distinctive features.

The combined use of geometrical features and texture features is proposed in [385]. In particular, Zernike moments are used as descriptors of the characteristics of the palmprint texture. A combined computational intelligence approach, based on Self-Organizing Maps (SOMs) and Backpropagation Neural Networks (BPNNs), is used to classify the features.

Different feature vectors extracted from several color spaces are used in [123] for palmprint recognition. For each colorspace used, the mean and entropy of each subregion of the image are extracted. The feature vectors corresponding to the same color spaces are compared using the Euclidean distance, and the match scores obtained by comparing the feature vectors from the different color spaces are combined using different fusion rules.

Coding-Based Approaches

The method described in [402] uses a Gabor filtering approach to extract the phase information relative to the direction of the palm lines. Then, the Gabor response is quantized to compute a bit string representing the information of the palmprint (PalmCode). The Hamming distance is used for comparison. A similar method using multiple Gabor filters is described in [194] (FusionCode). Specifically, the filter that produces the maximum intensity response is considered. In the method described in [197], the bitwise angular distance is used for comparison (Competitive Code). In the work described in [135], a Binary Orientation Co-occurrence Vector (BOCV) obtained by concatenating the normalized responses obtained using multiple Gabor filters is used as a feature.

A method based on a fuzzy C-means clustering algorithm is used in [396] to determine the best orientations of the Gabor filters to be applied on the image.

A similar coding scheme, called Robust Line Orientation Code (RLOC), is used in [176] to encode the orientation information of the image after an enhancement step based on the Radon transform.

Other Approaches

A correlation approach based on the phase information obtained by applying a modified Fourier transform of the image is used in [330] to match degraded palmprint images.

A representation of the palm lines based on a quad-tree decomposition is described in [183]. The decomposition splits the image into increasingly smaller blocks until the pixels within a block have an intensity value smaller than a certain threshold. Using this technique, it is possible to efficiently analyze the image using the required resolution only in the block that contains the information of interest.

The use of the contourlet transform is proposed in [242] to obtain the feature descriptors used for the recognition. The Euclidean distance is used for classification.

The combined use of the contourlet transform and fractal dimensions is described in [276]. In this method, the fractal dimension feature of an image is used as an indicator of the roughness of its texture. The Manhattan distance and the nearest-neighbor classifier are used for classification. Multifractal characteristics are also used in the method described in [323].

In the method described in [220], the Fourier response in the frequency domain is subdivided into several zones, and the intensity values of the different zones are used as features. Two feature sets are constructed by dividing the frequency image using either concentric rings or triangular sectors. Then, hierarchical matching is used to compare the similarity of the samples.

Features at different levels are extracted in [390]. Geometric features, global texture energy, palm lines, and local texture energy are used for recognition. A hierarchical matching method is used to accelerate identification from large databases. The Euclidean distance and angular distance between feature vectors are used as similarity measures.

The method described in [233] uses Gabor-based region covariance matrices, which contain information related to both the magnitude and phase of the Gabor response.

A method that combines the features extracted from a discrete wavelet transform with an estimate of the illumination quality is proposed in [292].

The method proposed in [358] is based on the enhancement of images using 2D Gabor wavelets, followed by the application of a Pulse-Coupled Neural Network (PCNN) to decompose the Gabor-filtered images into a series of binary images. The entropies of the binary images are used as features, and an SVM classifier is used for comparison. An efficient implementation designed for fast online palmprint identification is proposed in [359].

The use of SIFT features for palmprint matching is proposed in [16]. The Euclidean distance between SIFT descriptors is used as a measure of comparison between samples.

4.3.2   Three-Dimensional Touch-Based Palmprint Recognition

Three-dimensional touch-based palmprint recognition systems require the user to place the palm on a surface. These systems perform recognition using a three-dimensional model of the palmprint. These palmprint recognition systems usually use structured light illumination setups based on a CCD camera and a DLP projector. In addition to acquiring a three-dimensional image, a two-dimensional image of the palm of the hand is also captured.

In this section, methods that use touch-based three-dimensional acquisition methods are reviewed. The following four steps are analyzed: acquisition, segmentation and registration, image enhancement, and feature extraction and matching.

4.3.2.1   Acquisition

The majority of approaches that use a touch-based three-dimensional reconstruction of the palmprint [67, 219, 223, 383, 401, 404] use the acquisition system proposed in [219, 404]. This system is based on a structured light illumination setup and is composed of a CCD camera and a DLP projector (Fig. 4.35). The projector emits a series of shifted stripes onto the surface of the palm, and the CCD camera captures the images that are produced. A phase unwrapping technique is used to compute the depth information relative to each point in the image. The acquisition device has a resolution of 150 dpi, with an error of 1 mm for the estimation of the three-dimensional depth of the points. The device also captures a two-dimensional image similar to that captured by the system described in [402].

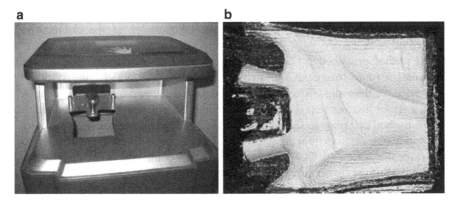

Fig. 4.35 The touch-based three-dimensional acquisition device described in [404]: (**a**) the device; (**b**) example of a three-dimensional acquisition (reproduced by permission of IEEE)

An enhanced version of the acquisition device, described in [401], incorporates infrared sensors to detect the placement of the hand on the sensor to automatically begin the acquisition. In addition, the stripes are projected on the palm with different brightness levels for each stripe, simplifying their distinction and the phase unwrapping process.

A database collected using this device is publicly available in [338].

4.3.2.2 Segmentation and Registration

As mentioned previously, in the method described in [219, 404], a two-dimensional acquisition is collected with the corresponding three-dimensional model. Because there is a point-to-point correspondence between the two acquisitions, the same methods used for the segmentation and registration of two-dimensional images can be used for three-dimensional palmprint models. The segmentation method described in [402] for two-dimensional, touch-based acquisitions is the most widely used technique for samples captured using the device described in [219, 404].

An improvement of the technique described in [402] is proposed in [222]. The ROI of both the two-dimensional and three-dimensional acquisitions is extracted using the method described in [402]. Then, the palm lines are extracted from the two-dimensional image, and an ICP algorithm is used to register both the two-dimensional image of the palm lines and the three-dimensional acquisition.

The method described in [227] segments the samples using the technique proposed in [402] and then uses a cross-correlation approach to refine the registration of the images.

4.3.2.3 Image Enhancement

In some cases, image enhancement algorithms are applied to the two-dimensional acquisitions. These algorithms are similar to those mentioned in Sect. 4.3.1.3 for touch-based two-dimensional systems, and Gabor filters are frequently used as a preliminary step [223, 401, 404] before the computation of the Competitive Code [197].

The method described in [221] computes a Mean Curvature Image (MCI) and a Gaussian Curvature Image (GCI) from the three-dimensional model of the palmprint to describe the three-dimensional shape of the palm using two-dimensional images. Then, a Gabor filtering step is applied to compute the Competitive Code.

The method described in [222] computes the MCI and GCI images and then uses a Radon transform to extract the palm lines from the two-dimensional acquisition and from the MCI and GCI images. A Gabor filtering step is applied for the computation of the Competitive Code.

4.3.2.4 Feature Extraction and Matching

The techniques for feature extraction and matching can be divided into methods used for two-dimensional images and methods used for three-dimensional models. In many cases, the methods used for two-dimensional images are similar to the methods described in Sect. 4.3.1.4. For example, the Competitive Code method is used in [401, 404] for feature extraction and matching of two-dimensional images.

The Competitive Code method is also used in [221, 222] to match MCI and GCI images, which use a two-dimensional representation of the three-dimensional shape of the palmprint.

In the method described in [404], MCI and GCI images are computed from the three-dimensional sample, along with the features that describe the local structure of the shape. The GCI and MCI images are matched using the AND operator, whereas the ST images are matched by considering their absolute difference. Various schemes for match score fusion are then tested.

A method based on PCA followed by a Two-Phase Test Sample Representation (TPTSR) is used in [67] to extract the features from both two-dimensional and three-dimensional samples. The TPTSR method uses a series of samples in a training phase and is based on the representation of the features of each sample as a linear combination of the features of all training samples. Then, the matching sample is sought among the nearest samples in the feature space.

The method described in [223] computes a binary image describing the palm lines from the MCI image and then uses the Competitive Code method to extract the orientation feature from the MCI. The AND operator is used to match the images describing the palm lines, whereas the angular distance between orientations is used in the Competitive Code method. Several match score fusion methods are tested.

A cross-correlation approach is used in [401] for matching MCI images.

A local contrast measure is used in [247] to extract the features from two-dimensional and three-dimensional samples of the palmprint, and PCA is used to reduce the dimensionality of the feature space. Then, a method based on hidden Markov models is used to model the feature vector, and the Log-likelihood measure is used as the match score.

A method based on LDA is used in [69] to extract the features from MCI images.

A method based on the analysis of the different depth levels of a three-dimensional model of the palmprint is described in [219]. In this method, a fixed number of isodepth curves is used to represent the sample, and the absolute difference between the values of the curves for each point of the shape is used as the match score.

4.4 Touchless Palmprint Recognition

In this section, the methods used to perform palmprint recognition using touchless acquisition devices are reviewed. For the purposes of this book, the acquisition procedure is considered touchless if the palm of the hand does not touch any surface. Some touchless systems do require the user to place the back of the hand on a fixed surface. In this section, touchless methods based on either two-dimensional images and three-dimensional models are described.

4.4.1 Two-Dimensional Touchless Palmprint Recognition

The methods used to perform the recognition of palmprint samples with a two-dimensional touchless acquisition system utilize CCD-based devices such as cameras or video cameras. These systems do not require contact between the palm and a sensor and can use partially constrained setups (e.g., placement of the back of the hand on a fixed support) or less-constrained setups (e.g., the hand does not touch any surface). Moreover, different constraints can be imposed regarding the position and orientation of the hand with respect to the camera. In this section, the four different steps involved in palmprint recognition by these devices are analyzed: acquisition, segmentation and registration, image enhancement, and feature extraction and matching.

4.4.1.1 Acquisition

Based on the type of illumination used, two-dimensional touchless acquisition techniques can be divided into two categories:

1. CCD-based acquisition using visible light;
2. CCD-based multispectral acquisition.

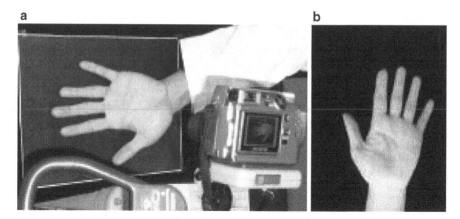

Fig. 4.36 The two-dimensional touchless acquisition device described in [205]: (**a**) the device; (**b**) example of a palmprint sample (reproduced by permission of Springer)

Fig. 4.37 Example of a two-dimensional touchless acquisition captured using the system described in [373] (reproduced by permission of IEEE)

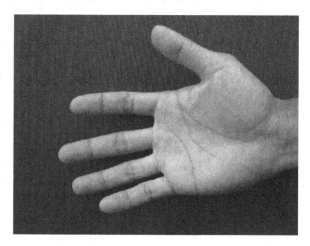

CCD-Based Acquisition Using Visible Light

A partially constrained touchless acquisition system is described in [205]. This system is based on a digital camera that captures images of the hand at a resolution of $1,280 \times 960$. For image acquisition, the back of the hand must be placed on a flat table with the fingers open. An image of the proposed system and an example of the corresponding touchless acquisition are shown in Fig. 4.36.

A similar acquisition method is used in [372, 373, 389]. In this method, the user must place the back of his hand on a flat surface with the fingers separated. A digital camera with a resolution of $1,024 \times 768$ is used to capture the images (Fig. 4.37).

The acquisition device used in [378] requires the user to place the back of his hand on a flat surface with a uniform background, and a digital camera placed in a fixed position is used to capture the sample. The device and an example of the corresponding acquisition are shown in Fig. 4.38.

A tripod-based device is described in [53, 201]. With this device, the acquisition is performed while the back of the user's hand is placed on the surface beneath the camera (Fig. 4.39).

The method described in [243] uses a dark-colored enclosure with a digital camera mounted on top (Fig. 4.40a). The user must place the back of his hand on a flat surface, and a ring illuminator is used to enhance the visibility of the details of the palm. The images are captured at a distance of 350 mm with 75 dpi resolution. An example of an acquisition is shown in Fig. 4.40b.

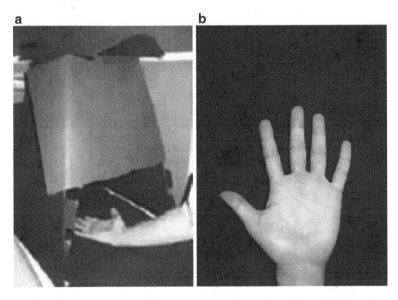

Fig. 4.38 The two-dimensional touchless acquisition device described in [378]: (**a**) the device; (**b**) example of a palmprint sample (reproduced by permission of IEEE)

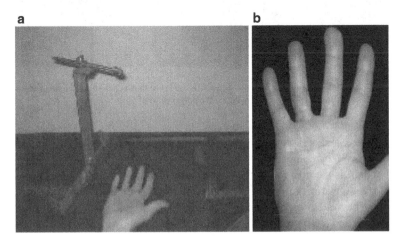

Fig. 4.39 The two-dimensional touchless acquisition device described in [53]: (**a**) the device; (**b**) example of a palmprint sample (reproduced by permission of IEEE)

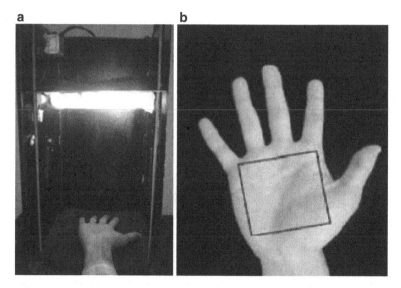

Fig. 4.40 The two-dimensional touchless acquisition device described in [243]: (**a**) the device; (**b**) example of a palmprint sample (reproduced by permission of IEEE)

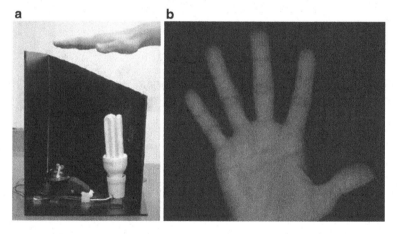

Fig. 4.41 The two-dimensional touchless acquisition device described in [255]: (**a**) the device; (**b**) example of a palmprint sample (reproduced by permission of Elsevier)

A touchless and less-constrained palmprint acquisition system is proposed in [255]. This system comprises a webcam, a light source, and an enclosure that partially controls the position of the user's hand. However, the hand does not touch any surface. A warm (yellow) light source is used to enhance the pattern of the palmprint. The system is designed to capture 640×480 images at 25 fps. An image of the system and a representative captured sample are shown in Fig. 4.41.

Fig. 4.42 Example of a
two-dimensional touchless
acquisition captured using the
system described in [103]
(reproduced by permission
of IEEE)

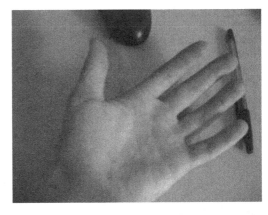

Fig. 4.43 Example of a
two-dimensional touchless
acquisition captured using the
system described in [291]
(reproduced by permission
of IEEE)

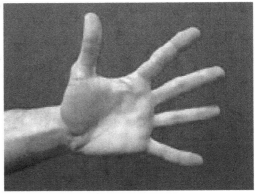

A webcam with 640×480 resolution is also used in the method described in [103, 105, 107], and an example of a captured sample is shown in Fig. 4.42.

A method based on the use of a webcam to collect frame sequences of a palm positioned in front of the camera is described in [250].

An unconstrained acquisition setup based on a webcam is described in [118]. This method uses a webcam with 640×480 resolution to collect images of the palm of the users. The position, orientation, and pose of the hand are unconstrained, and distances from 80 to 300 mm are possible. Moreover, the background and illumination are not controlled.

A method for the unconstrained acquisition of palmprints is also proposed in [24]. This method functions at distances of 300–500 mm with uncontrolled pose, background and illumination conditions. The imaging device has a resolution of $1,024 \times 768$.

The unconstrained acquisition setup described in [291] uses a webcam with $1,600 \times 1,200$ resolution and acquires the palmprint without requiring the user to place his hand at a specific distance. However, the hand must be placed horizontally with the fingers spread apart (Fig. 4.43).

Fig. 4.44 Example of a
two-dimensional touchless
acquisition captured using the
system described in [334]
(reproduced by permission
of IEEE)

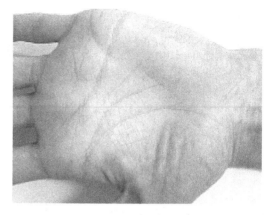

Fig. 4.45 Example of a
two-dimensional touchless
acquisition captured using the
system described in [394]
(reproduced by permission
of IEEE)

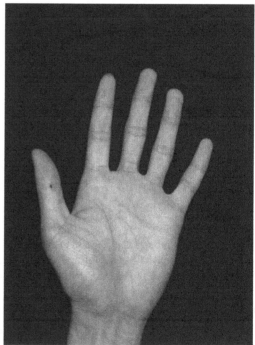

A digital camera-based acquisition device with a resolution of $1,792 \times 1,200$ is used in [334]. An example of a captured sample is shown in Fig. 4.44.

The method described in [391, 393, 394] uses images captured with a digital camera with a resolution of $2,048 \times 1,536$ (Fig. 4.45).

A method based on a digital camera and a ring-shaped led illuminator is proposed in [312]. A uniform dark background is used to facilitate the segmentation process. An example of an acquisition is shown in Fig. 4.46.

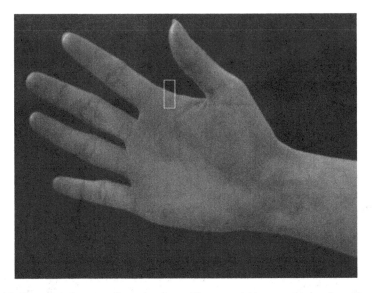

Fig. 4.46 Example of a two-dimensional touchless acquisition captured using the system described in [312] (reproduced by permission of IEEE)

A database of touchless palmprint acquisitions captured using an ad hoc designed device at 96 dpi with 640×480 resolution is available in [161]. Several methods in the literature [8, 17–20, 43, 112, 137, 296, 344, 352, 388, 431] use this database.

A database of palmprints captured using a touchless acquisition is available in [159]. In this database, the hands of the users are captured in different poses during the acquisition. The background and the illumination conditions are controlled. Specifically, a circular fluorescent light is used to illuminate the palms, and the images are captured at a resolution of 800×600. Several methods [156–158, 202, 236, 260, 261] use this database.

Mobile palmprint acquisition methods have also been described. For example, the use of a 100 dpi camera mounted on a PDA is proposed in [142]. A guided alignment procedure is used to capture images with the correct hand position. Experiments to evaluate palmprint recognition performance using images captured with different mobile phones are proposed in [52, 122, 175, 212]. The method proposed in [257] combines palmprint and knuckle print features for recognition using mobile devices.

Two-dimensional touchless palmprint acquisition systems have also been proposed in the context of multibiometric recognition systems.

The method proposed in [253, 254] captures both the palmprint and the finger knuckle using a low-cost webcam positioned with an upward orientation. The camera captures a video stream at 30 fps with 640×480 resolution. A real-time algorithm is used to extract the ROI from the image. The device and an example acquisition are shown in Fig. 4.47.

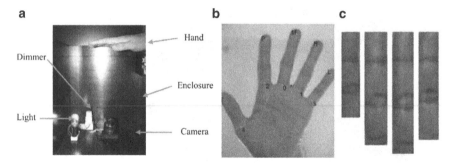

Fig. 4.47 The two-dimensional touchless acquisition device used in [253] to capture the palmprint and knuckle print: (**a**) the device; (**b**) example of a palmprint sample; (**c**) example of a knuckle print sample (reproduced by permission of Elsevier)

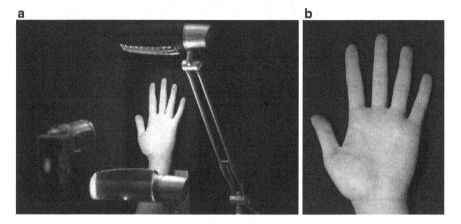

Fig. 4.48 The two-dimensional touchless acquisition device used in [44] to capture the palmprint and hand shape: (**a**) the device; (**b**) example of an acquisition (reproduced by permission of IEEE)

Several methods involving acquisition setups that capture both the palmprint and the hand shape have been proposed. In most cases, the hand shape can be captured without increasing the complexity of the acquisition system. Several methods use an acquisition setup composed of a downward-facing camera and require the user to place the back of his hand on a flat surface [205, 206, 376].

A less-constrained setup is described in [44] for the acquisition of the palmprint and hand shape. This setup requires the user to position his hand vertically in front of the camera. Two household light bulbs are used for illumination (Fig. 4.48).

The acquisition system described in [262] requires the user to pass his hand vertically up to down with the palm facing to the right while multiple images are captured (Fig. 4.49).

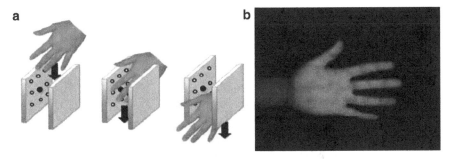

Fig. 4.49 The two-dimensional touchless acquisition device used in [262] to capture the palmprint and hand shape: (**a**) the device; (**b**) example of an acquisition (reproduced by permission of IEEE)

Some multibiometric systems have been proposed that combine palmprint features with features extracted from face [56, 291], fingerprint [46, 206], and finger geometry [392] acquisitions.

CCD-Based Multispectral Acquisition

An unconstrained touchless acquisition setup for capturing multispectral palmprint images is proposed in [141]. The acquisition system consists of two digital cameras: a CMOS camera that functions with natural illumination and an NIR camera. Both environmental lighting and an NIR illuminator are used. The palm must be placed at a distance of 350–500 mm facing the camera at a direct angle. The device and an example acquisition are shown in Fig. 4.50.

The method described in [143] uses six groups of LED illuminators ranging in wavelength from violet to near infrared and positioned in a circular fashion for uniform illumination. The different wavelengths are absorbed to different degrees by the skin and enhance different details of the palmprint pattern. A public database of multispectral acquisitions obtained using this device is available in [160]. Some methods described in the literature use this database [189, 191].

Two webcams, one operating with visible light and the other with IR light, are used in [119] for bispectral palmprint acquisition. The IR webcam is a normal webcam that has been modified by replacing the IR filter with a visible light filter. White LED and IR illumination are used during the acquisition. The device and an example acquisition are shown in Fig. 4.51. A database of bispectral acquisitions captured using this device is publicly available in [347].

Multibiometric systems based on multispectral palm acquisitions have also been described. In particular, methods that combine palmprint and palm vein images have been reported. The method proposed in [256] is based on a touchless multispectral acquisition device that uses two cameras, one for capturing images with visible light illumination and one for capturing images with IR illumination. The second camera is a normal low-cost camera modified with a visible light filter. Both visible light and

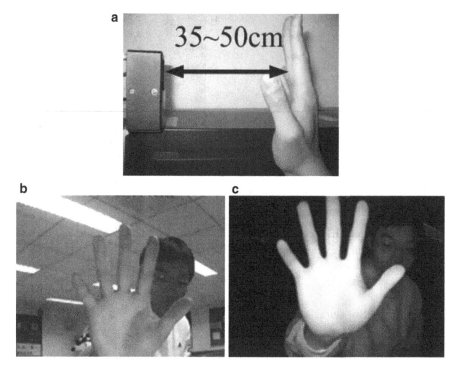

Fig. 4.50 The two-dimensional touchless multispectral acquisition device used in [141] to capture multispectral palmprint images: (**a**) the device; (**b**) example of a palmprint sample captured with the CMOS camera with environmental lighting; (**c**) example of a palmprint sample captured with the NIR camera (reproduced by permission of Springer)

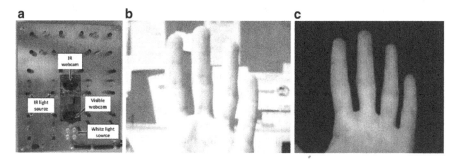

Fig. 4.51 The two-dimensional touchless multispectral acquisition device used in [119] to capture multispectral palmprint images: (**a**) the device; (**b**) example of a palmprint sample captured with visible light illumination; (**c**) example of a palmprint sample captured with the IR camera (reproduced by permission of IEEE)

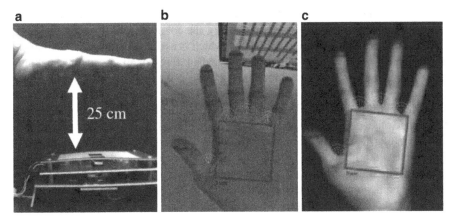

Fig. 4.52 The two-dimensional touchless multispectral acquisition device used in [256] to capture multispectral palmprint images: (**a**) the device; (**b**) example of a palmprint sample captured with visible light illumination; (**c**) example of a palmprint sample captured with the IR camera (reproduced by permission of IEEE)

IR illuminators are used, and diffuser paper is used to achieve uniform illumination. The device and an example of an acquisition are shown in Fig. 4.52.

4.4.1.2   Segmentation and Registration

Methods for the segmentation and registration of touchless palmprint acquisitions can be divided into those used with a uniform background and those used with an uncontrolled background. Methods for the registration and fusion of multispectral acquisitions have also been proposed.

Uniform Background

For acquisitions with a uniform background and the fingers spread apart, the segmentation and registration methods are generally similar to those described in Sect. 4.3.1.2 for two-dimensional touch-based acquisitions. In this context, the majority of segmentation methods are based on the application of a global threshold to obtain a binary image and contour-tracking algorithms to find the intersections between the fingers. These intersections are used as reference points to extract the central square region of the palmprint.

For example, the method described in [205] first binarizes the image using Otsu's threshold. An ellipse fitting method is then used to compute the major axis and the orientation of the hand. Then, a morphological erosion is performed, and the center of the eroded area is used as a reference point for the extraction of a square region containing the palm.

The method described in [255] uses a model of skin color to segment the hand image from the background. More specifically, the color of the skin is described by a Gaussian distribution of the color values, which is used to compute the likelihood of each pixel being a part of the background or foreground. A contourtracking algorithm is then used to detect the intersections of the fingers, which are used as reference points to extract the square region containing the palm.

A method based on Otsu's thresholding is described in [373]. After binarizing the image, the point corresponding to the middle of the wrist and the points corresponding to the intersection of the fingers are used to align the image and extract the central square ROI.

The method described in [378] computes the line that intersects the four main fingers at eight points. It then extracts the position of the valley points corresponding to the intersections of the fingers.

The method described in [236] binarizes the image using a threshold computed from a histogram of the image. It subsequently detects the valleys between the fingers and computes the line connecting the first and last valleys. The line is used as reference to extract the central square region of the palm.

Hysteresis thresholding is used in [243]. Then, the longest line passing through the palm is computed and used as a reference to align the image by comparing it with the direction of the major axis of the fitted ellipse. A fixed-size area is then extracted from the center of the hand by cropping the image.

The maximum inscribed circumference is used in [262] to determine the central region of the hand, followed by extraction of the inner square region.

The minimum circumscribed rectangle is used in [376] to segment the hand region in the image.

The method described in [44] binarizes the image using a threshold computed from a histogram. Then, a Sobel filter is used to detect and track the edge of the hand. The valleys between the fingers are used as reference points for the extraction of the central region of the palm.

In the method described in [291], images are captured on a green background, and a segmentation is performed in the red channel. A contour-tracking algorithm is used to detect the local minima and maxima of the border, corresponding to the fingertips and the valleys. The central region is then extracted accordingly.

After extracting the valley points, a variable-sized central region extraction is performed in [143] to account for differences in the size of the hand.

The method proposed in [189] binarizes the images and then uses a morphological closing operator to regularize the borders. A column-wise search for discontinuities is used to extract the position of the valleys. The central region of the palm is then extracted accordingly.

Uncontrolled Background

A method based on the extraction of reference points is used in [249] to align the hand images captured using an uncontrolled background. The method uses the intersections between the fingers as the initial reference points, which are expanded by sampling the points extracted using an edge detector. A RANSAC algorithm is used to compute the alignment between the set of points.

A method based on a Multi-Layer Perceptron (MLP) is used in [24] for the segmentation of hand images captured under unconstrained conditions and with an uncontrolled background.

A method based on neural networks is used in [103] to binarize input images. Then, a contour-tracking algorithm is used to detect the fingertips and the intersections between the fingers. These points are used to extract the center of the palm image.

A neural network approach based on the YCbCr color space is proposed in [306] for the segmentation of the hand in samples with a complex background.

The method described in [118] is proposed for the real-time segmentation of palmprint images from unsupervised acquisitions. First, an object detection algorithm is used to determine whether a hand is present in the image. Then, histogram models of skin and non-skin regions are computed, and the Bayesian maximum likelihood is used to compute the probability of a pixel belonging to the foreground. An edge detector-based method is used to compute the contour of the hand, even in the case of non-spread fingers. Then, a contour-tracking algorithm is used to find the positions of the valleys between open fingers and candidates for the valleys between closed fingers. An analysis of the neighboring points is performed to determine the correct points, and a shape context descriptor is used to discard the false keypoints. A central square region is then extracted based on the position of the computed keypoints.

The method proposed in [257] uses a set of rules for the R, G, B values to segment the skin from an uncontrolled background in hand images captured using a mobile camera. A contour-tracking algorithm is used to detect the fingertips and the valleys. The image is then aligned, and the central square region is extracted.

A method for the segmentation of palm images captured using mobile devices is proposed in [175]. The method first binarizes the image using Otsu's threshold. Then, the center of the wrist is computed, and the valleys between the fingers are detected. The position of the valleys is used to align the images to a horizontal orientation. A rectangle corresponding to the lower side of the hand is next extracted and enhanced using the Radon transform. The position of the maximum value of the enhanced region is used to normalize the images to the same scale. The center region of the palm image is then extracted.

The method described in [122] analyzes the central region of the images, which is supposed to be occupied by the hand, in the nRGB color space. The median and variance of the intensity of the pixels in the central region are computed and compared to the remaining pixels to determine whether the pixels belong to the foreground or background. Then, a preliminary detection of the valleys is performed, and the lines from each valley to the finger border are computed. The most frequent orientation is used as the reference orientation of the hand, which is used to align the image. The positions of the valleys are refined by searching a horizontal row with eight transitions. Finally, the central region of the hand is extracted based on the position of the valleys.

The center of gravity of palmprint images is extracted in the method described in [166]. A two-dimensional Hanning window is then used to extract the central region. The Fourier transform of the region is computed, and a correlation-based approach is used to align the images and normalize the scale.

A cascade classifier is used in [141] to segment hand regions in unconstrained acquisitions. In particular, hand acquisitions with excessive rotations must be rejected. The AdaBoost algorithm is used to select the most distinctive Haar features from the learning dataset. The orientation of the image is computed by calculating its moments. Then, a morphological erosion is used to remove the finger regions, and the central rectangular region is extracted.

Multispectral Acquisitions

The method proposed in [191] merges images captured using a multispectral acquisition setup to increase the recognition accuracy. The valleys between the fingers are used to coarsely align the images and extract the ROI. Then, the wavelet coefficients are merged to obtain a single image. A similar method is proposed in [143].

4.4.1.3 Image Enhancement

The majority of enhancement methods are based on derivative operators, Gabor filters, wavelet transforms, or Fourier transforms.

The Laplacian derivative operator, followed by a Gaussian low-pass filter, is used in [255] to enhance the details of the palm lines. The Sobel operator is used in [250, 255, 307, 372]. Other ad hoc line detectors are used in [205, 206]. A local ridge enhancement method based on a low-pass filter followed by a Laplacian operator is used in [256] to enhance palmprint and palm vein images.

Gabor filtering is used in [103, 250, 261, 291]. A circular Gabor filter is used in [105]. Gabor wavelets are used in [334].

Several wavelet transforms (Haar, Daubechies, Coiflets) are used in [373]. The Haar wavelet is used in [389]. The phase congruency of the wavelet response is used in [296] to enhance the edges and lines of the palm. Wavelet-based enhancement methods are used in [44, 157, 201, 236, 243, 256].

The Fourier transform is used in [166, 307, 378]. The DCT is used in [20, 156, 394, 421].

An enhancement method based on the combined use of the Fourier transform, logarithm, DCT, and wavelet transform is used in [112]. A regularization method based on partial differential equations (PDEs) is used in [107] to remove the noise in low-quality palmprint acquisitions. An adaptive histogram equalization technique based on a genetic algorithm is proposed in [274]. A combination of a wavelet transform and several Sobel operators with different orientations is used in [253].

A method for the correction of a non-uniform brightness in acquisitions is proposed in [18]. The method is based on dividing the images into subregions and computing the mean intensity value of each strip. The mean intensity map is interpolated for the entire image region to obtain a map of the reflections present. The obtained map is subsequently subtracted from the original image.

A force field transformation is used in [344]. The force field transformation represents each pixel as exerting a force that is directly proportional to its intensity and inversely proportional to the distance between the other pixels. For each pixel, the total force and orientation exerted by the remaining pixels are then computed.

4.4.1.4 Feature Extraction and Matching

The methods used for feature extraction and matching in two-dimensional touchless palmprint acquisitions can be divided according to a classification similar to the one used in Sect. 4.3.1.4. In particular, five categories can be distinguished:

1. Line-based approaches,
2. Subspace-based approaches,
3. Statistical approaches,
4. Coding-based approaches,
5. Other approaches.

Line-Based Approaches

The method proposed in [307] uses the Sobel operator to extract the palm lines. The endpoints and cross points of the lines are then computed and transformed in the frequency domain using the Fourier transform. The resulting coefficients are matched using the Euclidean distance measure.

Four different line detectors are used in [205] to enhance and extract the palm lines. The images are then merged, and the standard deviation of each subregion of the image is used to build the feature vector. The normalized correlation is used as a distance measure. A similar method that uses the cosine similarity measure is used in [206].

Subspace-Based Approaches

The variance of each subregion of the images is used in [53], in combination with the response of the Haar wavelet transform. A PCA-based approach is used to reduce the dimensionality of the feature vector.

The DCT is used in [394] to enhance the image and extract the features. Then, the PCA is used to reduce the dimensionality of the features. An RBF neural network is used for classification.

Palm shape features, variance values of the subregions of the images, and the wavelet response are used in [201]. A Karhunen–Loève transform is used to reduce the dimensionality of the feature vector.

An approach based on Generalized Discriminant Analysis (GDA) for feature extraction is used in [391].

A 2D PCA approach is used in [312] for the recognition of defocused palmprint acquisitions. A nearest neighbor classifier is used to match the templates.

A comparison of the use of PCA, GDA, and LDA for palmprint recognition is presented in [393].

LDA is used in [392] to extract the features from palmprint acquisitions. Then, a correlation-based approach is used to merge the palmprint features with features related to the finger geometry. The Euclidean distance is used for matching.

The 2D-DWT is used in [157] to enhance the image and extract the features, which are reduced using PCA. The average sum of the squares of the distances between the feature vectors is used as the comparison measure.

Statistical Approaches

LBPs are extracted from Sobel-enhanced images in the method described in [255]. A PNN is used to classify the results.

A method based on the characteristic matrix as the distinctive feature for recognition is used in [333].

The energy values extracted from different wavelet transforms applied to the image are used as the distinctive features in [373]. A neural network is used to compute the distance between different feature vectors.

In the method described in [107], a normalization approach is applied to each subregion of the image. The intensity values of each region are then used as features and are classified using an SVM-based method.

The energy values computed from the Haar wavelet transform of the image are used in [389]. The Euclidean distance is used to compare the features.

The entropy measure is used in [376] to characterize the statistical grayscale distribution of the images and as a distinctive feature. Both global and local entropy values for each subregion are computed. The Euclidean distance is used to measure the similarity between feature vectors.

Cohort information obtained using multiple template comparisons per user is used in [202] to enhance the recognition accuracy of the matching method for ordinal features.

Coding-Based Approaches

A method based on matching the quantized responses of Gabor-filtered images as proposed in [402] is frequently used [249, 250, 291] to match touchless palmprint acquisitions.

The binarized response of different Sobel operators is used in [372] to represent a map of the dominant orientations of the palmprint images. The Hamming distance is used to compare different samples. A similar method is applied in [256] for both palmprint and palm vein images after decomposing the image using a wavelet transform. An SVM classifier is used to combine the match scores obtained for the two images.

The method described in [253] enhances the images using the wavelet transform. The binarized response of the Sobel operator is used as the bit string for matching.

A wavelet transform is used in [44] to enhance the details of the lines of the palmprint, and the response is encoded according to the local orientation. The Hamming distance is used for matching.

The use of Orthogonal Line Ordinal Features (OLOF) is described in [262]. Briefly, orthogonal filters with different phase values are used to extract the orientation information of the palmprint. Then, the filter response is binarized and matched using the Hamming distance. Ordinal features are also used in [119, 141] for the recognition of palmprints captured using an unconstrained, multispectral setup.

Steerable filters based on a linear combination of oriented filters are used in [431] to enhance the orientation of the palm lines. Then, the innovative distance measure proposed in [137] is used to match palmprint acquisitions. Both the bitwise angular distance and the Hamming distance are shown to be specific cases of the proposed distance measure.

A symbolic representation of palmprint images is proposed in [43] to efficiently encode the acquisitions. The proposed Symbolic Aggregate Approximation (SAX) converts a signal into a string of discrete symbols. The different symbols are generated with the same probability by choosing threshold values that follow a Gaussian distribution. An ad hoc distance measurement function is used to compare the resulting templates.

The method described in [18] segments the palmprint image into overlapping circular strips, which are averaged along their radial direction to obtain a one-dimensional signal. Then, the Stockwell transform is applied to the signal, and the phase differences between adjacent strips at the same location are extracted and binarized. The Hamming distance is used for matching.

The method proposed in [20] extracts overlapping rectangular blocks with a particular orientation from the palmprint images and then averages their intensities across the height to obtain a one-dimensional signal. The DCT transform is applied to each block. The differences in the DCT coefficients in adjacent blocks are then extracted and binarized. The Hamming distance is used as a measure of comparison.

A similar method that uses the phase difference information computed from adjacent square blocks is used in [19].

The contourlet transform is used in [189] for palmprint recognition. The contourlet transform enhances the directional frequency information present in the image. Then, the dominant orientation at each image location is encoded. The templates are matched by counting the number of positive bits in common.

Other Approaches

The method described in [112] enhances images using a combination of the Fourier transform and logarithm operator. The amplitudes of the DCT and the Haar wavelet transform are used as features, and a neural approach is used to match the feature vectors from different acquisitions.

A feature extraction and matching method based on SIFT and OLOF is used in [261]. The Euclidean distance is used to match the two sets of feature vectors, and a weighted sum is used to combine the two match scores. A similar method that also compares different color spaces is described in [263].

In the method described in [103], the Gabor-filtered image is convoluted with the features related to the shape of the hand. The result is binarized and the Hamming distance is used for matching.

A combination of Gabor Wavelet Networks (GWN) and PNNs is used in [334] for touchless palmprint recognition.

A string-matching algorithm is used in [105] to match the palmprint acquisitions after enhancement using Gabor filters.

The Fourier transform is used in [378] to enhance images and extract the features of the palmprint. A method based on Radial Basis K-means and a hierarchical SVM classifier is then used for classification.

A combination of wavelet features and fuzzy features is used in [236]. In particular, the fuzzy features are related to the cumulative difference between the intensity of the pixels in each subregion and the average intensity of each region.

The DCT is used in [421] to extract the features from several different color spaces. The nearest-neighbor classifier is used to match the feature vectors. A method based on 2D-DCT is used in [156].

The features extracted from several wavelet transform are concatenated in the method described in [243], and the Euclidean distance is used as a measure of comparison.

A set of three value functions is used in [52, 257] to project the palmprint image onto the respective feature spaces. The dot product of each function and the palmprint is computed, and the results compose the feature vector. Generation of the functions using the random method, manual method, and PCA method is tested.

A comparison of subspace-based approaches (PCA, LDA), correlation approaches, and coding-based approaches (ordinal code, Competitive Code, and line orientation code) is proposed in [175] for the recognition of palmprints captured using mobile devices.

SIFT features are used in the method described in [8], which uses a matching procedure based on a KNN classifier to compare the feature vectors.

A correlation-based method is used in [166] to match the phase information obtained by computing the DFT of the palmprint images.

A force field transformation is computed in [344] to enhance the details of the palmprint. The orientation information of the force field is then used as a distinctive feature. More specifically, the local structure tensor is used to describe the information related to the local orientation present in the image. A matching method based on the Euclidean distance is used to compare different acquisitions.

4.4.2 Three-Dimensional Touchless Palmprint Recognition

Only a few methods for three-dimensional touchless palmprint recognition have been proposed. Methods that use three-dimensional laser scanners and methods based on structured light illumination have been described. The principal advantage of three-dimensional touchless methods is that they perform less-constrained recognition because the position of the hand can be determined in the metric space and variations in the distance and orientation can be accurately measured. Moreover, compared to two-dimensional touchless systems, the accuracy of recognition is increased due to the information derived from a three-dimensional model of the hand. However, the acquisition setups are more complex and more expensive than those of two-dimensional acquisition systems.

A framework for touchless recognition using hand features is described in [186]. The method described uses both two-dimensional and three-dimensional features related to the palmprint, hand geometry, and finger geometry. The acquisition device consists of a commercial three-dimensional digitizer, which is based on an illumination beam that is used to capture the light reflected from the surface. A triangulation procedure is used to compute the three-dimensional model, and a color image is simultaneously captured (Fig. 4.53).

The images and the models are captured under uncontrolled illumination conditions, and the position of the hand is unconstrained. However, the subject is asked to place his hand parallel to the image plane of the digitizer. A uniform background is used to facilitate the segmentation process. A size of 640×480 is used for both the color images and three-dimensional models.

The color image is binarized using Otsu's threshold, and a contour-tracking algorithm is used to extract the positions of the local minima and maxima of the boundary, which correspond to the valleys and fingertips, respectively. Based on the positions of the valleys, a rectangular ROI of the palmprint is extracted from both the color image and the three-dimensional model.

Using the information for the three-dimensional shape of the palmprint, a principal curvature map of the palmprint is computed by fitting a surface over a local neighborhood of the image. The minimum and maximum values of the partial derivatives are computed and used to construct a Shape Index (SI). Based on the SI, nine possible surface categories can be defined. Then, the SI relative to each pixel is encoded using a 4-bit string. This representation is called SurfaceCode, and a method based on the Hamming distance is used to compare different acquisitions.

The Competitive Code [197] feature extraction scheme is then used to extract the characteristics from the two-dimensional color image.

A similar acquisition and recognition method is proposed in [185], and a technique for normalization of the hand pose and orientation in three-dimensional space is also introduced. To perform the normalization, the center of the palm is located by computing the distance transform of the pixels of the segmented image, and an ROI with a fixed size is extracted. A plane is fitted to the three-dimensional points of the ROI and is used to determine the orientation of the hand. Then, a

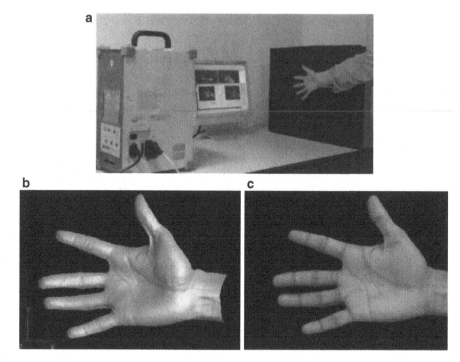

Fig. 4.53 The three-dimensional touchless acquisition device used in [186]: (**a**) the device; (**b**) example of a three-dimensional model; (**c**) corresponding color image (reproduced by permission of IEEE)

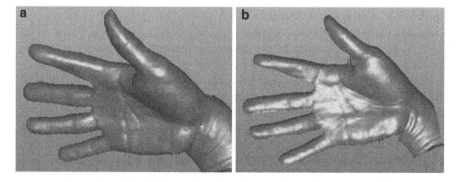

Fig. 4.54 The three-dimensional pose normalization method proposed in [186]: (**a**) three-dimensional model of the hand before normalization and (**b**) after normalization (reproduced by permission of IEEE)

rotation is applied to both the three-dimensional model and the image. An example of a model before and after the normalization of the hand pose is shown in Fig. 4.54.

An embedded three-dimensional surface measurement system is proposed in [235] for the touchless three-dimensional acquisition of a palmprint. The proposed

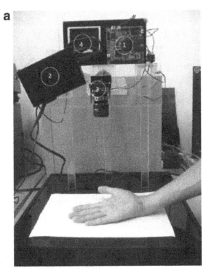

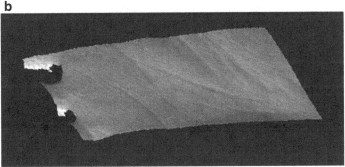

Fig. 4.55 The three-dimensional touchless acquisition device used in [235]: (**a**) the device; (**b**) example of a three-dimensional model (reproduced by permission of IEEE)

system uses a digital camera and a projector, and the reconstruction method is based on a structured light illumination technique. However, the hand of the user must be placed against a flat surface (Fig. 4.55).

4.5 Quality Estimation of Palmprint Samples

Only a few methods for estimating the quality of palmprint acquisitions have been proposed.

The method described in [411] determines the least significant (fragile) bits of the computed templates using coding-based palmprint recognition approaches. Fragile bits are present when the inner product between the filter and a region

Fig. 4.56 The three regions
of the palmprint with
different quality, as defined in
[418]. Region 3, near the
thumb (the thenar region),
often has lower quality
(reproduced by permission of
IEEE)

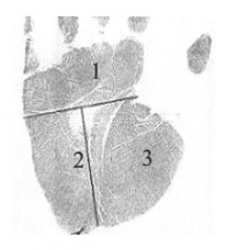

of the image produces an output with a small magnitude. These fragile bits can
be caused by the particular structure of the palmprint region, the filtering scheme
used, the quantization method, or a combination of these factors. To identify fragile
bits, the method analyzes the recognition accuracy obtained using the binary co-
occurrence vector (BCOV) coding scheme [135]. Recognition accuracy is increased
by removing the fragile bits.

A method for the quality estimation of palmprint samples captured using inked
impressions or optical devices is proposed in [418]. Quality estimation techniques
for touch-based palmprint samples are particularly useful because very different
pressures are applied by the different regions of the palm. For example, the region
near the thumb often exhibits lower quality due to the higher applied pressure
(Fig. 4.56).

The method divides the images into a set of blocks and computes quality indices
for each block. The indices used are based on ridge continuity, ridge thickness
uniformity, smudginess, dryness, orientation certainty, ridge-valley frequency, and
the special region index. A final quality value for each block is computed using a
weighted sum, and the weights are computed using a linear regression technique.

4.6   Palmprint Classification

Palmprint samples are classified to reduce the size of the database of samples
needed for comparison to perform recognition. Efficient classification methods are
particularly useful for identification purposes. In addition, accurate classification
methods can help increase the recognition accuracy of biometric systems working
in the authentication modality. In this section, techniques used for the classification
of palmprint samples are reviewed.

The use of correlation filters for palmprint classification is proposed in [146].
Correlation filters produce a sharp peak when applied to a sample of the corresponding class but a noisy output if the sample is of a different class. The method uses

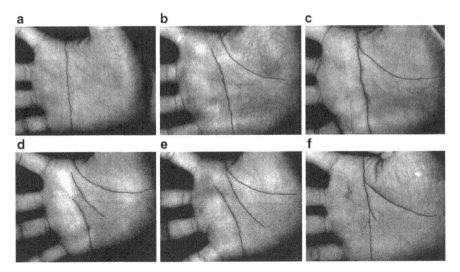

Fig. 4.57 Examples of the six palmprint categories defined in [398]: (**a**) Category 1; (**b**) Category 2; (**c**) Category 3; (**d**) Category 4; (**e**) Category 5; (**f**) Category 6 (reproduced by permission of Springer)

a line-based ROI extraction method and then extracts the lines of the palm using a phase-symmetry approach. The energy output of the image containing the palm lines is computed, and the images with the highest energy are chosen for each class to train the correlation filters.

A classification method based on the global features of three-dimensional palmprints is used in [397]. Three global features are used for classification. The first feature is related to the maximum depth of the three-dimensional palmprint with respect to the reference plane, whose depth is calculated as the mean depth of the three-dimensional palmprint. The second feature is computed by slicing the three-dimensional palmprint with horizontal planes at different depths. The area enclosed by the level curve in each slice is used as a feature. The third feature is computed by extracting the distance between each point lying on the contour of the level curve to the corresponding centroid. This feature is used to describe the contour of each level curve. An LDA-based method is used to reduce the dimensionality of the feature vector, and an SVM-based method is used to classify the features.

An online palmprint classification scheme based on the principal lines is described in [398]. First, the palmprint image is segmented, and the main principal lines and their intersections are extracted using an edge detector-based method. The number of principal lines and the number of intersections among them are used to classify the palmprint into one of six categories (Fig. 4.57). However, because category 5 is the most common, a method for the sub-classification of palmprints belonging to category 5 is proposed in [114].

A classification method based on the heart line (Fig. 4.4) is used in [267]. In particular, an edge detector based on the Sobel operator is used to extract the position of the heart line. The palm image is subsequently divided into subregions, and the regions in which the heart line is present are extracted and sorted. The set of regions crossed by the heart line is used as a feature vector for classification.

A method based on the curvature and intersections of the heart and life lines is described in [310]. Six categories are defined by considering three possible curvatures of the heart lines and the presence or absence of an intersection between the heart and life lines.

The method proposed in [178] extracts the principal lines and a set of keypoints along the direction of the main lines. The position, direction, and energy of the keypoints are used to retrieve a set of similar palmprint samples. Moreover, a preliminary distinction between left and right palms is used to further reduce the set of possible matches.

A ridge-based method for palmprint classification is proposed in [387]. First, the palmprint image is registered according to a set of reference orientations. Ridge orientation and ridge density maps are then used for palmprint classification.

4.7   Generation of Synthetic Palmprint Samples

A preliminary study of a method for generating synthetic palmprint samples has been proposed in [370]. Importantly, the generation of synthetic palmprint samples can reduce the time and cost needed for the collection of large databases. The proposed method is based on the extraction of the principal palm lines from a real palmprint image. Then, the wrinkles and ridges are synthesized and combined with the principal lines to produce a synthetic sample. Multiple images are generated starting from an obtained image. Thus, several acquisitions are computed for the same individual.

First, a Canny edge detector is used to extract the principal lines from a real palmprint image. If the image has a low contrast or is too noisy, it is discarded. The real palmprint image is blurred to eliminate the principal lines, and a set of patches is extracted from the image. The patches are combined in different ways to generate different synthetic images, which are then combined with the extracted principal lines.

To simulate different acquisitions of the same synthetic individual with intra-class variations, deformation meshes are used to shift the position of the pixels in the image. The grayscale values are shifted to simulate changes in the illumination, while Gaussian noise is used to simulate defects in the acquisition procedure.

4.8   Summary

Palmprint recognition systems are a specific type of hand-based biometric system with the advantages of good speed, good accuracy, and low intrusiveness. In contrast to fingerprints, palmprint features can be extracted even from the elderly or manual laborers. In addition, palmprint recognition systems have a relatively large usable area for feature extraction and can be implemented with low-cost hardware.

Applications for palmprint recognition systems exist in forensic and law enforcement scenarios, as well as in civil applications for access control, mobile authentication, and unconstrained recognition.

Depending on the level of detail, different features can be used for palmprint recognition, including shape features, principal lines, wrinkles, singular points, or minutiae.

Palmprint recognition systems are usually based on five modules, which perform the acquisition, segmentation and registration, enhancement, feature extraction, and matching.

Based on the technique used in the feature extraction module, palmprint recognition methods can be divided into ridge-based approaches, line-based approaches, subspace-based approaches, statistical methods, and coding-based approaches.

Palmprint recognition methods can also be classified according to the type of acquisition device. In particular, touch-based and touchless techniques can be distinguished, and each category can be divided according to the use of two-dimensional images or three-dimensional models.

Two-dimensional touch-based acquisition methods can use ink-based acquisitions, latent palmprint lifting techniques, optical devices, digital scanners, or CCD-based acquisitions, both in visible and non-visible light. Structured light illumination systems based on a CCD camera and a projector are used for three-dimensional touch-based acquisitions. Touchless acquisition methods are based on CCD cameras that use both visible and IR light, and three-dimensional touchless acquisition methods are based on laser scanners. The methods used for segmentation, registration, enhancement, feature extraction and matching have been reviewed for each type of acquisition device.

Quality estimation techniques based on the intensity of the Gabor filter response or maps of the ridge orientation and frequency have been described in the literature.

Methods for palmprint classification have been proposed to accelerate the recognition process, particularly for identification scenarios. Specifically, methods based on correlation filters, three-dimensional shape features, and the position and orientation of principal lines have been described.

A preliminary study of the generation of synthetic palmprint samples has also been proposed.

Chapter 5
Innovative Methods for Touchless and Less-Constrained Palmprint Recognition

In this chapter, innovative methods for touchless, less-constrained palmprint recognition are described. In particular, these palmprint recognition systems do not require contact of the hand with any surface or the use of a fixed positioning system. The only constraint imposed on the user is that the hand must be placed open, facing the CCD cameras, and inside the field of view of the cameras. Three-dimensional models are used to compute a representation that is independent of the acquisition position.

After an overview of innovative methods for palmprint recognition, this chapter describes palmprint recognition methods in detail. First, a feasibility study for touchless and less-constrained recognition based on acquisitions performed at a fixed distance is described. Then, innovative methods for less-constrained recognition using acquisitions at uncontrolled distances are detailed. The specific steps involved in palmprint recognition are described, including acquisition, segmentation, three-dimensional reconstruction, three-dimensional model processing, image enhancement, and feature extraction and matching.

5.1 Overview of the Methods

The main feature of the innovative methods described in this chapter is that, by not requiring a surface for the placement of the hand, problems related to distortion, latent impressions, dirt, hygiene, or cultural aspects can be avoided. Moreover, eliminating the need for a fixed hand position increases social acceptance and decreases the time needed for each acquisition. In contrast to some reported methods, users do not need to spread their fingers open to facilitate the segmentation process. The use of three-dimensional reconstruction techniques permits the computation of a metric representation of the palmprint that is independent of the distance and pose of the hand with respect to the camera.

© Springer International Publishing Switzerland 2014   111
A. Genovese et al., *Touchless Palmprint Recognition Systems*,
Advances in Information Security 60, DOI 10.1007/978-3-319-10365-5_5

Currently, both touch-based and touchless three-dimensional palmprint recognition methods are described in the literature. Touch-based three-dimensional methods use a structured light illumination setup, which consists of a CCD camera and a projector. Pegs are used to guide the hand into the correct position. By contrast, touchless three-dimensional methods are based on a laser scanner.

Compared to the touch-based three-dimensional palmprint recognition systems described in the literature, the methods described here use an original acquisition technique. Furthermore, they do not require the use of pegs to constrain the position of the hand, they do not have problems related to contact of the palm with the sensor (distortion, dirt, latent impressions), and they are based on a simpler hardware setup with a lower cost (a projector is not required). The speed of image capture is also faster. Compared to the touchless three-dimensional methods presented in the literature, the methods described here use a lower-cost acquisition setup (a laser scanner is not required) and have superior image capture speed. The described methods achieve touchless three-dimensional acquisition using an innovative setup that is based on a simple two-view acquisition system and LED illumination.

First, a feasibility study was conducted on samples captured by placing the back of the hand on a flat surface to control the acquisition distance from the camera. An innovative, touchless, less-constrained biometric system for palmprint recognition was subsequently studied and implemented. Importantly, this approach does not require a flat surface and requires only that the palm be placed inside an acquisition volume. Moreover, the methods described in this book are more general than those studied for fingerprint recognition and can be extended to include features related to fingerprints, the finger knuckle, and hand shape. An outline of the methods described is shown in Fig. 5.1.

5.2 Feasibility Study for Touchless and Less-Constrained Palmprint Recognition: A Method Based on a Fixed Distance

In this section, a feasibility study for touchless palmprint recognition using acquisitions performed at a fixed distance is described. The methods described in this section are low cost and do not use complex hardware but require that the hand be positioned on a flat surface with a high degree of precision and cooperation.

The described methods can be divided into several steps. First, the cameras used in the acquisition setup are calibrated. Then, a multiple-view touchless acquisition is performed. The images are preprocessed to segment the palm region, and a cross-correlation-based method is used to compute a three-dimensional model of the palmprint. The corresponding texture images are enhanced. Subsequently, the two-dimensional features are extracted and matched. A three-dimensional feature extraction and matching step is used to further increase the matching accuracy. An outline of these steps is shown in Fig. 5.2.

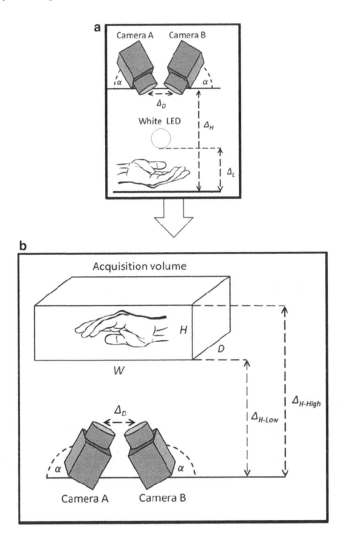

Fig. 5.1 Outline of the described methods: (**a**) feasibility study for touchless, less-constrained palmprint recognition using acquisitions performed at a fixed distance; (**b**) fully contactless, less-constrained palmprint recognition at an uncontrolled distance

5.2.1 Camera Calibration

Calibration of the cameras for the multiple-view setup is performed offline prior to the acquisition. A chessboard captured in multiple orientations is used as a calibration object, and a corner detector algorithm is used to extract the corners of the chessboard for each orientation [31]. Then, the algorithms described in [145, 415] are used to compute the intrinsic and extrinsic parameters. A DLT method [144] is used to compute the homography matrix H and a RANSAC algorithm is used to compute the fundamental matrix F [200].

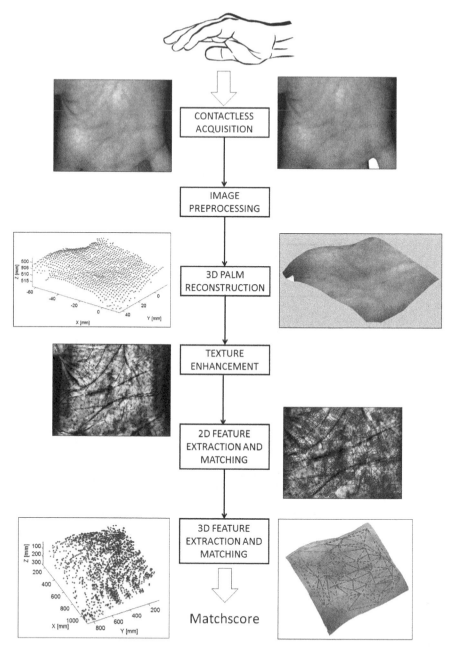

Fig. 5.2 Schematic of the feasibility study for touchless, less-constrained palmprint recognition using acquisitions performed with the hand positioned at a fixed distance

Fig. 5.3 Schematic of the
touchless acquisition setup
with the hand positioned at a
fixed distance

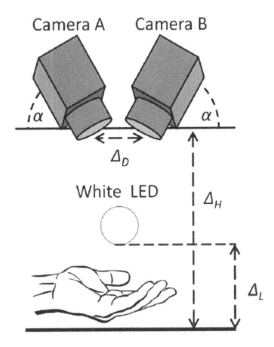

5.2.2   *Acquisition*

The touchless acquisition setup is depicted in Fig. 5.3. This setup consists of two
CCD color cameras mounted at a fixed distance Δ_H from a flat surface with a dark
uniform color and a white LED illuminator positioned at a distance Δ_L from the flat
surface. The cameras are oriented at an angle α with respect to the surface and are
placed at a distance Δ_D between the centers of the optics. The illuminator is placed
so that the light is emitted almost perpendicularly to the surface to be captured.

The setup requires the user to place his hand on the flat surface at a fixed distance
from the cameras. The palm of his hand must also be positioned in the overlapping
fields of view of the two cameras. Then, a two-view acquisition is used to capture a
pair of images I_A and I_B. A trigger mechanism is used to synchronize the cameras.
The shutter time is fixed and is chosen experimentally to enhance the details of the
palm without saturating the image. An example of an acquisition consisting of a pair
of two-view corresponding images is shown in Fig. 5.4.

5.2.3   *Image Preprocessing*

The two captured images are segmented to remove the background. Because a
surface with a uniform color is used, a thresholding operation is used to extract
the foreground:

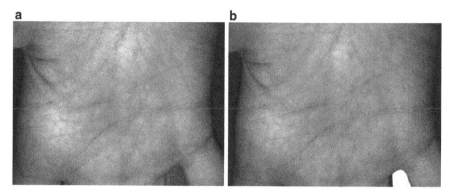

Fig. 5.4 Example of a pair of images captured at a fixed distance from the camera using the described setup: (**a**) left image I_A; (**b**) right image I_B

$$I_s(x,y) = \begin{cases} 1 \text{ if } I(x,y) > t_s \\ 0 \text{ otherwise} \end{cases}, \tag{5.1}$$

where $I_s(x,y)$ is the binary segmented mask and ts is an experimentally estimated threshold value. To eliminate points outside the boundary that could possibly be segmented as foreground, a morphological opening operation is applied, followed by a closing operation. Then, only the largest connected component is extracted. An example of this segmentation operation is shown in Fig. 5.5.

5.2.4   Three-Dimensional Palm Reconstruction

The method used for the computation of the three-dimensional model of the palm is based on the extraction of a set of equally spaced reference points, which are matched using a cross-correlation approach. A method based on the normalized cross-correlation is used because, as described in [87], the illumination can be considered uniform and similar in the two images captured with the two-view acquisition, and only small differences in the orientations of the cameras are present.

Then, the calibration information of the cameras is used to triangulate the matching points in three-dimensional space. A method for the refinement of the point cloud is applied. Linear interpolation techniques are then used to compute a three-dimensional surface model describing the palm and the corresponding texture image. An outline of the three-dimensional reconstruction technique is shown in Fig. 5.6.

The three-dimensional reconstruction method can be divided into several steps:

1. Extraction and matching of the reference points;
2. Triangulation of the matched points;

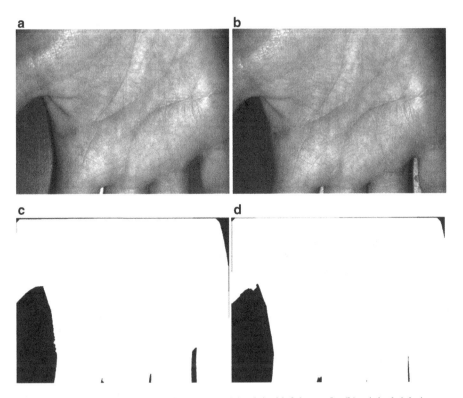

Fig. 5.5 Example of the segmentation process: (**a**) original left image I_A; (**b**) original right image I_B; (**c**) segmented left image; (**d**) segmented right image

3. Point cloud filtering;
4. Surface estimation and texture mapping.

5.2.4.1 Extraction and Matching of the Reference Points

A downsampling procedure with a fixed step s_{ds} is used to extract a set of N_P reference points from the left image I_A. An adaptive procedure is used to compute the downsample step s_{ds} according to the desired number of points N_P to be matched.

Then, for each extracted point, a preliminary match is computed. For each point x_A pertaining to a set of reference points extracted from I_A, the search for the matching point in the second image is performed using the homography matrix:

$$X_B' = H X_A \ , \tag{5.2}$$

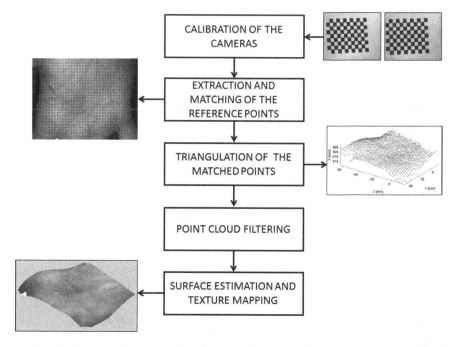

Fig. 5.6 Outline of the three-dimensional reconstruction method

where H represents a 3×3 homography matrix, X_A is the point x_A converted into homogeneous coordinates:

$$X_A = \begin{bmatrix} x_A \\ y_A \\ 1 \end{bmatrix} \quad , \tag{5.3}$$

and X_B' is the preliminary matching point expressed in homogeneous coordinates:

$$X_B' = \begin{bmatrix} X_B \\ Y_B \\ W_B \end{bmatrix} \quad . \tag{5.4}$$

A Cartesian representation of the point X_B' is computed as:

$$x_B' = \begin{bmatrix} \frac{X_B}{W_B} \\ \frac{Y_B}{W_B} \end{bmatrix} \quad . \tag{5.5}$$

A series of possible matching points adjacent to x'_B are extracted in a rectangular region centered on x'_B. The possible matching points are considered if:

$$d_x(x^i_B, x'_B) < \Delta_x$$
$$d_y(x^i_B, x'_B) < \Delta_y \ , \tag{5.6}$$

where x^i_B is the i-th adjacent point, d_x and d_y represent the distances in the x and y directions, and Δ_x and Δ_y are the dimensions of the rectangular area.

For each point x_A, the set of possible matching points lies on the corresponding epipolar line in the image I_B. In particular, the distance of each possible matching point x^i_B from the corresponding epipolar line is computed as:

$$d^i_{ep} = \frac{(X^i_B)^T F X_A}{\sqrt{(l_1)^2 + (l_2)^2}} \ , \tag{5.7}$$

where d^i_{ep} is the epipolar distance, X^i_B is the i-th adjacent point expressed in homogeneous coordinates, F is the fundamental matrix, l_1 and l_2 are the first two components of the epipolar line l, which is calculated using:

$$l = F X_A \ . \tag{5.8}$$

The distance of the possible matching points from the corresponding epipolar line must be inferior to a threshold t_{ep}:

$$d^i_{ep} < t_{ep} \ . \tag{5.9}$$

The Canny edge detector is applied to the two images I_A and I_B and used to verify the consistency of the possible matching points. Only the candidate matching points with corresponding values in the binary edge images are considered:

$$C_A(x_A) = C_B(x^i_B) \ , \tag{5.10}$$

where C_A, C_B are the images resulting from the application of the Canny edge detector to I_A and I_B.

If the aforementioned conditions are met, the set of the possible matching points x^i_B corresponding to the point x_A are inserted into the list V_B of valid points to be verified:

$$x^i_B \in V_B \text{ if } \begin{cases} d^i_{ep} < t_{ep} \ , \\ d_x(x^i_B, x'_B) < \Delta_x \ , \\ d_y(x^i_B, x'_B) < \Delta_y \ , \\ C_A(x_A) = C_B(x^i_B) \end{cases} \ . \tag{5.11}$$

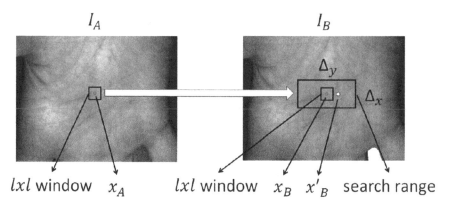

Fig. 5.7 Illustration of the method used to search for the corresponding points. An $l \times l$ window is centered on point x_A in the image I_A as well as every point of V_B in the image I_B

The actual matching point is computed by performing the normalized cross-correlation of two $l \times l$ windows, one centered on x_A, and the other centered on every point of V_B (Fig. 5.7). The normalized cross-correlation coefficient of the two windows is computed as follows:

$$r = \frac{\sum_m \sum_n (A_{mn} - \bar{A})(B_{mn} - \bar{B})}{\sqrt{(\sum_m \sum_n (A_{mn} - \bar{A})^2)(\sum_m \sum_n (B_{mn} - \bar{B})^2)}} \quad ,$$

$$1 < m < l, \quad 1 < n < l \;, \tag{5.12}$$

where A and B are the two windows of size $l \times l$. The coefficient is computed on the Y, R, G, B channels separately, and the maximum coefficient is considered:

$$r_m = \max(r_Y, r_R, r_G, r_B) \;, \tag{5.13}$$

where r_m is the maximum cross-correlation coefficient and r_Y, r_R, r_G, r_B are the cross-correlation coefficients computed for the Y, R, G, B channels of the images, respectively.

The final matching point x_B is chosen as the point in V_B corresponding to the window that produces the highest cross-correlation coefficient r_m:

$$x_B = \underset{r_m}{\mathrm{argmax}}(x_B^i) \;. \tag{5.14}$$

Intensity maps for a sample pair of acquisitions, depicting the cross-correlation values along the epipolar line for different points, are shown in Fig. 5.8.

An example of a two-view acquisition and the computed matching points is shown in Fig. 5.9.

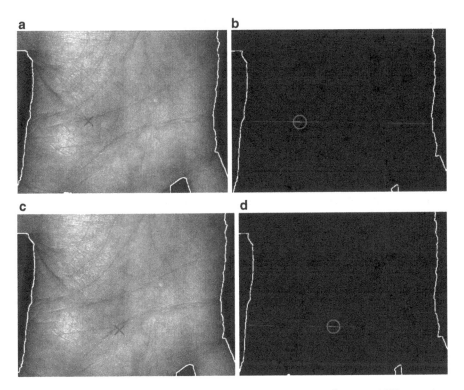

Fig. 5.8 Example of intensity maps along the epipolar lines, corresponding to two different points in the same image: (**a**, **c**) image I_A and the point to be matched; (**b**, **d**) intensities along the corresponding epipolar line in the image I_B and the matched point. The matched point is chosen as the point with the maximum intensity, and the results show that the method is capable of computing the correct position of the corresponding point

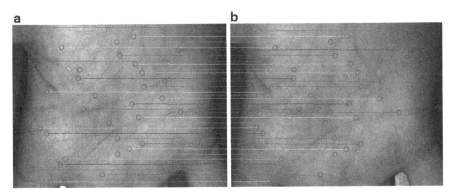

Fig. 5.9 Example of matched points in two images: (**a**) left image I_A; (**b**) right image I_B. The results indicate that the method can correctly match the corresponding points in the two images

5.2.4.2   Triangulation of the Matched Points

The two-dimensional coordinates of the matching points are normalized using a rectification procedure. The three-dimensional coordinates corresponding to each pair of matching points are then computed using the triangulation formula [31]:

$$z = \frac{fT}{x_A - x_B} \tag{5.15}$$

where f is the focal length of the two cameras, T is the baseline distance between the rectified position of the two cameras, and x_A and x_B are the two matched points. The three-dimensional coordinates of the points are adjusted using a common reference system. Reference systems centered on both Camera A and Camera B are considered, producing two point clouds (X_A, Y_A, Z_A) and (X_B, Y_B, Z_B). Point cloud (X_B, Y_B, Z_B) is related to point cloud (X_A, Y_A, Z_A) by a rotation R and a translation t:

$$\begin{bmatrix} X_B \\ Y_B \\ Z_B \end{bmatrix} = R \begin{bmatrix} X_A \\ Y_A \\ Z_A \end{bmatrix} + t \ , \tag{5.16}$$

where R and t are computed in the calibration step and describe the rotation and translation of Camera B with respect to Camera A.

5.2.4.3   Point Cloud Filtering

A point cloud filtering procedure is separately applied to the point clouds (X_A, Y_A, Z_A) and (X_B, Y_B, Z_B).

Because the matched points are obtained using a downsampling method with a constant step s_{ds} and the surface is sufficiently smooth, the three-dimensional point clouds of the reconstructed models present a regular distribution of the points.

An initial check for outliers is performed by removing the points that are too distant from the mean Z coordinate of the point cloud:

$$(z_i - \overline{Z}) < (\sigma_Z t_s) \tag{5.17}$$

where z_i is the Z coordinate of the i-th three-dimensional point, $\overline{Z}$ is the mean Z coordinate of the point cloud, σ_Z is the standard deviation of the Z coordinate of the point cloud, and t_s is a fixed parameter.

A further search for outliers is performed by removing the three-dimensional points that are not close to any other point in the point cloud. The distance from each point to the points comprising its 4-neighborhood must be inferior to a threshold t_d:

$$d((x_i, y_i, z_i), (x_{i+j}, y_{i+j}, z_{i+j})) < t_d$$
$$1 \le j \le 4, \tag{5.18}$$

where (x_i, y_i, z_i) is the i-th three-dimensional point, $(x_{i+j}, y_{i+j}, z_{i+j})$ are the points in its 4-neighborhood, and $d(\cdot)$ represents the Euclidean distance. The threshold t_d is calculated as twice the minimum distance between adjacent three-dimensional points:

$$t_d = 2 \min_{i=1...N} \left(d((x_i, y_i, z_i), (x_{i+1}, y_{i+1}, z_{i+1})) \right) \quad , \tag{5.19}$$

where N is the number of three-dimensional points.

5.2.4.4 Surface Estimation and Texture Mapping

The surface relative to the point cloud (X_A, Y_A, Z_A) is estimated by first storing the intensity values of the original image I_A in the vector C_A. Then, from the vectors X_A and Y_A, the maps S_{Ax} and S_{Ay} are computed as a mesh with a constant step s_{interp}. A surface map S_{Az} and a texture intensity map S_{Ac} are obtained by applying a bilinear interpolation to the vectors Z_A and C_A at the coordinates described by the meshed maps S_{Ax} and S_{Ay}. The coordinates of the surface maps S_{Ax} and S_{Ay} are adjusted to match the coordinates of the image I_A.

Surface estimation of the point cloud (X_B, Y_B, Z_B) is performed similarly to obtain the maps S_{Bx}, S_{By}, S_{Bz}, and S_{Bc}. Then, the coordinates of the surface maps S_{Bx} and S_{By} are adjusted to match the coordinates of the image I_B.

Examples of reconstructed point clouds with the relative estimated surfaces and textures are shown in Fig. 5.10.

5.2.5 Texture Enhancement

The quality of the ridge pattern in the touchless acquisitions is very different for each individual, and for some, the ridge pattern is hardly visible. Thus, in the described texture enhancement method, the details of the ridge pattern are not extracted.

The texture enhancement method can be divided into several steps. First, an adaptive histogram equalization procedure is used. Then, the background I_B containing the skin of the palm is estimated using a morphological operation and removed from the original image. The resulting image I_R is inverted and processed using a logarithm operator to reduce the noise:

$$I_L(x, y) = \log((1 - I_R(x, y)) + \varepsilon) \quad , \tag{5.20}$$

where a small value ε is needed to avoid the computation of the logarithm of 0. The resulting image is normalized by subtracting the minimum intensity value and divided by the maximum value to adjust the intensity range to the interval $[0, 1]$:

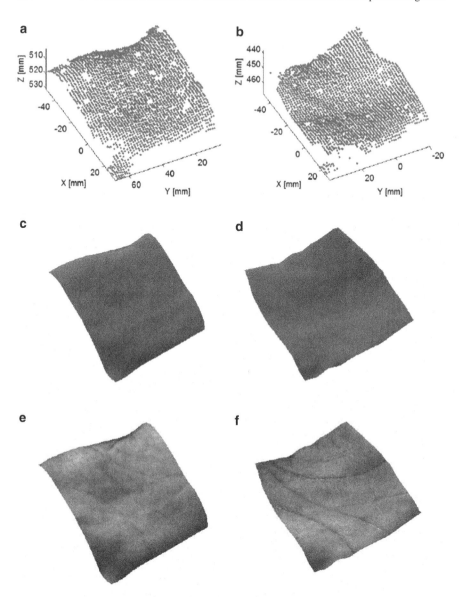

Fig. 5.10 Example of reconstructed three-dimensional palmprint models: (**a**, **b**) filtered point clouds; (**c**, **d**) interpolated surfaces; (**e**, **f**) texture images. The method is capable of computing an accurate three-dimensional representation of the palmprint

$$I_N(x,y) = \frac{I_L(x,y) - \min(I_L(x,y))}{\max(I_L(x,y))} \quad . \tag{5.21}$$

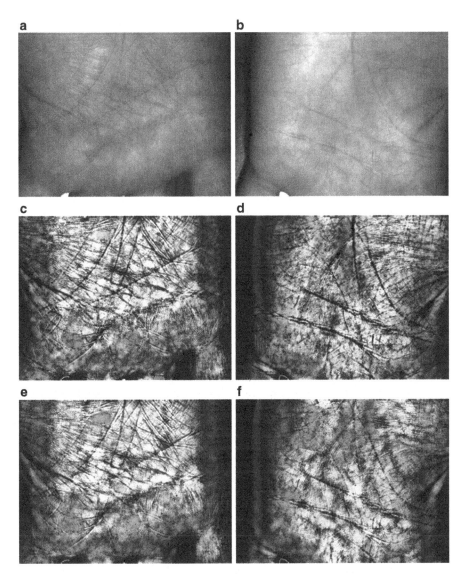

Fig. 5.11 Example of enhanced texture images: (**a**, **b**) original left images from two different individuals; (**c**, **d**) enhanced textures obtained from the B channel; (**e**, **f**) enhanced textures obtained from the R channel

Then, the inverse of the histogram equalized image is computed, and the image I_E is obtained.

The same enhancement procedure is performed separately on the R and B channels of the image and on both the images I_A and I_B. Examples of enhanced textures are shown in Fig. 5.11.

Table 5.1 Summary of the images considered for each palmprint sample

Notation	Description
I_{A_R}	R channel of the left texture image I_A
I_{A_B}	B channel of the left texture image I_A
I_{AE_R}	Enhanced texture computed from the R channel of the left texture image I_A
I_{AE_B}	Enhanced texture computed from the B channel of the left texture image I_A
I_{B_R}	R channel of the right texture image I_B
I_{B_B}	B channel of the right texture image I_B
I_{BE_R}	Enhanced texture computed from the R channel of the right texture image I_B
I_{BE_B}	Enhanced texture computed from the B channel of the right texture image I_B

5.2.6 Two-Dimensional Feature Extraction and Matching

For each palmprint sample, eight images are considered to build the corresponding template. The images used are summarized in Table 5.1, where the notation I_A, I_B is used to indicate the images belonging to the first template, and the notation I'_A, I'_B is used to indicate the images belonging to the second template.

The two-dimensional feature extraction and matching procedure can be divided into several steps. First, the corresponding images in the two templates to be compared are aligned using an intensity-based transformation. Then, a method based on the use of SIFT features is used to extract and match the distinctive points. A procedure based on point collinearity is used to refine the extracted points. An outline of the two-dimensional feature extraction and matching method is shown in Fig. 5.12.

5.2.6.1 Image Alignment

Because the palm images captured at a fixed distance and with the back of the hand placed on a flat surface using the method described in Sect. 5.2.2 are nearly flat, the three-dimensional models do not present sufficient information for a robust registration of the samples. For this reason, a two-dimensional alignment procedure is used. More specifically, an intensity-based alignment procedure is used to register the corresponding images in the two templates to be compared. Because the acquisition distance is fixed and the back of the hand is placed against a surface, preventing rotation of the hand, only rigid transformations, consisting of a rotation and a translation, are considered. Transformation mapping of the second image onto the first is performed using a gradient descent algorithm, and a linear interpolation is used to calculate the intensity values in the rotated image.

An example of an image after the alignment step is shown in Fig. 5.13.

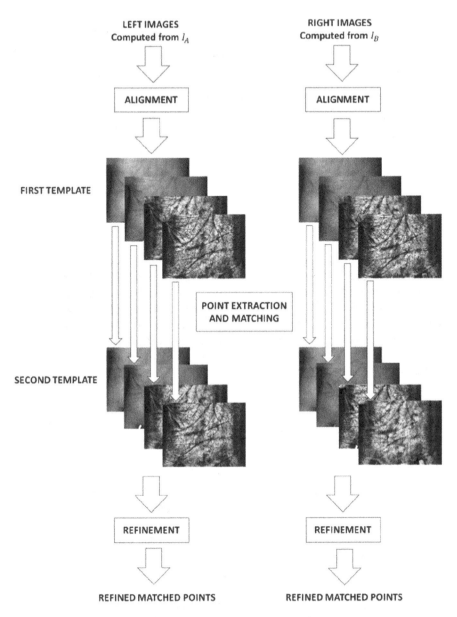

Fig. 5.12 Outline of the two-dimensional feature extraction and matching method. Each template is composed of eight images: four left images are computed from image I_A, and four right images are computed from image I_B

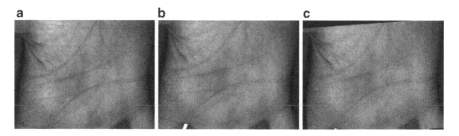

Fig. 5.13 Example of the image alignment: (**a**) B channel extracted from the first image I_A; (**b**) B channel extracted from the second image I'_A; (**c**) second image aligned according to the first. Only rigid transformations are considered

5.2.6.2   Point Extraction and Matching

The central region of the palm images corresponding to $3/4$ of the image size is extracted to discard potentially noisy regions, including the bases and valleys of the fingers and the border of the hand. The images are resized by a factor $1/2$.

A Gaussian low-pass filter is applied to remove the high-frequency information for the palm. Then, the SIFT feature points and descriptors [229] are extracted from the images to be compared [349]. The SIFT points are extracted from the eight considered images of the first template to be compared, for a total of eight sets of points $P_{1,\ldots,8}$.

$$
\begin{array}{llll}
I_{A_R} \rightarrow_{SIFT} P_1 & ; & I_{B_R} \rightarrow_{SIFT} P_5 & ; \\
I_{AE_R} \rightarrow_{SIFT} P_2 & ; & I_{BE_R} \rightarrow_{SIFT} P_6 & ; \\
I_{A_B} \rightarrow_{SIFT} P_3 & ; & I_{B_B} \rightarrow_{SIFT} P_7 & ; \\
I_{AE_B} \rightarrow_{SIFT} P_4 & ; & I_{BE_B} \rightarrow_{SIFT} P_8 & ,
\end{array}
\tag{5.22}
$$

where $\rightarrow_{SIFT}$ refers to the SIFT point extraction procedure.

The number of points in each set is variable. For each point, a descriptor $D(f_1,\ldots,f_{128})$ consisting of 128 features, is computed. The same procedure is used to extract the sets of points $P'_{1,\ldots,8}$ and descriptors from the images pertaining to the second template.

The procedure based on the Euclidean distance described in [229] is used to match the corresponding sets of descriptors obtained from the two templates. In particular, considering a set of points P_i corresponding to the first template and the corresponding set of points P'_i for the second template, the Euclidean distance between each pair of descriptors is calculated. Then, a descriptor D_m is considered as matched to a descriptor D'_n only if their distance multiplied by a fixed threshold is less than the maximum distance between D_m and the other descriptors:

$$
d(D_m, D'_n) \cdot t_{SIFT} \leq \max_{p=1,\ldots,N'} (d(D_m, D'_p))
\tag{5.23}
$$

where $d(\cdot)$ represent the Euclidean distance, t_{SIFT} is a fixed threshold, and N' is the number of points from the considered image to be compared with the second template. The sets of matching points obtained, which correspond to the matched descriptors, are referred to as $M_{1,...,8}$ and $M'_{1,...,8}$.

5.2.6.3 Refinement of the Matched Points

Because the palmprint images are captured in a horizontal position, the palm region of the hand can be considered almost flat. Moreover, because the images have been previously aligned, the lines connecting the matched points must be parallel. Thus, a method based on the collinearity of the pairs of matched points is used to remove erroneous matches.

First, the eight sets of matching points $M_{1,...,8}$ corresponding to the first template are merged in two sets. This merging is achieved by distinguishing the matched points pertaining to the left images and the matched points pertaining to the right images, to obtain the sets M_{At} and M_{Bt}. Similarly, the sets of points corresponding to the second template are merged in the sets M'_{At} and M'_{Bt}.

Then, the width W of the first image I_A is added to the X coordinates of the matched points belonging to M'_{At} and M'_{Bt} to ideally translate them to the right of the corresponding points in the images of the first template.

The Euclidean distances between the pairs of matching points are computed, and only the pairs whose distance does not exceed a threshold are considered:

$$d(p(x,y), p'(x,y)) < t_f \quad , \tag{5.24}$$

where $d(\cdot)$ represent the Euclidean distance, $(p(x,y), p'(x,y))$ is a pair of matching points, and the threshold t_f is defined as:

$$t_f = W + \frac{1}{10}W \tag{5.25}$$

where W is the width of the image.

Then, the derivative of the line connecting each pair of points is calculated. First, the points belonging to M_{At} and M'_{At} are considered:

$$D_i = \frac{d_y(p_i(x,y), p'_i(x,y))}{d_x(p_i(x,y), p'_i(x,y))} \quad , \tag{5.26}$$

where D_i represents the derivative of the line connecting the point $p_i(x,y)$ belonging to M_{At} and the point $p'_i(x,y)$ belonging to M'_{At}. The values d_x and d_y represent the Euclidean distances along the x and y axes, respectively. The pairs of points corresponding to the most diffused derivative value are considered valid matching points. Similarly, the derivatives of the pairs of points in M_{Bt} and M'_{Bt} are computed, and only the pairs of points corresponding to the most diffused derivative value are considered as valid matching points.

Duplicate points are removed, and the resulting points are stored in the point sets M_{Af}, M'_{Af}, and M_{Bf}, M'_{Bf}. An example of the matched points before and after refinement is shown in Fig. 5.14.

5.2.7 Three-Dimensional Feature Extraction and Matching

The three-dimensional feature extraction and matching step can be divided into several steps. First, the three-dimensional coordinates of the refined matching points are determined. Then, the corresponding point clouds are registered using an ICP algorithm. A three-dimensional template based on the Delaunay triangulation is computed. Finally, the number of similar triangles is extracted.

5.2.7.1 Computation of the Three-Dimensional Coordinates

The three-dimensional coordinates of the refined matching points M_{Af}, M_{Bf} corresponding to the first template are computed using the surface maps S_{Ax}, S_{Ay}, S_{Az}, S_{Bx}, S_{By}, and S_{Bz}, which are estimated as described in Sect. 5.2.4.4:

$$X_{Af} = S_{Ax}(x_{Af}, y_{Af}) \;\; ; \;\; X_{Bf} = S_{Bx}(x_{Bf}, y_{Bf}) \;\; ;$$
$$Y_{Af} = S_{Ay}(x_{Af}, y_{Af}) \;\; ; \;\; Y_{Bf} = S_{By}(x_{Bf}, y_{Bf}) \;\; ;$$
$$Z_{Af} = S_{Az}(x_{Af}, y_{Af}) \;\; ; \;\; Z_{Bf} = S_{Bz}(x_{Bf}, y_{Bf}) \;\; , \tag{5.27}$$

where (x_{Af}, y_{Af}) and (x_{Bf}, y_{Bf}) are the coordinates of the points belonging to M_{Af} and M_{Bf}, respectively, while (X_{Af}, Y_{Af}, Z_{Af}) and (X_{Bf}, Y_{Bf}, Z_{Bf}) are the corresponding three-dimensional coordinates.

Similarly, the three-dimensional coordinates of the points belonging to M'_{Af} and M'_{Bf} are computed to obtain the point clouds $(X'_{Af}, Y'_{Af}, Z'_{Af})$ and $(X'_{Bf}, Y'_{Bf}, Z'_{Bf})$.

5.2.7.2 Registration of the Point Clouds

An ICP algorithm [25] is used to register the point clouds. The three-dimensional points (X_{Af}, Y_{Af}, Z_{Af}) and (X_{Bf}, Y_{Bf}, Z_{Bf}) are respectively registered with the points $(X'_{Af}, Y'_{Af}, Z'_{Af})$ and $(X'_{Bf}, Y'_{Bf}, Z'_{Bf})$.

An example of three-dimensional point clouds before and after registration is shown in Fig. 5.15.

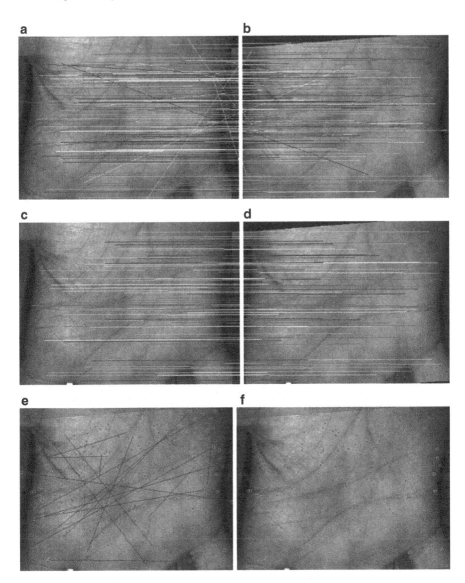

Fig. 5.14 Example of point refinement based on collinearity: (**a**, **b**) matching points between the first and second images before refinement; (**c**, **d**) matching points after the refinement; (**e**) superimposition of the first and second images before refinement, in which the matching points are connected using a *blue line*; (**f**) superimposition of the first and second images after refinement, in which the matching points are connected by a *blue line*. The results indicate that the majority of erroneously matched points are removed

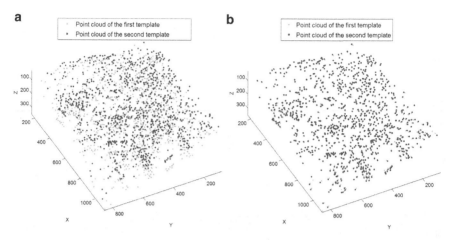

Fig. 5.15 Example of three-dimensional point cloud registration based on the ICP algorithm: (**a**) point cloud (X_{Af}, Y_{Af}, Z_{Af}) (*orange*) and $(X'_{Af}, Y'_{Af}, Z'_{Af})$ (*blue*) before registration; (**b**) point clouds after registration. In this case, the point clouds are computed from different acquisitions of the same palm and are correctly registered

Fig. 5.16 Example of a Delaunay triangulation using the refined matched points

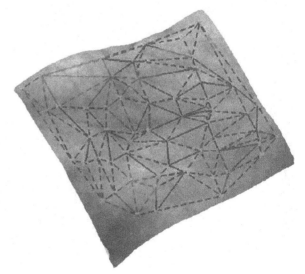

5.2.7.3 Computation of the Three-Dimensional Template

First, the two-dimensional Delaunay triangulation of the point clouds is computed by considering only the X and Y coordinates. The Z coordinate is subsequently added to each vertex of the computed triangles (Fig. 5.16), and the lengths of the sides of the triangles in three-dimensional space are computed:

$$L_{1i} = \sqrt{(X_{1i} - X_{2i})^2 + (Y_{1i} - Y_{2i})^2 + (Z_{1i} - Z_{2i})^2} \; ;$$

$$L_{2i} = \sqrt{(X_{2i} - X_{3i})^2 + (Y_{2i} - Y_{3i})^2 + (Z_{2i} - Z_{3i})^2} \; ;$$

$$L_{3i} = \sqrt{(X_{1i} - X_{3i})^2 + (Y_{1i} - Y_{3i})^2 + (Z_{1i} - Z_{3i})^2} \; , \tag{5.28}$$

where $(X_{1i}, Y_{1i}, Z_{1i}), (X_{2i}, Y_{2i}, Z_{2i}), (X_{3i}, Y_{3i}, Z_{3i})$ are the three-dimensional coordinates of the three vertices of the i-th triangle and L_{1i}, L_{2i}, L_{3i} are the lengths of the sides of the i-th triangle.

5.2.7.4 Extraction of Similar Triangles and Computation of the Match Score

The triangles pertaining to the first and second templates are compared by analyzing the lengths of the sides of the triangles. Each triangle in the first template is compared to every triangle in the second template to determine if the three sides have similar lengths:

$$L_{1i} - L'_{1j} < (t_D L_{1i}) \; ;$$

$$L_{2i} - L'_{2j} < (t_D L_{2i}) \; ;$$

$$L_{3i} - L'_{3j} < (t_D L_{3i}) \; , \tag{5.29}$$

where L_{1i}, L_{2i}, L_{3i} are the lengths of the three sides of the i-th triangle in the first template, $L'_{1j}, L'_{2j}, L'_{3j}$ are the lengths of the three sides of the j-th triangle in the second template, and t_D is a fixed threshold that is determined experimentally.

The number of similar triangles is used as the match score.

5.3 Fully Touchless and Less-Constrained Palmprint Recognition with Uncontrolled Distance

The results obtained in the feasibility study for touchless recognition based on acquisitions performed at a fixed distance enabled the extension of the described methods for an innovative, fully touchless and less-constrained acquisition.

In this section, innovative methods based on acquisitions at uncontrolled distances are described. These methods are able to achieve touchless palmprint recognition with a reduced number of constraints compared to previously reported approaches. Specifically, the hand does not touch any surface, and the user is only required to place his hand horizontally inside a volume corresponding to the intersecting areas of the fields of view of the cameras that are sufficiently close to

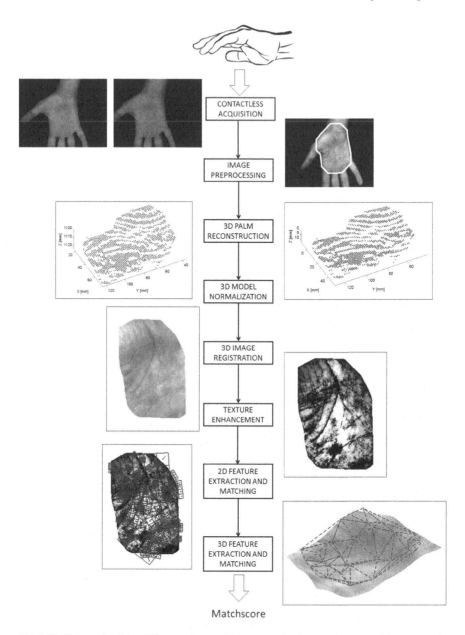

Fig. 5.17 Schematic of the fully touchless and less-constrained palmprint recognition system in which acquisitions are performed with the hand positioned at an uncontrolled distance

the illumination. Moreover, the user is not required to spread his fingers or open his hand in a specific way. The use of three-dimensional reconstruction techniques permits a description of the palm that is invariant to the pose of the hand and the acquisition distance. Compared to proposed touchless three-dimensional palmprint recognition methods [185, 186], the described methods perform a faster acquisition and are based on an innovative low-cost setup consisting of a two-view acquisition system and LED illumination.

The method described for palmprint recognition using acquisitions performed at uncontrolled distances can be divided into several steps. First, the acquisition setup is calibrated. Then, a multiple-view, less-constrained touchless acquisition is performed using uniform LED illumination. The images are preprocessed to segment the palm region. Three-dimensional processing of the palmprint is subsequently performed by reconstructing a three-dimensional model of the palmprint and then registering the model to normalize the pose and the distance according to a common reference position. Three-dimensional image registration is performed by reprojecting the models onto the image plane using the calibration data. The corresponding texture images are enhanced, and the two-dimensional features are then extracted and matched. A three-dimensional feature extraction and matching step is also used to further refine the matching. An outline of this method is shown in Fig. 5.17.

5.3.1 Camera Calibration

The method described in Sect. 5.2.1 is used to calibrate the cameras. The intrinsic and extrinsic parameters of the cameras are computed, along with the homography matrix H and the fundamental matrix F.

5.3.2 Acquisition

The touchless acquisition setup used to capture the palmprint images at an uncontrolled distance is depicted in Fig. 5.18 and consists of a two-view acquisition system and LED illumination. Specifically, two CCD color cameras are mounted facing upward. The user's hand must only be placed inside an acquisition volume, which is defined by the field of view of the cameras, their depth of focus, and the region with uniform illumination. Moreover, the user is not required to spread his fingers to facilitate the segmentation process, and a relaxed position of the hand is sufficient to perform the recognition.

The acquisition volume, which has size $W \times H \times D$, considers all of the space in which the hand can be placed to perform a correct acquisition and is placed at a distance Δ_{H-Low} from the cameras. A surface with a uniform color is placed at a distance Δ_{H-High} to delimit the superior part of the acquisition volume.

The illumination is designed to be uniform, and differences in the position, distance, and orientation of the hand inside the acquisition volume produce limited differences in the visibility of details on different parts of the palm. However, the

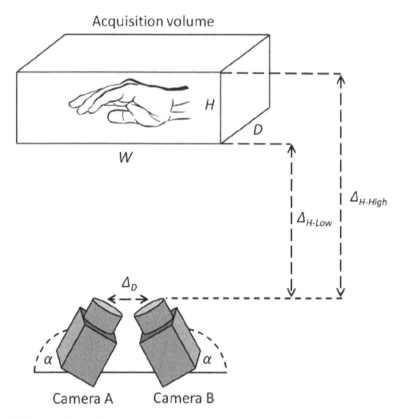

Fig. 5.18 Acquisition volume

possible presence of regions with non-uniform illumination (e.g., reflections or shadows) does not influence the position and structure of palmprint details and at most can only partially reduce the usable area.

Three types of illuminations, referred to as Method 1, Method 2, and Method 3, are considered to achieve the most uniform illumination possible inside the acquisition volume:

- *Method 1*: two white LED bars are mounted at the sides of the acquisition volume at a distance Δ_L from the cameras, and with a distance Δ_W between them. The bars are inclined toward the acquisition volume at an angle β (Fig. 5.19). This method provides uniform illumination within the acquisition volume
- *Method 2*: three downlight illuminators with white LEDs are mounted at the same distance Δ_L from the cameras and arranged equispaced in a circular fashion around the acquisition volume. The downlights are inclined toward the acquisition volume at an angle β (Fig. 5.20). Compared to Method 1, this method provides higher intensity illumination.

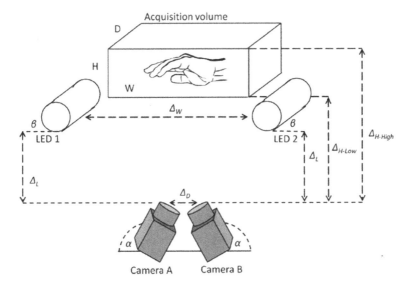

Fig. 5.19 Schematic of the illumination used in Method 1

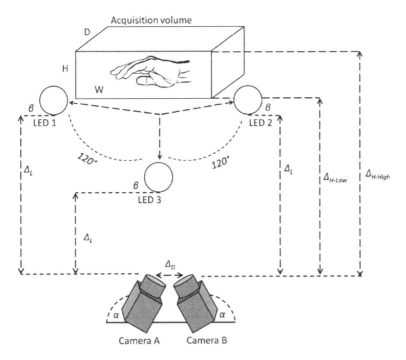

Fig. 5.20 Schematic of the illumination used in Method 2

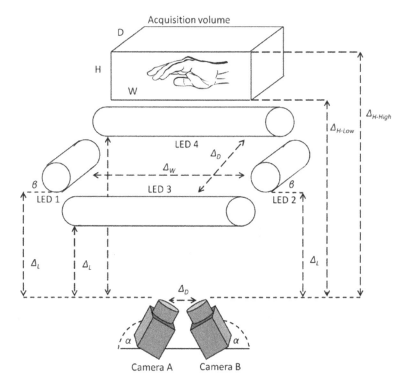

Fig. 5.21 Schematic of the illumination used in Method 3

- *Method 3*: four blue LED bars are mounted at a distance Δ_L from the cameras. The bars are arranged around the acquisition volume with a distance Δ_W between the lateral bars and a distance Δ_D between the front and rear bars. The bars are inclined toward the acquisition volume at an angle β (Fig. 5.21). This method provides uniform illumination, and the blue light enhances the details of the palmprint. However, the R channel of the captured images contains little information.

To capture a palmprint sample, the user is required to place his hand inside the acquisition volume. A synchronized two-view acquisition is then performed. The orientation and pose of the hand are not constrained, and the user is only required to place his hand in a way that makes the palmprint visible to the acquisition system.

A relaxed position of the hand is possible, with uncontrolled yaw orientations (Fig. 5.22). Small rotations along the pitch and roll angles can also be tolerated.

An adaptive shutter adjustment scheme is used to capture images with a similar average brightness and to cope with changes in the ambient light and variations in the reflectivity of the skin of different people:

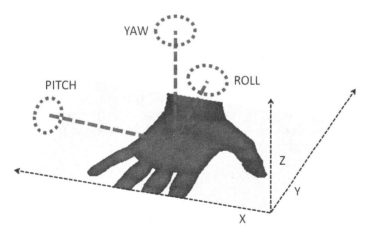

Fig. 5.22 Schematic of the three possible rotations of the hand

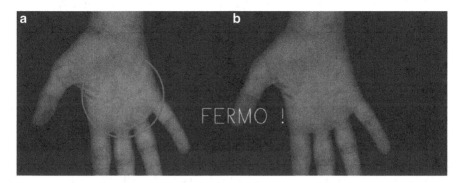

Fig. 5.23 Example of the user interface showing the live feed from the two-view camera setup: (**a**) left camera; (**b**) right camera

$$
t_{Shutter} = \begin{cases} t_{Shutter} + 1 & \text{if } \overline{I(x,y)} < t_M \text{ and } \max{(I(x,y))} < 250 \\ t_{Shutter} - 1 & \text{if } \overline{I(x,y)} > t_M \\ t_{Shutter} & \text{if } \overline{I(x,y)} = t_M \end{cases} , \tag{5.30}
$$

where t_M is an experimentally chosen value and the value of 250 is used to avoid saturation effects.

To increase the ease of use of the acquisition device, a user interface is designed to show a live feed of the field of view of the cameras. In addition, a circle is superimposed on the live image (Fig. 5.23), and the acquisition is performed when the palm of the user is placed within the circle.

The live image is segmented as follows:

$$I_s(x,y) = \begin{cases} 1 \text{ if } I(x,y) > t_s \\ 0 \text{ otherwise} \end{cases} , \tag{5.31}$$

where $I_s(x,y)$ is the binary segmented mask and t_s is an experimentally estimated threshold value. Moreover, to verify the presence of the palm inside the circle, a circular ROI mask $C(x,y)$ is defined and centered on the image. The *AND* operator is used to combine the masks $I_s(x,y)$ and $C(x,y)$:

$$K(x,y) = I_s(x,y) \cap C(x,y) , \tag{5.32}$$

where $K(x,y)$ is the resulting image. If $K(x,y) = C(x,y)$, the central region of the hand corresponding to the palm is placed over the circle in the central area of the image. Text is then superimposed on the live feed to direct the user to remain steady. After a short period of time required to avoid motion blur, the acquisition is automatically performed.

Examples of acquisitions using the three described illumination methods are shown in Fig. 5.24.

5.3.3   Image Preprocessing

The purpose of the image preprocessing step is to segment the palm region of the hand in the acquisitions.

First, the two color images are converted to single-channel images. For acquisitions performed using Method 1 and Method 2, a grayscale image is computed. For acquisitions performed using Method 3, the blue B channel of the image is considered. Then, the images are segmented to remove the background. Because a surface with a uniform color is used, the thresholding operation described in (5.31) is used to extract the foreground and obtain the image $I_s(x,y)$.

To eliminate points outside the boundary that could potentially be segmented as foreground, a morphological opening operation is applied, followed by a closing operation. Then, only the largest connected component is extracted.

The fingers are removed with a morphological opening operation using a structural element with a circular shape and a fixed size, and the points lying on the computed boundary are extracted.

A two-dimensional ellipse is fitted to the extracted points by solving a minimization problem:

$$\min \left(\log \left(\det A \right) \right) , \tag{5.33}$$

where A is the 2×2 matrix of the ellipse equation, expressed in the form:

$$(x - c_e)^T A (x - c_e) = 1 , \tag{5.34}$$

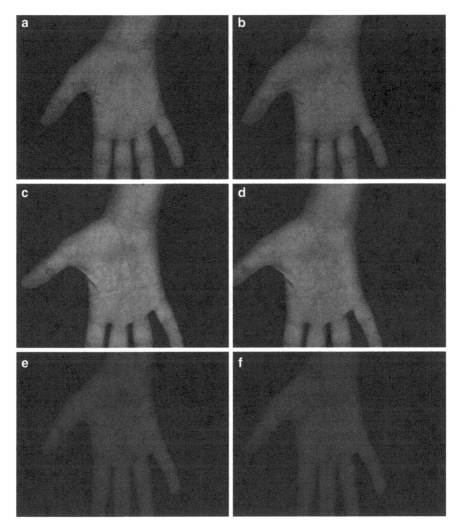

Fig. 5.24 Examples of touchless two-view acquisitions performed at an uncontrolled hand distance: (**a, b**) acquisition performed using Method 1; (**c, d**) acquisition performed using Method 2; (**e, f**) acquisition performed using Method 3

where c_e is the vector containing the coordinates of the center of the ellipse. The minimization problem is subject to the following constraints:

$$(p_i - c_e)^T A (p_i - c_e) \leq 1 \ , \tag{5.35}$$

where p_i is the i-th extracted point lying on the boundary.

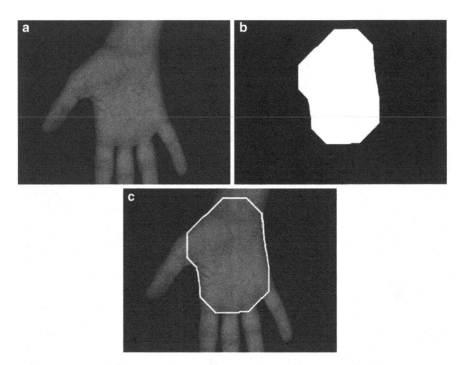

Fig. 5.25 Example of the segmentation step: (**a**) grayscale image captured using Method 1; (**b**) segmented image; (**c**) edge of the segmented image superimposed on the grayscale image. Only the region corresponding to the palm is extracted

Then, the singular value decomposition of the matrix A is computed as follows:

$$[U \ Q \ V] = \text{svd}(A) \ . \tag{5.36}$$

The radii r_1, r_2 of the fitted ellipse are then computed as follows:

$$r_1 = \frac{1}{\sqrt{Q_{(1,1)}}} \quad ; \quad r_2 = \frac{1}{\sqrt{Q_{(2,2)}}} \ . \tag{5.37}$$

A morphological opening operation is performed to extract the central palm region using a structural element with a circular shape and a size s_e, which is computed based on the radii of the fitted ellipse:

$$s_e = k_e \min(r_1, r_2) \ , \tag{5.38}$$

where k_e is a fixed parameter chosen experimentally.

An example of the segmentation operation is shown in Fig. 5.25.

5.3.4 Three-Dimensional Palmprint Processing

The three-dimensional processing of the palmprint can be divided into three steps. First, the three-dimensional model of the palm is reconstructed using the two-view acquisitions and the calibration data. Then, the model is normalized in three-dimensional space. Finally, a three-dimensional image registration is performed by reprojecting the model onto the image plane using the calibration data.

5.3.4.1 Three-Dimensional Palmprint Reconstruction

The method described in Sect. 5.2.4, which is based on a cross-correlation approach, is used to compute the three-dimensional model of the palmprint described by the point cloud (X_A, Y_A, Z_A). A similar procedure is used to compute the corresponding surfaces and textures S_{Ax}, S_{Ay}, S_{Az}, and S_{Ac}.

Examples of reconstructed point clouds with the relative estimated surfaces and textures are shown in Fig. 5.26.

5.3.4.2 Three-Dimensional Model Normalization

The three-dimensional point cloud (X_A, Y_A, Z_A) is registered to normalize its position and orientation in three-dimensional space. The pitch and roll rotations are corrected (Fig. 5.22) to obtain a model that is oriented primarily in the XY plane.

First, the point cloud is centered in the origin of the axes by subtracting the corresponding mean coordinates from the point cloud:

$$X_{Am} = X_A - \frac{1}{N} \sum_{i=1}^{N} X_{A_i} \; ;$$

$$Y_{Am} = Y_A - \frac{1}{N} \sum_{i=1}^{N} Y_{A_i} \; ;$$

$$Z_{Am} = Z_A - \frac{1}{N} \sum_{i=1}^{N} Z_{A_i} \; , \tag{5.39}$$

where N is the number of points in the point cloud. Then, a linear interpolation is used to fit a plane to the points, and the point cloud (X_p, Y_p, Z_p) is produced. The fitted plane is used to estimate the orientation of the palm in the three-dimensional space. In particular, the ranges of the values of the fitted plane in the X, Y, and Z directions are considered as the catheti of two right triangles, and trigonometric formulas are used to estimate the pitch and roll angles (Fig. 5.27).

The ranges of the values of the plane along the x and z directions are computed as:

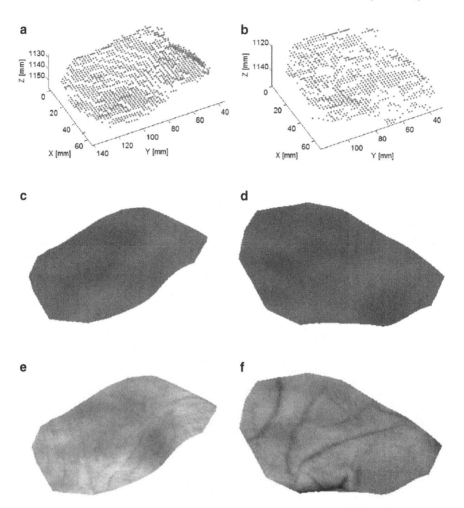

Fig. 5.26 Examples of reconstructed three-dimensional palmprint models: (**a, b**) filtered point clouds; (**c, d**) interpolated surfaces; (**e, f**) texture images. The described method can reconstruct three-dimensional palmprint models with good accuracy

$$x_r = \max X_p - \min X_p \;\; ;$$

$$z_r = \max Z_p - \min Z_p \;\; ; \tag{5.40}$$

where x_r is the range of the values of the fitted plane along the X axis and z_r is the range of the values of the fitted plane along the Z axis. Using the ranges z_r, x_r as the catheti of a right triangle, the hypotenuse a_r is computed as the following:

$$a_r = \sqrt{x_r^2 + z_r^2} \;\; . \tag{5.41}$$

Fig. 5.27 Computation of the roll and pitch angles using the fitted plane. The ranges of the values of the plane on the X, Y, Z axes are considered as the catheti of two right triangles, and trigonometric formulas are used to estimate the pitch and roll angles

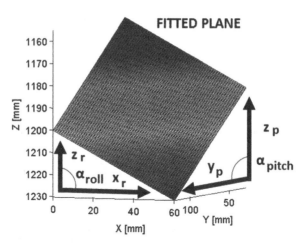

The roll angle α_{roll} is then estimated using the trigonometric formula:

$$\alpha_{roll} = \sin^{-1} \frac{z_r}{a_r} \; . \tag{5.42}$$

The rotation matrix corresponding to α_{roll} is computed as:

$$R_{roll} = \begin{bmatrix} \cos(\alpha_{roll}) & 0 & \sin(\alpha_{roll}) \\ 0 & 1 & 0 \\ -\sin(\alpha_{roll}) & 0 & \cos(\alpha_{roll}) \end{bmatrix} . \tag{5.43}$$

This rotation is applied to the points belonging to the reconstructed model of the palm:

$$\begin{bmatrix} X_{roll} \\ Y_{roll} \\ Z_{roll} \end{bmatrix} = R_{roll} \begin{bmatrix} X_{Am} \\ Y_{Am} \\ Z_{Am} \end{bmatrix} , \tag{5.44}$$

where $(X_{roll}, Y_{roll}, Z_{roll})$ is the point cloud after compensating for the roll angle.

Similarly, the pitch angle is compensated for by first estimating the ranges of the values of the fitted plane along the Y and Z axes:

$$y_p = \max Y_p - \min Y_p \; ;$$
$$z_p = \max Z_p - \min Z_p \; , \tag{5.45}$$

where y_p is the range of the values of the fitted plane along the Y axis and z_p is the range of the values of the fitted plane along the Z axis. The hypotenuse a_p is computed as follows:

$$a_p = \sqrt{y_p^2 + z_p^2} \; , \tag{5.46}$$

and the pitch angle α_{pitch} is estimated using the following trigonometric formula:

$$\alpha_{pitch} = \sin^{-1} \frac{z_p}{a_p} \; . \tag{5.47}$$

The rotation matrix corresponding to α_{pitch} is computed as follows:

$$R_{pitch} = \begin{bmatrix} \cos(\alpha_{pitch}) & 0 & \sin(\alpha_{pitch}) \\ 0 & 1 & 0 \\ -\sin(\alpha_{pitch}) & 0 & \cos(\alpha_{pitch}) \end{bmatrix} \; . \tag{5.48}$$

This rotation is then applied to the points obtained after the correction for the roll angle:

$$\begin{bmatrix} X_{pitch} \\ Y_{pitch} \\ Z_{pitch} \end{bmatrix} = R_{pitch} \begin{bmatrix} X_{roll} \\ Y_{roll} \\ Z_{roll} \end{bmatrix} \; , \tag{5.49}$$

where $(X_{pitch}, Y_{pitch}, Z_{pitch})$ is the point cloud after compensating for the pitch angle.

The obtained point cloud is centered at the origin of the axes by subtracting the corresponding mean coordinates:

$$X_{norm} = X_{pitch} - \frac{1}{N} \sum_{i=1}^{N} X_{pitch_i} \; ;$$

$$Y_{norm} = Y_{pitch} - \frac{1}{N} \sum_{i=1}^{N} Y_{pitch_i} \; ;$$

$$Z_{norm} = Z_{pitch} - \frac{1}{N} \sum_{i=1}^{N} Z_{pitch_i} \; , \tag{5.50}$$

Examples of normalized point clouds are shown in Fig. 5.28.

5.3.4.3   Three-Dimensional Image Registration

The purpose of the three-dimensional image registration step is to reproject the normalized models onto the image plane to obtain two-dimensional images as if they are captured in the same position and with the same orientation, even if the acquisitions of the hand are performed at different distances and with different orientations.

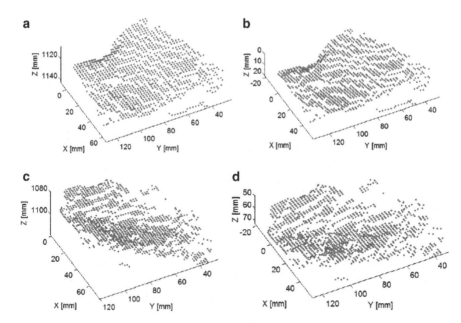

Fig. 5.28 Example of three-dimensional normalized models obtained from acquisitions performed using Method 1: (**a**, **c**) three-dimensional models before normalization; (**b**, **d**) three-dimensional models after normalization. The compensation for the pitch and roll rotations is apparent, and the normalized models lie on the XY plane

The calibration data and the method described in Sect. 5.3.1 are used to project the normalized model onto the image plane according to the method described in [92]:

$$
\begin{bmatrix} u \\ v \\ 1 \end{bmatrix} = K[R|t] \begin{bmatrix} X_{norm} \\ Y_{norm} \\ Z_{norm} \\ 1 \end{bmatrix} , \tag{5.51}
$$

where (u, v) are the projected pixel coordinates, K is the intrinsic camera matrix, R and t are the rotation matrix and translation vector that describe the position of the object with respect to the camera, and $(X_{norm}, Y_{norm}, Z_{norm})$ is the normalized three-dimensional point cloud.

To project every model in the same manner, fixed values for R and t are used. Moreover, two different values are used to project the model in two positions, maintaining the same relative difference between the two registered images as that between the original images I_A and I_B:

$$R_L = \begin{bmatrix} 1 & 0 & 0 \\ 0 & 1 & 0 \\ 0 & 0 & 1 \end{bmatrix} \quad ; \quad t_L = \begin{bmatrix} t_x \\ t_y \\ t_z \end{bmatrix} \quad ;$$

$$R_R = R_c \quad ; \quad t_R = (R_R \, t_L) + t_C \quad , \tag{5.52}$$

where R_L, and t_L are the parameters used to project the model in the first position, R_R, and t_R are the parameters used to project the model in the second position, t_x, t_y, and t_z are fixed values, and R_C and t_C are the parameters obtained from the calibration of the acquisition setup that describe the relative position of the right Camera B with respect to the left Camera A.

The resulting images are computed using a linear interpolation of the images I_A and I_B at the new positions (u, v), producing the registered images I_{Ar} and I_{Br}.

The method described in Sect. 5.2.4.4 is used to compute the surface maps S'_{Ax}, S'_{Ay}, S'_{Az} from the normalized point cloud $(X_{norm}, Y_{norm}, Z_{norm})$. Then, the coordinates of the surface maps S'_{Ax}, S'_{Ay} are adjusted to match the coordinates of the image I_{Ar}.

Similarly, the surface maps S'_{Bx}, S'_{By}, S'_{Bz} are obtained by adjusting the coordinates of the computed surface maps to match the coordinates of the image I_{Br}.

5.3.5   Texture Enhancement

A texture enhancement procedure similar to the procedure described in Sect. 5.2.5 is used to enhance the images obtained after three-dimensional registration. The method involves background subtraction, a logarithm operator, and a histogram equalization procedure.

In the case of palmprint samples captured using Method 1 or Method 2, the same enhancement procedure is performed on the R and B channels separately for both the left and right images I_{Ar} and I_{Br}. In the case of palmprint samples captured using Method 3, the enhancement procedure is performed only on the B channel of the left and right images. Examples of enhanced textures are shown in Fig. 5.29.

5.3.6   Two-Dimensional Feature Extraction and Matching

For each palmprint sample captured using Method 1 or Method 2, 8 images are considered to build the corresponding template. Table 5.2 summarizes the images that are considered. For palmprint samples captured using Method 3, only four images, which are summarized in Table 5.3, are used.

In this section, the method used for extracting and matching the two-dimensional features of two templates is described. In particular, the notation I_A, I_B is used to indicate the images corresponding to the first template, while the notation I'_A, I'_B is used to indicate the images corresponding to the second template.

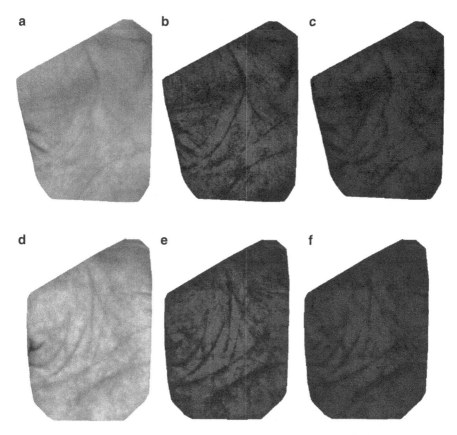

Fig. 5.29 Examples of enhanced texture images captured using Method 1: (**a**, **d**) original left images from two different individuals; (**b**, **e**) enhanced textures obtained from the B channel; (**c**, **f**) enhanced textures obtained from the R channel

The two-dimensional feature extraction and matching method can be divided into three steps. First, the images to be compared are aligned. Then, a method similar to the one described in Sect. 5.2.6, based on the SIFT features, is used to extract and match the distinctive points. Finally, a procedure based on point collinearity is used to refine the extracted points.

5.3.6.1 Image Alignment

An image alignment procedure is used to minimize the differences between the images being compared. However, because the region of interest of the palms captured using the method described in Sect. 5.3.2 is almost flat, the corresponding three-dimensional models present little information for registering the models, and accurate alignment would not be possible using only the three-dimensional

Table 5.2 Summary of the images considered for each palmprint sample captured using Method 1 or Method 2

Notation	Description
I_{A_R}	R channel of the left texture image
I_{A_B}	B channel of the left texture image
I_{AE_R}	Enhanced texture computed from the R channel of the left texture image
I_{AE_B}	Enhanced texture computed from the B channel of the left texture image
I_{B_R}	R channel of the right texture image
I_{B_B}	B channel of the right texture image
I_{BE_R}	Enhanced texture computed from the R channel of the right texture image
I_{BE_B}	Enhanced texture computed from the B channel of the right texture image

Table 5.3 Summary of the images considered for each palmprint sample captured using Method 3

Notation	Description
I_{A_B}	B channel of the left texture image
I_{AE_B}	Enhanced texture computed from the B channel of the left texture image
I_{B_B}	B channel of the right texture image
I_{BE_B}	Enhanced texture computed from the B channel of the right texture image

information. For this reason, a two-dimensional alignment procedure is used. Specifically, a SIFT-based method [349] is used to align the images corresponding to the templates to be compared. For samples captured using Method 1 and Method 2, the SIFT feature points are extracted from the enhanced images of the first template $I_{AE_R}, I_{AE_B}, I_{BE_R}, I_{BE_B}$:

$$I_{AE_R} \to_{SIFT} S_1 \quad ; \quad I_{BE_R} \to_{SIFT} S_3 \quad ;$$
$$I_{AE_B} \to_{SIFT} S_2 \quad ; \quad I_{BE_B} \to_{SIFT} S_4 \quad . \tag{5.53}$$

Similarly, the SIFT feature points are extracted from the images $I'_{AE_R}, I'_{AE_B}, I'_{BE_R}, I'_{BE_B}$ for the second template. For samples captured using Method 3, only the images I_{AE_B}, I_{BE_B} pertaining to the first template and I'_{AE_B}, I'_{BE_B} pertaining to the second template are considered.

The number of points extracted from each image is variable, and a descriptor $D(f_1, \ldots, f_{128})$ comprising 128 features is computed for each point.

A procedure based on the Euclidean distance is used to match the sets of descriptors extracted from the corresponding images of the two templates. In particular, a descriptor D_m is matched to a descriptor D'_n only if their distance, multiplied by a fixed threshold, is less than the maximum distance between D_m and the other descriptors:

$$d(D_m, D'_n) \cdot t_{SIFT} \leq \max_{p=1,\dots,N'} (d(D_m, D'_p)) \ , \tag{5.54}$$

where $d(\cdot)$ represents the Euclidean distance and N' is the number of points in the image to be compared in the second template. The coordinates of the matching points corresponding to the matched descriptors are referred to as $M_{1,\dots,4}$ and $M'_{1,\dots,4}$.

Then, the sets of matching points $M_{1,\dots,4}$ relative to the first template are merged in two sets. The matched points corresponding to the left images I_{AE_R}, I_{AE_B} and the right images I_{BE_R}, I_{BE_B} are distinguished to obtain the sets M_{At}, M_{Bt}. Similarly, the sets of points relative to the images pertaining to the second template are merged in the sets M'_{At}, M'_{Bt}.

The sets of matched points M_{At}, M'_{At} are used to compute the non-reflective similarity transformation between the left images of the first template I_{A_R}, I_{A_B}, I_{AE_R}, I_{AE_B} and the left images of the second template I'_{A_R}, I'_{A_B}, I'_{AE_R}, I'_{AE_B}. A non-reflective similarity transformation is a subset of affine transformations that may include rotation, translation, and scaling. In non-reflective similarity transformations, shapes and angles are preserved, parallel lines remain parallel, and straight lines remain straight. Here, a RANSAC-based algorithm is used to estimate the transformation T_A, described by a 3×2 matrix, which transforms the point locations M'_{At} in the locations M_{At}.

Similarly, the sets M_{Bt}, M'_{Bt} are used to compute the non-reflective similarity transformation between the right images of the first template I_{B_R}, I_{B_B}, I_{BE_R}, I_{BE_B} and the right images I'_{B_R}, I'_{B_B}, I'_{BE_R}, I'_{BE_B} of the second template. The transformation is described by the matrix T_B, which maps the points M'_{Bt} to the points M_{Bt}.

Then, the computed transformation matrix T_A is applied to the left images of the second template I'_{A_R}, I'_{A_B}, I'_{AE_R}, I'_{AE_B} to obtain the aligned images I''_{A_R}, I''_{A_B}, I''_{AE_R}, I''_{AE_B}. Similarly, the transformation T_B is applied to the right images of the second template I'_{B_R}, I'_{B_B}, I'_{BE_R}, I'_{BE_B} to obtain the aligned images I''_{B_R}, I''_{B_B}, I''_{BE_R}, I''_{BE_B}.

An example image alignment is shown in Fig. 5.30.

5.3.6.2 Point Extraction and Matching

A method based on the SIFT feature points similar to the method described in Sect. 5.2.6.2 is used to extract and match the points from the images corresponding to the two templates to be compared. However, in contrast to the method described in Sect. 5.2.6.2, the entire image is considered, and the images are not resized.

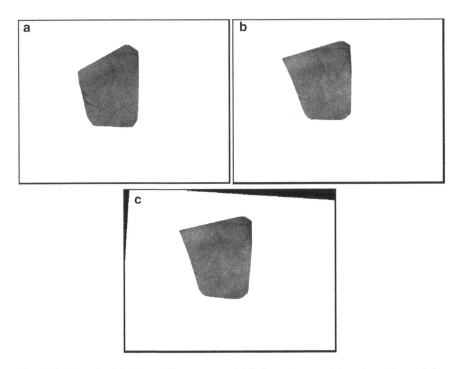

Fig. 5.30 Example of the image alignment step: (**a**) B channel extracted from image I_A pertaining to the first template to be compared; (**b**) B channel extracted from image I'_A pertaining to the second template to be compared; (**c**) alignment of image I''_A with image I_A to minimize the differences between the images to be compared

5.3.6.3   Refinement of the Matched Points

Because the images have been previously aligned, the method based on collinearity of the matched points described in Sect. 5.2.6.3 is used to refine the obtained sets of matching points. An example of the matched points before and after refinement is shown in Fig. 5.31.

5.3.7   *Three-Dimensional Feature Extraction and Matching*

The method described in Sect. 5.2.7 is used to extract and match three-dimensional features. The method is based on computation of the three-dimensional coordinates of the matching points using the surface maps computed in Sect. 5.3.4.1, combined with the use of the ICP algorithm to register the obtained point clouds. Then, a Delaunay triangulation is applied, and the number of similar triangles is used as the match score.

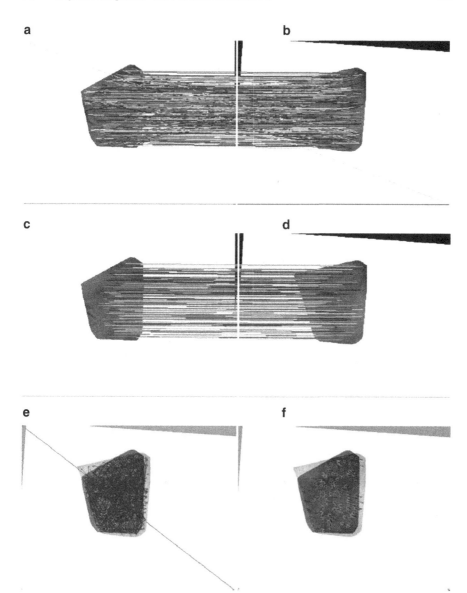

Fig. 5.31 Example of point refinement based on collinearity: (**a**, **b**) matching points between the first and second images before refinement; (**c**, **d**) matching points after refinement; (**e**) superimposition of the first and second images before the refinement in which the matching points are connected with a blue line; (**f**) superimposition of the first and second images after refinement in which the matching points are connected with a blue line. The results indicate that the majority of erroneous matches have been removed

5.4   Summary

Innovative methods for touchless and less-constrained palmprint recognition were described. The approaches described do not require the user to place his palm on any surface, thus avoiding hygiene problems, increasing user acceptability, and decreasing the acquisition time. Compared to other reported touchless three-dimensional acquisition methods, the methods described here are novel because they enable a fully touchless acquisition with a shorter capture time and at lower cost.

Two different touchless palmprint recognition methods were described. The first method, which was developed to study feasibility, requires the hand to be placed against a fixed surface, while the second method is fully touchless and does not require a fixed position of the hand or a support. A three-dimensional metric reconstruction of the palm is used to achieve a representation that is invariant with respect to the pose as well as the acquisition distance.

First, the method that requires a fixed position of the hand was described. In this method, the back of the hand must be placed on a fixed surface, and a two-view touchless acquisition is performed. LED illumination is used to enhance the visibility of the details. The captured images are segmented. Then, a method based on cross-correlation is used to obtain a set of matching points, which are triangulated in three-dimensional space using the camera calibration information. A point cloud filtering procedure is applied. The three-dimensional surface is then computed, along with the corresponding texture. The texture is enhanced using a method based on background subtraction, logarithmic transformation, and adaptive histogram equalization.

A SIFT-based method is used to extract and match the distinctive points in the images. The points are subsequently refined, and the corresponding three-dimensional coordinates are computed. The ICP algorithm is used to register the three-dimensional points of different samples, and the Delaunay triangulation is then computed. The number of similar triangles in the three-dimensional space is used as the match score.

A fully touchless and less-constrained method was also described. Importantly, the method does not require a fixed position of the hand and uses an original touchless acquisition procedure that defines an acquisition volume in which the hand is free to be positioned. The user is not required to spread the fingers to facilitate the segmentation process. Innovative illumination methods based on LEDs with different colors and positions are used to achieve uniform illumination and enhance the details of the palmprint.

The acquisitions are segmented using morphological operators and methods based on ellipse fitting. Three-dimensional models are then reconstructed. A normalization of the models in three-dimensional space is performed to compensate for differences in orientation and acquisition distance. The models are reprojected onto the image plane using the same parameters to obtain two-dimensional images, as if they were captured at the same position and with the same orientation.

Then, the resulting textures are enhanced and aligned, and a SIFT method is used to extract and match the distinctive points. A method based on ICP registration is used to register the point clouds. The Delaunay triangulation is then performed, and the number of similar triangles is used as the match score.

Chapter 6
Application and Experimental Evaluation of Methods

This chapter discusses the application of the innovative methods described in Chap. 5 and their experimental evaluation. The methods were tested to evaluate the different biometric aspects of the implemented techniques, including accuracy, robustness, speed, cost, interoperability, usability, acceptability, security, and privacy. However, particular emphasis was given to the evaluation of the accuracy of the described palmprint recognition systems because accuracy is commonly considered the most important aspect of biometric systems. The evaluation procedures used and figures of merit are described in Sect. 2.4.

The results are presented relative to those obtained using methods based on acquisitions at a fixed distance. A description of the acquisition of test datasets, a summary of the parameters used, an evaluation of the three-dimensional models produced, and a description of the recognition accuracy performances are given. In additions, the results of the methods based on acquisitions at an uncontrolled distance are presented and described. The acquisition of test datasets is described, the parameters used are summarized, and the three-dimensional models produced are evaluated. The achieved recognition accuracy is discussed. The robustness to hand orientation and variations in environmental illumination are considered. Other biometric aspects are also analyzed. A comparison of the described methods with the most recent approaches reported in the literature is presented. Some final considerations regarding the obtained results conclude the chapter.

6.1 Methods Based on Acquisitions at a Fixed Distance

In this section, the experimental evaluation of the methods based on acquisitions performed at a fixed distance described in Sect. 5.2 is presented. First, the collection of the test datasets is described in detail, including the hardware setup and the procedure used for sample collection. The acquisition parameters used, the acquisition

© Springer International Publishing Switzerland 2014
A. Genovese et al., *Touchless Palmprint Recognition Systems*,
Advances in Information Security 60, DOI 10.1007/978-3-319-10365-5_6

conditions, and the types of samples captured are also described. The parameters used to experimentally tune the algorithms are reported. Then, an evaluation of the three-dimensional reconstruction step is presented to determine the accuracy of the reconstruction method. Finally, the recognition accuracy is evaluated using the procedures and figures of merit described in Sect. 2.4.

6.1.1 Collection of the Test Datasets

The acquisition procedure described in Sect. 5.2.2 was used to collect the test dataset. The acquisition setup used (Fig. 6.1) consisted of two Sony XCD-SX90CR CCD color cameras with a 25 mm focal length that captured images at 15 fps and $1{,}280 \times 960$ resolution. The cameras were synchronized using a trigger mechanism and oriented at an angle $\alpha = 85°$ with respect to the surface, and the distance between the center of the optics was $\Delta_D = 100$ mm. The distance from the optics to the surface was $\Delta_H = 485$ mm, and the distance from the illumination source to the surface was $\Delta_H = 250$ mm.

The system was calibrated using a two-dimensional rigid chessboard composed of 12×9 squares, with each square having a size of 2.8×2.8 mm. The chessboard was captured in 15 different positions using synchronized two-view acquisitions.

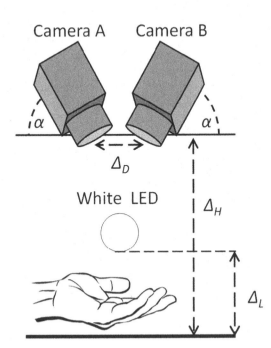

Fig. 6.1 Schematic of the touchless acquisition setup with the hand positioned at a fixed distance

These acquisitions were used to calibrate the two-view acquisition system, and a reconstruction error equal to 0.03 mm was obtained. The reconstruction error was computed by triangulating the positions of the corners of the squares in three-dimensional space using the formula described in Sect. 5.2.4.2 and fitting a plane through the points. The standard deviation of the distances between the points and the fitted plane is assumed to be a measure of the reconstruction error, similar to the method described in [132].

The dataset PF, which was used in the evaluation of the described method, was collected by capturing the 2 palms of 13 individuals to obtain a total of 26 different palms. For each palm, 8 different two-view acquisitions were performed, resulting in a total of 208 two-view acquisitions. Between different acquisitions, the user was required to remove his hand and then place it back on the surface so that a different sample was captured each time. The acquisitions corresponding to each user were performed in a single session. The volunteers were both male and female of different ethnicities and ranged in age from 25 to 45 years. Some examples of acquisitions for different individuals are shown in Fig. 6.2.

6.1.2 Parameters Used

The threshold used in the segmentation step was $t_s = 50$. The number of extracted points was $N_P = 10,000$. In the three-dimensional reconstruction step, the size of the rectangular search area was $\Delta_x = 150, \Delta_y = 10$, the epipolar distance threshold used was $t_{ep} = 2$, and the size of the cross-correlation window was $l \times l = 15 \times 15$. The parameter in the point cloud filtering step was $t_s = 5$. The threshold in the two-dimensional feature extraction and matching step was $t_{SIFT} = 1.5$. The threshold for comparing the triangles in the three-dimensional feature extraction and matching step was $t_D = 0.2$.

6.1.3 Evaluation of the Three-Dimensional Reconstruction

To evaluate the accuracy of the three-dimensional reconstruction process, the percentage of correctly reconstructed points was determined for each reconstructed model. Specifically, the ratio of the final number of points obtained after the point cloud filtering step to the number of points extracted from image I_A was calculated. The mean ratio and the standard deviation computed using all the samples in the database are reported in Table 6.1. These data indicate that the majority of the extracted points were correctly matched.

The percentage and spatial distribution of the matched points influence the accuracy of the computed template. For example, a smaller percentage of matched points can result in a smaller usable area for recognition because the corresponding three-dimensional information will not be available for some areas of the palmprint.

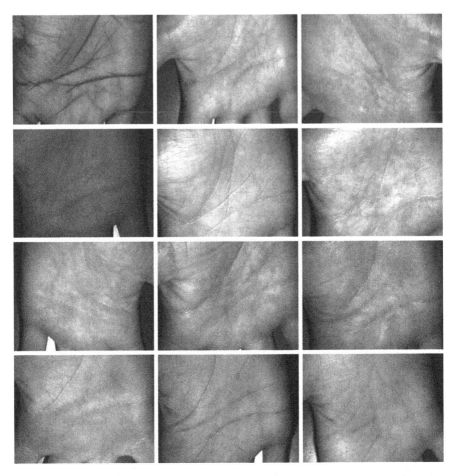

Fig. 6.2 Examples of acquisitions of palmprints captured at a fixed distance. The palms were captured from people of different ethnicities, both male and female, with an age range of 25–45 years

Table 6.1 Percentage of the correctly reconstructed points, expressed as the ratio of the number of points after the point cloud filtering step to the number of extracted points from the image I_A

	Ratio	
Dataset	Mean	Std
PF	89.37 %	3.49 %

The results indicate that the majority of the points are correctly matched

Moreover, areas with a smaller spatial distribution of matched points yield a coarser three-dimensional model, which provides less information and can decrease the recognition accuracy. However, in our experiments, a correct three-dimensional model consisting of a sufficient number of points was always reconstructed.

Examples of the reconstructed three-dimensional models computed using the method described in Sect. 5.2.4 are shown in Fig. 6.3, along with the corresponding interpolated surfaces and textures. These results indicate that the three-dimensional reconstruction method can compute accurate models that describe the shape of the depicted hand region. However, the resolution of the imaging system is not sufficient for the computation of information related to the three-dimensional depth of the palm lines.

6.1.4 Recognition Accuracy

The described feature extraction and matching method consisting of the two-dimensional and three-dimensional feature extraction and matching methods described in Sect. 5.2.6 and in Sect. 5.2.7 was applied to the computed three-dimensional models and the corresponding textures.

An ROC curve describing the recognition accuracy of the method is shown in Fig. 6.4, and Table 6.2 summarizes the obtained FMR and FNMR values at different points of the curve. Notably, the described recognition method achieved an EER value equal to 0.25 %. Thus, the described method was able to perform an accurate recognition comparable to that of previously described touchless palmprint recognition systems, which are summarized in Sect. 6.2.7. Moreover, the data in Table 6.2 indicate that the method obtained low percentages of false non-matches, similar to the EER value, with thresholds of the matching scores that resulted in small numbers of false matches, suggesting that the system could be used in high-security applications. In addition, the system produced low percentages of false matches, in agreement with the EER value, with threshold values that produced small numbers of false non-matches, suggesting that the system could also be used for low and medium security applications.

The number of individuals in the tested dataset was not sufficient for more general considerations regarding the recognition accuracy. However, the results obtained permitted the extension of the method to acquisitions performed at an uncontrolled distance.

6.2 Methods Based on Acquisitions with Uncontrolled Distance

In this section, experiments testing the methods based on acquisitions with uncontrolled distance described in Sect. 5.3 are described. First, the collection of the test datasets is described, including the hardware setup and the procedure used for the collection of the dataset. The acquisition parameters used, the acquisition conditions, and the types of samples captured are also described. The parameters

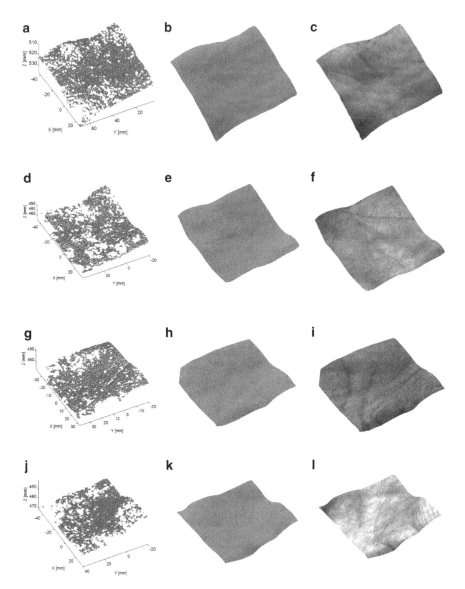

Fig. 6.3 Examples of three-dimensional palmprint models reconstructed using the method described in Sect. 5.2.4: (**a, d, g, j**) filtered point clouds; (**b, e, h, j**) interpolated surfaces; (**c, f, i, l**) corresponding textures. These results indicate that the described method can compute accurate three-dimensional models of the palmprint

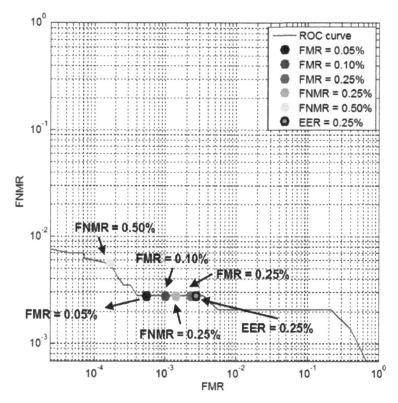

Fig. 6.4 ROC curve of the described palmprint recognition method based on acquisitions performed at a fixed distance. The points corresponding to the EER and to significant values of FMR and FNMR are *highlighted*

used to experimentally tune the algorithms are reported. Then, an evaluation of the three-dimensional reconstruction step is presented to determine the accuracy of the reconstruction method. The recognition accuracy is analyzed using the procedures and figures of merit described in Sect. 2.4. Moreover, the recognition accuracy obtained using multiple comparisons is also presented, and the robustness of the method to hand orientations and variations in environmental illumination is analyzed. Other biometric aspects, including speed, cost, interoperability, usability, acceptability, security, and privacy are analyzed using the most common practices. A comparison with the most recent approaches described in the literature is presented. Finally, an overall summary of the results is described.

Table 6.2 FMR and FNMR obtained by the described palmprint recognition method based on acquisitions performed at a fixed distance

	FNMR @FMR =0.05 %	FNMR @FMR =0.10 %	FNMR @FMR =0.25 %	FMR @FNMR =0.25 %	FMR @FNMR =0.50 %
EER (%)					
0.25	0.27 %	0.27 %	0.27 %	0.14 %	0.02 %

Fig. 6.5 Acquisition volume

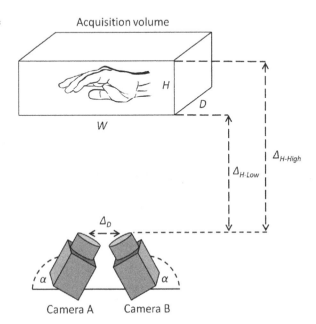

Acquisition volume

6.2.1 Collection of the Test Datasets

The acquisition procedure described in Sect. 5.3.2 was used to collect the datasets used. The acquisition setup used (Fig. 6.5) consisted of two Sony XCD-SX90CR CCD color cameras with a 25 mm focal length that captured images at 15 fps and $1{,}280 \times 960$ resolution. The cameras were synchronized using a trigger mechanism. The cameras were oriented at an angle $\alpha = 87°$ with respect to the surface, and the distance between the center of the optics was $\Delta_D = 100$ mm. The distances from the optics of the cameras to the lowest and highest points of the acquisition volume were $\Delta_{H-Low} = 1{,}080$ mm and $\Delta_{H-High} = 1{,}380$ mm, respectively. The size of the acquisition volume was $W = 225$ mm, $H = 300$ mm, and $D = 155$ mm. The value t_M used for controlling the shutter time was $t_M = 100$.

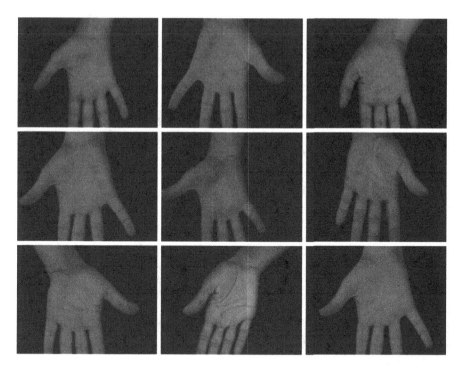

Fig. 6.6 Examples of acquisitions of palmprints captured with uncontrolled distance using Method 1. The palms were captured from people of different ethnicities, both male and female, with ages ranging from 25 to 45 years

For calibration, a two-dimensional rigid chessboard consisting of 12×9 squares, in which each square had a size of 7×7 mm, was used. The chessboard was captured in 15 different positions using synchronized two-view acquisitions performed with the described setup. These acquisitions were used to calibrate the two-view acquisition system, and a reconstruction error equal to 0.12 mm was obtained. The reconstruction error was computed by triangulating the positions of the corners of the squares in three-dimensional space using the formula described in Sect. 5.2.4.2 and fitting a plane through the points. The standard deviation of the distances between the points and the fitted plane was used as the reconstruction error measure, similar to the method described in [132].

The parameters used to implement the different illumination setups were as follows:

- *Method 1*: The LED bars were mounted at a distance $\Delta_L = 960$ mm from the cameras and with a distance $\Delta_W = 240$ mm between them. The bars were inclined toward the acquisition volume at an angle $\beta = 45°$. Examples of acquisitions captured using Method 1 are shown in Fig. 6.6.

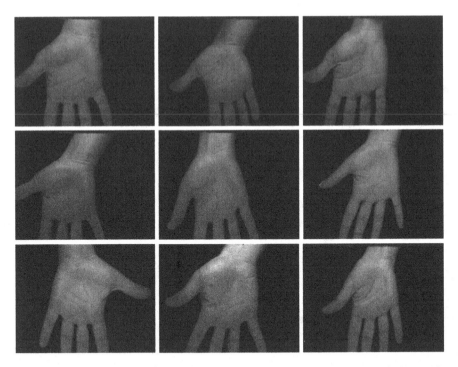

Fig. 6.7 Examples of palmprint acquisitions captured at uncontrolled distances using Method 2. The palmprints were captured from people of different ethnicities, both male and female, with ages ranging from 25 to 45 years

- *Method 2*: The downlight illuminations with white LEDs were mounted at a distance $\Delta_L = 960$ mm from the cameras and inclined toward the acquisition volume at an angle $\beta = 45°$. Examples of acquisitions captured using Method 2 are shown in Fig. 6.7.
- *Method 3*: The blue LED bars were mounted at a distance $\Delta_L = 960$ mm from the cameras, with a distance $\Delta_W = 290$ mm between the lateral bars and a distance $\Delta_D = 300$ mm between the front and rear bars. The bars were positioned horizontally ($\beta = 0°$). Examples of acquisitions captured using Method 3 are shown in Fig. 6.8.

The three different illumination methods were used to collect two datasets *PA* and *PB*. Each dataset contained the samples of individuals captured using two different illumination methods. First, the dataset *PA*, which contained the samples from individuals captured using Methods 1 and 3, was collected to assess the differences between white and blue illumination. The results obtained drove us to collect a second dataset *PB*, which contained the samples from individuals captured using Methods 2 and 3, which allowed us to evaluate the effectiveness of higher intensity white illumination compared with blue illumination.

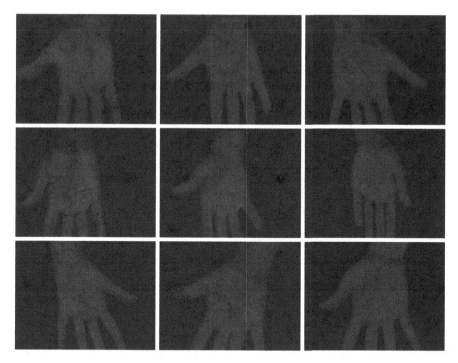

Fig. 6.8 Examples of palmprint acquisitions captured at uncontrolled distances using Method 3. The palmprints were captured from people of different ethnicities, both male and female, with ages ranging from 25 to 45 years

Two datasets were collected because illumination Methods 1 and 2 were implemented at different times and it was not possible to collect the samples from the same individuals. The two datasets *PA* and *PB* are summarized as follows:

- *Dataset PA*: This dataset was collected using Methods 1 and 3 to capture images of the 2 palms of 9 individuals to obtain a total of 18 different palms. For each palm, 10 different two-view acquisitions were performed, resulting in a total of 180 two-view acquisitions.
- *Dataset PB*: This dataset was collected using Methods 2 and 3 to capture images of the 2 palms of 32 individuals to obtain a total of 64 different palms. For each palm, 10 different two-view acquisitions were performed, resulting in a total of 640 two-view acquisitions.

Between different acquisitions, each user was required to remove his hand and then place it back on the surface. This process ensured that a different sample was captured each time. A minimum amount of instructions was given to the users. They were only required to extend the open hand in a relaxed position inside the

acquisition volume and place the palm over the circle superimposed on the live feed
(Fig. 5.23). The volunteers were both male and female of different ethnicities and
ranged in age from 25 to 45 years.

The acquisitions corresponding to each user were performed in a single session.
The entire acquisition procedure for each sample took approximately 5 s, including
the time required to position the hand, adapt the shutter duration, and ensure that the
hand was still (approximately 2 s). The actual capture of the image was performed
almost instantly, with shutter times ranging from 0.02 to 0.03 s.

Separate acquisition procedures were performed to capture the samples using
illumination Methods 2 and 3. However, a method for the quasi-simultaneous
capture of the images using both illumination methods could be easily implemented
using a small hardware circuit. In that case, the total capture time of the images
would simply be the sum of the two respective capture times, which would be no
greater than 0.06 s.

6.2.2 Parameters Used

The threshold in the segmentation step was $t_s = 50$, and the parameter for extracting
the central region of the palm was $k_e = 0.6$. The number of extracted points was
$N_P = 2,000$. In the three-dimensional reconstruction step, the size of the rectangular
search area was $\Delta_x = 90$ and $\Delta_y = 2$, the epipolar distance threshold was $t_{ep} = 2$, and
the size of the cross-correlation window was $l \times l = 30 \times 30$. The parameter in the
point cloud filtering step was $t_s = 1$. The threshold in the alignment step and the two-
dimensional feature extraction and matching step was $t_{SIFT} = 1.5$. The threshold for
comparing the triangles in the three-dimensional feature extraction and matching
step was $t_D = 0.2$.

6.2.3 Evaluation of the Three-Dimensional Reconstruction

To evaluate the accuracy of the three-dimensional reconstruction process, the ratio
of the final number of points obtained after the point cloud filtering step to the
number of extracted points from the image I_A was computed for each reconstructed
model. The mean ratio and its standard deviation were computed for each dataset
using all of the samples and are reported in Table 6.3. These data indicate that the
majority of points were correctly matched.

As mentioned in Sect. 6.1.3, the percentage and spatial distribution of the
matched points influence the accuracy of the computed template. For example, a
smaller percentage of matched points can result in a smaller usable area for recognition because some areas of the palmprint will not have the corresponding three-
dimensional information. Moreover, the normalization of the three-dimensional
model and the corresponding three-dimensional registration of the image could be
less precise. In our experiments, the thumb region of the hand (or the thenar region),

Table 6.3 Percentage of correctly reconstructed points, expressed as the ratio of the number of points after the point cloud filtering step to the number of extracted points from the image I_A

Dataset	Ratio	
	Mean	Std
PA—Method 1	66.72 %	13.71 %
PA—Method 3	74.44 %	15.23 %
PB—Method 2	70.50 %	12.99 %
PB—Method 3	70.94 %	15.25 %

The results indicate that the majority of the points were correctly matched

whose depth differs significantly from that of other regions of the hand, was not always reconstructed by the described three-dimensional reconstruction algorithm. However, the thenar area is of minor significance for palmprint recognition because only a small percentage of the details of the palmprint are contained in this region.

Areas with a smaller spatial distribution of matched points result in a coarser three-dimensional model, which provides less information and can decrease the recognition accuracy. However, in our experiments, a redundancy of points was extracted to ensure a sufficient number of points to correctly describe the three-dimensional model.

Examples of reconstructed three-dimensional models computed using acquisitions performed using Method 1 described in Sect. 5.3.4.1 are shown in Fig. 6.9, along with the corresponding interpolated surfaces. Examples of reconstructed models computed using acquisitions performed using Method 2 are shown in Fig. 6.10. Examples of reconstructed models computed using acquisitions performed using Method 3 are shown in Fig. 6.11. From the figures, it is evident that the three-dimensional reconstruction method computed accurate models and described the shape of the considered hand region. However, the resolution of the imaging system was not sufficient to compute the three-dimensional depth of the palm lines.

6.2.4 Recognition Accuracy

The tests performed to measure the recognition accuracy were divided according to the two datasets described in Sect. 6.2.1. First, the recognition accuracy using the dataset *PA* was tested to compare acquisition Methods 1 and 3. Then, the recognition accuracy using the dataset *PB* was evaluated to compare acquisition Methods 2 and 3.

6.2.4.1 Dataset PA

First, the accuracy of the described palmprint recognition method was tested with the dataset *PA*, which contained samples from individuals captured using Methods 1 and 3. The obtained results were compared to determine which illumination method performed best. The obtained match scores corresponding to the two illumination methods were combined using different fusion rules.

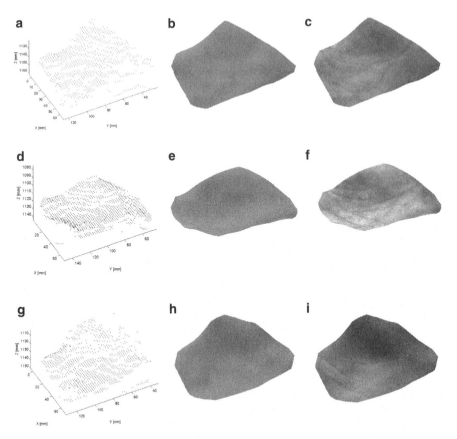

Fig. 6.9 Examples of three-dimensional palmprint models captured using Method 1 and reconstructed using the method described in Sect. 5.2.4: (**a, d, g**) filtered point clouds; (**b, e, h**) interpolated surfaces; (**c, f, i**) corresponding textures. These results indicate that the described method can compute accurate three-dimensional models of the palmprint

The ROC curves corresponding to the dataset *PA* are shown in Fig. 6.12. Using the samples captured with Method 1, the system achieved an EER value of 2.36 %, whereas the samples captured with Method 3 yielded an EER value of 1.71 %. Thus, both methods could perform accurate recognition. However, using the samples captured using Method 3 yielded a lower EER value, and the corresponding ROC curve exhibited better performance over nearly the entire range of the curve.

In addition, the potential integration of Methods 1 and 3 was evaluated using different fusion schemes at the match score level, expressed as follows:

$$m_s(i, j) = \text{mean}\,(m_1(i, j), m_3(i, j))\;;\qquad\qquad (6.1)$$

$$m_s(i, j) = \min\,(m_1(i, j), m_3(i, j))\;;\qquad\qquad (6.2)$$

$$m_s(i, j) = \max\,(m_1(i, j), m_3(i, j))\;,\qquad\qquad (6.3)$$

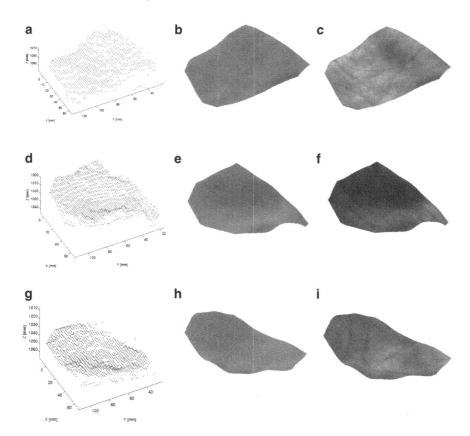

Fig. 6.10 Examples of three-dimensional palmprint models captured using Method 2 and reconstructed using the method described in Sect. 5.2.4: (**a, d, g**) filtered point clouds; (**b, e, h**) interpolated surfaces; (**c, f, i**) corresponding textures. These results indicate that the described method can compute accurate three-dimensional models of the palmprint

where $m_1(i, j)$ is the match score corresponding to the comparison of samples from individuals i and j in the dataset *PA* captured using Method 1 and $m_3(i, j)$ is the match score corresponding to the comparison of the samples from individuals i and j in the dataset *PA* captured using Method 3.

The corresponding ROC curves are presented in Fig. 6.13. Notably, the fusion scheme based on the computation of the mean match score using (6.1) obtained the best results and increased the recognition accuracy to EER = 0.42 %. Moreover, the corresponding ROC curve exhibited better performance over nearly the entire range of the curve.

The FMR and FNMR values obtained at different points of the curve for the fusion scheme based on the computation of the mean match score are reported in Table 6.4. Based on the average match score, the system exhibited low percentages of false non-matches, in agreement with the EER value, with thresholds of the

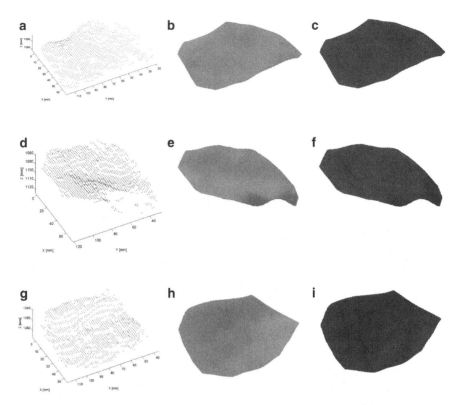

Fig. 6.11 Examples of three-dimensional palmprint models captured using Method 3 and reconstructed using the method described in Sect. 5.2.4: (**a**, **d**, **g**) filtered point clouds; (**b**, **e**, **h**) interpolated surfaces; (**c**, **f**, **i**) corresponding textures. These results indicate that the described method can compute accurate three-dimensional models of the palmprint

matching scores resulting in small numbers of false matches. This result suggests that the system could be used in high-security applications. Furthermore, the system had low percentages of false matches, in agreement with the EER value, also with threshold values that resulted in small numbers of false non-matches. Thus, the system could also be used for low- and medium-security applications.

However, the illumination performed using Method 1 did not have sufficient intensity for a real-time acquisition procedure and could easily produce samples affected by motion blur. These aspects limited the accuracy and usability of the system, and the supervision of an expert operator during the collection of the dataset *PA* was necessary. For this reason, a white illumination with more intensity was considered, and the larger dataset *PB* was collected using illumination Methods 2 and 3.

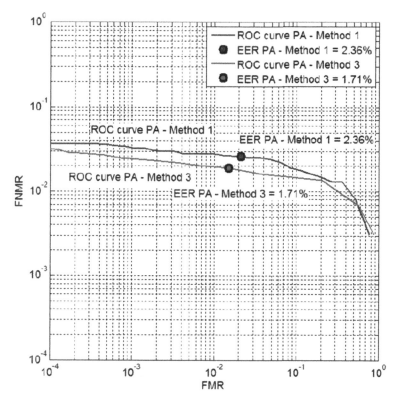

Fig. 6.12 ROC curves for the dataset *PA*, corresponding to the samples captured using Methods 1 and 3

Table 6.4 FMR and FNMR values for the dataset *PA*, obtained by calculating the mean of the results for the samples captured using Methods 1 and 3

Dataset	Fusion scheme	EER (%)	FNMR @FMR =0.25 %	FNMR @FMR =0.50 %	FNMR @FMR =0.75 %	FMR @FNMR =0.50 %	FMR @FNMR =0.75 %
PA	Mean	0.42	0.49 %	0.43 %	0.38 %	0.18 %	0.06 %

6.2.4.2   Dataset PB

The accuracy of the described palmprint recognition method was tested using the dataset *PB*, which was captured using illumination Methods 2 and 3. The results obtained were compared to determine which illumination method performed best. The results obtained by comparing each biometric template with three templates were also computed, and the best result was considered the match score. Moreover, the obtained match scores corresponding to the two illumination methods were combined using different fusion rules, and the corresponding confidence was estimated.

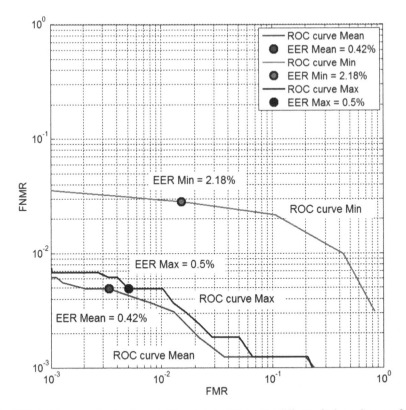

Fig. 6.13 ROC curves for the dataset *PA* corresponding to the different fusion schemes of the results for the samples captured using Methods 1 and 3

The ROC curves corresponding to the dataset *PB* are shown in Fig. 6.14. Using the samples captured with Method 2, the system achieved an EER value of 4.13 %, whereas the samples captured with Method 3 achieved an EER value of 2.53 %. Thus, better results were obtained using the samples captured using Method 3, and the corresponding ROC curve exhibited better performance over the entire range of the curve.

The potential integration of Methods 2 and 3 was tested using different fusion schemes at the match score level, computed using (6.1)–(6.3).

The corresponding ROC curves are reported in Fig. 6.15. The results show that the fusion scheme based on the computation of the mean match score produced the best results and permitted an increase in the recognition accuracy, with EER $= 0.66 \%$. Moreover, better performances were obtained over the entire range of the ROC curve compared to the other fusion methods.

The obtained FMR and FNMR values at different points in the curve are reported in Table 6.5. The system exhibited low percentages of false non-matches,

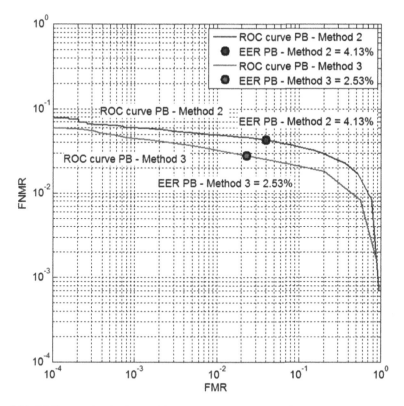

Fig. 6.14 ROC curves for the dataset *PB*, corresponding to the samples captured using Methods 2 and 3

in agreement with the EER value, with thresholds of the matching scores resulting in small numbers of false matches that could permit use of the system in high-security applications. Moreover, the system yielded low percentages of false matches, in agreement with the EER value, and the matching scores corresponded to small numbers of false non-matches.

Analysis of the genuine and impostor distributions of the dataset *PB* (Fig. 6.16) revealed that whereas the distributions of the impostors were condensed in a limited range of values ($[0, \sim 20]$), the match scores of the genuine comparisons were spread over a much wider range of values ($[0, \sim 7,000]$). Notably, some genuine comparisons produced low match scores, which caused the distributions of the genuine comparisons to overlap with the impostor distributions. This result occurred because the less-constrained acquisition procedure produced variation in the quality of the samples, and thus some lower-quality samples were captured that were not correctly matched to the other samples of the same individual.

To mitigate this problem and increase the accuracy and robustness of the biometric system, multiple comparisons could be performed for each recognition

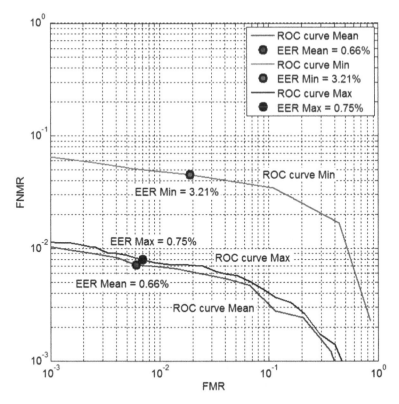

Fig. 6.15 ROC curves for the dataset *PB*, corresponding to the different fusion schemes of the results corresponding to the samples captured using Methods 2 and 3

Table 6.5 FMR and FNMR values for the dataset *PB* obtained by computing the mean of the results corresponding to the samples captured using Methods 2 and 3

Dataset	Fusion scheme	EER (%)	FNMR @FMR =0.25 %	FNMR @FMR =0.50 %	FNMR @FMR =0.75 %	FMR @FNMR =0.75 %
PB	Mean	0.66	1.02 %	0.86 %	0.79 %	0.88 %

attempt, followed by selection of the best result. This strategy has been proposed in several documents describing best practices for the evaluation of biometric recognition systems [239, 240].

The accuracy of the described palmprint recognition method was tested using the dataset *PB* by performing three comparisons for each recognition attempt, and then selecting the maximum match score. The ROC curves corresponding to the samples of the dataset *PB* captured using Method 2, considering one comparison as well as three comparisons, are shown in Fig. 6.17. By considering three comparisons, the

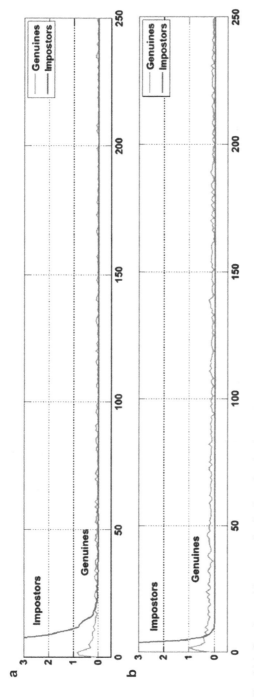

Fig. 6.16 Genuine and impostor distributions for the dataset *PB*. The plots are magnified in the overlapping areas of the distributions. (**a**) Genuine and impostor distributions corresponding to the samples captured using Method 2; (**b**) genuine and impostor distributions corresponding to the samples captured using Method 3. The distributions of the impostors are condensed in a limited range of values ([0,~20]), while the match scores of the genuine comparisons are distributed over a much wider range of values ([0,~7,000]). The wide range of match scores is the result of variation in the quality of the samples due to the less-constrained acquisition procedure, which resulted in the capture of some lower-quality samples that were not correctly matched to the other captured samples for the same individual

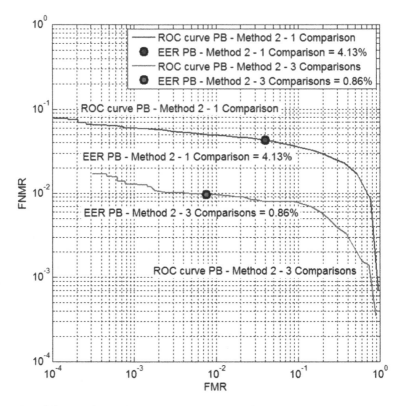

Fig. 6.17 ROC curves for the dataset *PB*, corresponding to the samples captured using Method 2, considering both one comparison and three comparisons

recognition accuracy was significantly increased. The EER was reduced from 4.13 to 0.86 %. The ROC curves corresponding to the samples of the dataset *PB* captured using Method 3 for both one comparison and three comparisons are shown in Fig. 6.18. The recognition accuracy was increased by considering three comparisons because the EER was reduced from 2.53 to 0.64 %.

In addition, the obtained match scores corresponding to the samples captured using Methods 2 and 3 were combined using the fusion rule based on the mean match score described in (6.1). The corresponding ROC curve is shown in Fig. 6.19. By considering three comparisons and computing the average match score for the samples captured using Methods 2 and 3, a lower EER value of 0.08 % was obtained.

The obtained FMR and FNMR values for different points of the curve are reported in Table 6.6. The system exhibited low percentages of false non-matches, in agreement with the EER value, with thresholds of the matching scores resulting in small numbers of false matches, again suggesting that the system could be used in high-security applications. Moreover, the system yielded low percentages of false matches, in agreement with the EER value, with thresholds corresponding to small numbers of false non-matches.

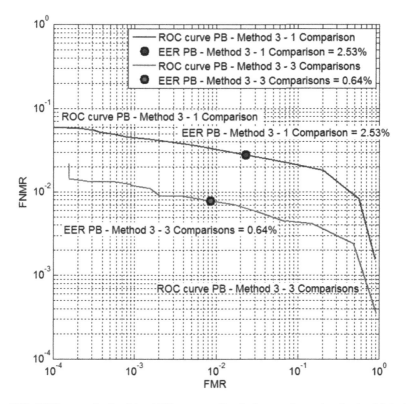

Fig. 6.18 ROC curves for the dataset *PB* corresponding to the samples captured using Method 3, considering both one comparison and three comparisons

Because it is not possible to collect databases of palmprints from the entire population, the confidence of the performed accuracy measurements must be estimated to test the applicability of the described biometric system in a real scenario. For this purpose, the two techniques for confidence estimation described in Sect. 2.4.3.4 were used. The first technique was based on the assumption that the obtained data follows a normal distribution, and the second technique was based on a bootstrap approach. Both techniques used a confidence level of 90 %, and the bootstrap method was applied using 1,000 iterations.

The confidence boundaries for the accuracy of the dataset *PB* were obtained by computing the mean of the results corresponding to the samples captured using Methods 2 and 3 and considering three comparisons. The ROC curves obtained, along with the corresponding confidence boundaries, are shown in Fig. 6.20. These results demonstrate that the confidence boundaries of the proposed system are small, indicating that the described system could be effectively used for a larger dataset.

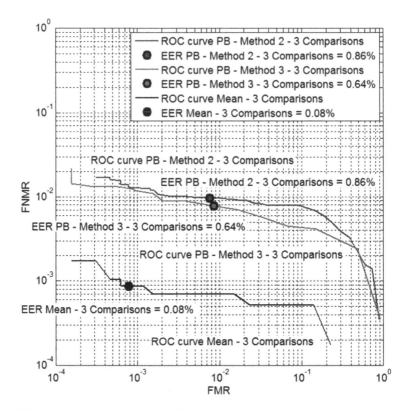

Fig. 6.19 ROC curves for the dataset *PB*, obtained by computing the mean of the results corresponding to the samples captured using Methods 2 and 3 and considering three comparisons

Table 6.6 FMR and FNMR values for the dataset *PB*, obtained by computing the mean of the results corresponding to the samples captured using Methods 2 and 3 and considering three comparisons

Dataset	Fusion scheme	EER (%)	FNMR @FMR =0.05 %	FNMR @FMR =0.10 %	FNMR @FMR =0.25 %	FMR @FNMR =0.10 %	FMR @FNMR =0.25 %
PB	Mean	0.08	0.10 %	0.09 %	0.07 %	0.06 %	0.00 %

Note: The average match score for three comparisons is considered

6.2.5 Robustness to Hand Orientation and Environmental Illumination

To test the robustness of the proposed method, the performance of the proposed method was tested for varying hand orientations and environmental illumination conditions during the acquisition.

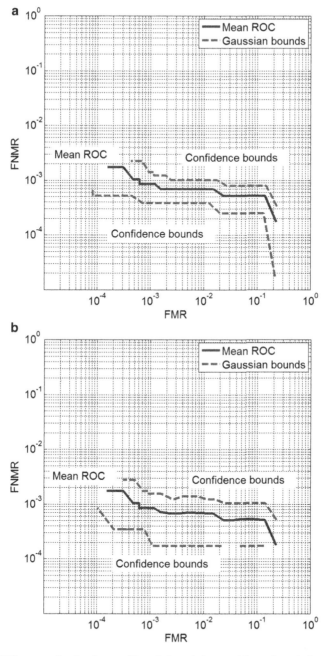

Fig. 6.20 ROC curves for the dataset *PB* and the relative confidence boundaries obtained by computing the mean of the results corresponding to the samples captured using Methods 2 and 3 and considering three comparisons: (**a**) confidence boundaries computed assuming a normal distribution of the data; (**b**) confidence boundaries computed using the bootstrap method. The results demonstrate that the confidence boundaries of the proposed system are small, indicating that the described system can be effectively used for a larger dataset

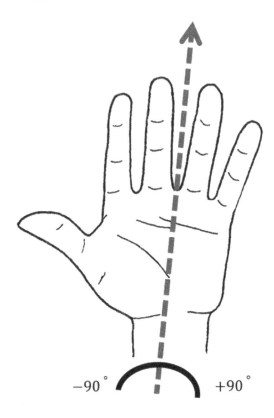

The robustness to hand orientation was tested by capturing a reduced dataset of palms with different roll orientations (Fig. 5.22), computing the biometric templates using the described method, and performing biometric matching of the templates. The results were then analyzed to determine how the genuine and impostor match scores were affected by the differences in the respective orientations of the samples.

Two palms were captured with 20 different orientations each, ranging from, $-90°$ to $+90°$ (Fig. 6.21), using both illumination Methods 2 and 3. Examples of the captured palmprints are shown in Figs. 6.22 and 6.23.

Then, each sample corresponding to a palm was processed using the described method and compared with the other samples for the same palm. The resulting match scores for the samples captured using illumination Methods 2 and 3 are reported in the tables in Figs. 6.24 and 6.25, respectively.

The results demonstrate that the method described here for fully touchless and less-constrained palmprint recognition exhibits tolerance in matching different samples pertaining to the same palm when captured with a similar roll orientation. This result is evident from an analysis of the match scores near the main diagonal of the table in Fig. 6.24. In the majority of cases, these match scores were greater than 58, which is the maximum impostor match score for the acquisitions in dataset *PB* performed using Method 2. Similarly, the majority of the match scores near the

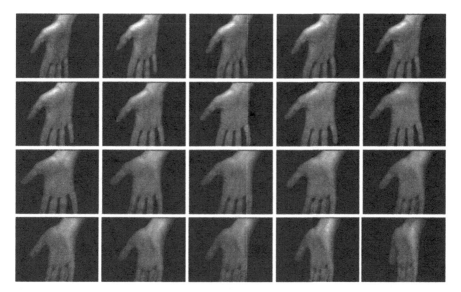

Fig. 6.22 Examples of palmprints captured in different orientations using illumination Method 2

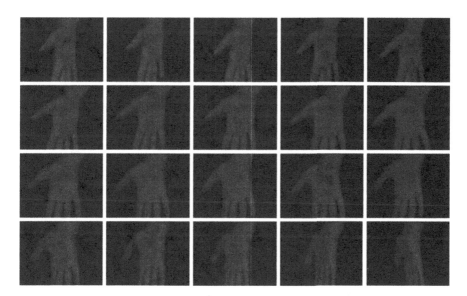

Fig. 6.23 Examples of palmprints captured in different orientations using illumination Method 3

Samples

Samples	01	02	03	04	05	06	07	08	09	10	11	12	13	14	15	16	17	18	19	20
01	-	1760.5	1563.5	1782.5	1410	955	538	231.5	29	2.5	2.5	1	2.5	2	1.5	2	1.5	2	2	3.5
02	1607.5	-	2165	863.5	1335.5	678.5	458	204.5	21.5	0.5	1.5	2	3	1	2	4	2.5	1	2.5	3.5
03	1394	1079	-	3360	1792.5	1287	1312	414	49	3	1.5	2	2.5	1.5	1.5	2	3	1.5	0.5	2.5
04	1375.5	1075	2754.5	-	4102.5	2325	1119.5	806	87	5	3	4	1.5	2.5	1.5	5	1	1.5	1.5	8
05	1365.5	1993	1973	3268.5	-	2943	2426.5	1422	305	1.5	1	2.5	8.5	3.5	2.5	2	5.5	2	3	0.5
06	895.5	1024.5	1970.5	2684.5	2189	-	3384.5	1967.5	954	1.5	1.5	1.5	2	0.5	4.5	3	4	3	2	2
07	342.5	1115	1265.5	1967.5	3601.5	4302	-	2823	1964	8	1.5	2	3	1	2.5	2.5	2.5	2	4	2
08	132.5	265.5	844.5	1411	1713.5	2295	2273.5	-	3059.5	106	3	1.5	2	3	3.5	2	3	6.5	1.5	4
09	5.5	1	75	169	317.5	609.5	2514.5	3503	-	637.5	3	1	3	1	1	2	1.5	1	1.5	1.5
10	2	3	4	5.5	2.5	7.5	19	27	441.5	-	1011.5	57	21.5	1.5	6	5.5	6.5	4	1	3.5
11	2.5	6.5	2.5	2	4.5	3	5.5	5.5	3	1490.5	-	893.5	422.5	41.5	2.5	5	2.5	4	4	3
12	2	5	2	1.5	3	7	2.5	2.5	0.5	88.5	574.5	-	2288	1037.5	210	642	24	21.5	18	3.5
13	2	1	3	2	4	4	5.5	4	9	37	79.5	2566	-	1086	531.5	789.5	115	98.5	17	7
14	1	8	4	2.5	5	2	3.5	2.5	1.5	4	39	1128	888	-	1412.5	1318.5	1056	7.5	84	2
15	0.5	2.5	4	2	7	2.5	4.5	3.5	3.5	2.5	4	192	355	1940	-	2050	4457.5	2477	701	23
16	3	3.5	2.5	3.5	2	2.5	13	2.5	3	5	11	469.5	876	1193.5	2911.5	-	3390.5	3493.5	1284	10.5
17	2	1	4	2	4.5	1.5	1	2	1.5	4.5	2	116	75.5	1524	3531	2744.5	-	3490	670.5	8
18	2.5	4.5	2	3	7	1.5	6	4.5	6.5	2.5	3.5	183.5	119.5	78	2297	2497	2205	-	3367	70.5
19	2	1.5	2.5	2	10.5	1.5	7	1	1.5	2	5.5	1	26	214	558.5	1138	884	2397.5	-	685
20	1	2.5	1.5	2	2.5	6.5	3	2	3	3	2	1.5	4	5	6	14	9	102	296.5	-

Fig. 6.24 Match scores between samples captured using Method 2 with different roll orientations. The match scores greater than the maximum impostor match score are *colored*. The results demonstrate that the described method exhibits tolerance in matching different samples corresponding to the same palm when captured with a similar roll orientation

Samples

	01	02	03	04	05	06	07	08	09	10	11	12	13	14	15	16	17	18	19	20
01	-	1142	1888.5	1504	488	370.5	32	46	2.5	2	0.5	2.5	1.5	2	1	2	2	2	1.5	2.5
02	884	-	701	678	637	669	225	132	3.5	1	1	2	1.5	2	1	4	2	1	1	3
03	1233	932	-	3120	1608.5	447	173.5	26	2.5	2.5	1	2.5	2	2.5	0.5	2	1.5	1	2	1
04	1757	640.5	2604.5	-	2985	2017.5	671.5	86	2.5	1.5	1.5	2	2	2	1.5	1.5	2	3	1	2
05	359	887.5	2101	3199	-	4391.5	1889.5	390	35.5	2	2	2	2	2.5	2	1.5	0.5	0.5	1	2.5
06	292	491	474.5	1885	3036	-	2400.5	1720	134	2	2	1.5	2	1.5	2.5	1	0.5	1	2	1.5
07	90.5	341.5	189.5	521	1165	2484	-	2867.5	250.5	8.5	3	1.5	1	2	3	1	1.5	1.5	2.5	2
08	25.5	119	33.5	111	358	1376.5	3856	-	2866.5	16	21	2	3	2	1.5	1	1	2	3	1.5
09	5	3.5	3.5	20	47	189	391.5	2691	-	1009	281.5	3	2.5	2	2	2	2	1	1	1
10	1	1	2	0.5	1	2	5.5	38	1120	-	2086.5	67	37	22	4	2.5	2.5	1	1.5	1.5
11	2	0.5	1.5	1.5	1.5	1	6.5	23	400.5	1543.5	-	440.5	146.5	30.5	5	1	2.5	1.5	2	2
12	2	1.5	2	2.5	2	1	1.5	0.5	7.5	99	352.5	-	4122.5	1402.5	623.5	314	29.5	7	54.5	26.5
13	1	2	1.5	2	2.5	1.5	2.5	1	3.5	41.5	163	3250.5	-	2970	2104.5	799.5	144.5	26	287.5	141
14	0.5	2.5	2	2	2.5	2.5	2	2.5	2	13	15.5	1407	2426.5	-	1856	3432	343	342.5	854	221
15	1	4	1	2	1	2.5	1.5	1.5	2	4.5	4	969.5	1526.5	2403.5	-	3528.5	356.5	265	1137.5	470.5
16	1.5	2.5	2.5	1.5	1.5	2	1.5	1.5	1.5	1.5	8.5	226	864.5	3403.5	2411	-	1758.5	244.5	2657	2316.5
17	2.5	1.5	2	1.5	2.5	3	2	1	2	2.5	1	23	70	269	434.5	2442	-	2163.5	1167	144.5
18	0.5	1	2	1	1.5	2	2	1.5	2	4	0.5	15.5	22	151.5	262	208.5	3117.5	-	842.5	51.5
19	2	2	2	1.5	0.5	0	2	2.5	0.5	0.5	2	58	167.5	756	1049.5	2047	369	717	-	837
20	1.5	0.5	1	1	0.5	1.5	1.5	2	1.5	1.5	1	52.5	230	409.5	575	2898	193.5	186	1303.5	-

Samples

Fig. 6.25 Match scores between samples captured using Method 3 with different roll orientations. The match scores greater than the maximum impostor match score are *colored*. The results demonstrate that the described method exhibits tolerance in matching different samples corresponding to the same palm when captured with a similar roll orientation

main diagonal of the table in Fig. 6.24 are greater than 28, which is the maximum impostor match score for the acquisitions in dataset PB performed using Method 3. However, excessive differences in the roll orientations during sample acquisition can result in unrecognizable samples.

A similar experiment was performed to test the robustness of the proposed method under different environmental illumination conditions. Specifically, ten samples each from two palms were captured under several illumination situations:

1. *Standard Laboratory Acquisition*: The room curtains are closed and the room illumination systems (neons or lamps) are turned off. This is the most controlled situation.
2. *Morning Light*: The acquisitions are performed in the morning, with the room curtains open to allow sunlight to enter the room. The windows of the laboratory face west. Thus, the sunlight does not directly hit the palm during the acquisition. The room illumination systems (neons or lamps) are turned off.
3. *Afternoon Light*: The acquisitions are performed in the afternoon, with the room curtains open to allow sunlight to enter the room. Because the windows of the laboratory face west, the sunlight directly hits the palm during the acquisition. The room illumination systems (neons or lamps) are turned off.
4. *Artificial Light*: The acquisitions are performed in the evening, when there is no sunlight entering the room. The room illumination systems (neons or lamps) are turned on.

For each illumination situation, the acquisitions were performed using Method 2 and Method 3. The templates computed from the corresponding samples were then matched, and the average match score of genuine and impostor comparisons was computed. The results for Method 2 and Method 3 are presented in Tables 6.7 and 6.8, respectively. Similar values for genuine and impostor match scores were obtained under the different illumination conditions, indicating that the described method for fully touchless and less-constrained palmprint recognition is robust to changes in environmental illumination.

6.2.6 Evaluation of Other Biometric Aspects

In this section, other biometric aspects that must be considered are evaluated, including computational speed, cost, interoperability, usability, social acceptance, security, and privacy.

6.2.6.1 Computational Speed

Two different times were considered in the evaluation of the computational speed of the described method: the acquisition time and the processing time.

Table 6.7   Average match scores of genuine and impostor comparisons for the samples captured using Method 2 and different environmental illumination conditions

	Match scores			
	Genuine	Comparisons	Impostor	Comparisons
Illumination Situation	Mean	Std	Mean	Std
Standard laboratory acquisition	3,179.8	942.1	3.3	1.8
Morning light	2,677.4	941.6	2	0.8
Afternoon light	2,748.9	903.2	2	0.8
Artificial light	2,770.9	876.8	2	0.8

The results demonstrate that similar values for genuine and impostor match scores were obtained under the different illumination conditions, indicating that the described method for fully touchless and less-constrained palmprint recognition is robust to changes in environmental illumination

Table 6.8   Average match scores of genuine and impostor comparisons for the samples captured using Method 3 and different environmental illumination conditions

	Match scores			
	Genuine	Comparisons	Impostor	Comparisons
Illumination Situation	Mean	Std	Mean	Std
Standard laboratory acquisition	2,743.4	1,405.7	1.6	0.9
Morning light	2,566.3	1,347.4	2.1	1.3
Afternoon light	3,156.7	1,141.5	1.4	1.3
Artificial light	2,936.5	1,212.2	1.4	1.3

The results demonstrate that similar values for genuine and impostor match scores were obtained under the different illumination conditions, indicating that the described method for fully touchless and less-constrained palmprint recognition is robust to changes environmental illumination

First, the acquisition time was considered to evaluate the usability of the proposed method. The acquisition time can be further divided into the time needed to position the hand and the time needed to capture the image. As mentioned in Sect. 6.2.1, approximately 5 s is required to position the hand, including the time needed for the user to place his hand inside the acquisition volume, the time needed for the shutter duration to adapt, and the time required to ensure that the hand is still (approximately 2 s). The actual capture of the image is performed almost instantly, and the time needed to capture the image is related to the shutter time, which ranged between 0.02 and 0.03 s. If a system for the simultaneous acquisition of images using both Methods 2 and 3 was implemented, the corresponding capture time would be no greater than 0.06 s.

Previous studies have not reported total acquisition times or the time needed to correctly position the hand. This time depends heavily on the type of acquisition device used, the operational conditions, and the familiarity of each user with the specific device or biometric systems in general.

The time required by our system for image capture is similar to those of other reported methods based on CCD acquisitions and considerably shorter than those of other methods using touch-based three-dimensional acquisitions [219] and touchless three-dimensional acquisitions, which require capture times as long as 2.5 s [2, 186].

The processing time was evaluated by implementing the described methods using Matlab R2013a and an Intel Xeon 3.30 GHz processor with 8 GB of RAM. The operating system was Windows 7 Professional 64 bit. The processing times included the time needed to create the biometric template from a sample (the three-dimensional model and the enhanced texture) and the time needed for a biometric comparison (the feature extraction and matching step). In our experiments, the computational time required to compute a template using the described method was approximately 200 s, while the computational time required for one biometric comparison was approximately 10 s.

The Matlab language is a prototype development system and is optimized for coding simplicity rather than runtime speed. An increase in computational speed of up to 100-fold has been reported for the use of OpenCV libraries [4] written in C++ compared to the corresponding Matlab implementations for image processing applications [246].

Moreover, many steps of the methods are highly parallelizable. For example, the three-dimensional reconstruction step can be easily parallelized to compute several matching points at the same time, and the feature extraction and matching steps can be executed in parallel for the 8 images considered. For these reasons, the use of a multi-core parallel architecture, such as the CUDA architecture [6], could greatly reduce the computational time needed for the steps of the biometric recognition system. Studies have demonstrated an increase in computational speed of up to 30-fold using an OpenCV implementation that takes advantage of the CUDA architecture [295] compared to a CPU-based OpenCV implementation. Therefore, a parallel C/C++ implementation using the OpenCV libraries and the CUDA architecture would greatly reduce the processing times and would likely enable the use of the described methods in a real-time live biometric system.

A comparison of the times needed for the creation of the template with other reported methods is not presented because those times are seldom reported. Moreover, implementing some of the most recent methods reported in the literature using Matlab would require a substantial amount of time as well as the purchase and assembly of the necessary hardware. Such a comparison would also be beyond the scope of this book. Similarly, a comparison of the times needed to perform a biometric comparison is not presented. However, optimized implementations of SIFT-based matching methods for image processing have been shown to operate in real-time [47].

6.2.6.2   Cost

Many proposed methods for palmprint recognition are currently oriented toward the use of low-cost sensors, such as flatbed scanners or low-resolution cameras (e.g., webcams). In contrast to fingerprint recognition systems, which require a resolution of 500 dpi, palmprint recognition systems can use resolutions as low as 75 dpi.

However, reported systems for performing three-dimensional acquisitions use complex and expensive setups. The methods for touch-based three-dimensional acquisitions [219, 404] require a complex structured light illumination setup, while the methods that perform touchless three-dimensional acquisition [185, 186] use an expensive three-dimensional laser scanner [2], which can cost several thousands of dollars.

By contrast, the methods described here use a simpler two-view acquisition setup that is based on two CCD cameras and LED illumination. Two Sony XCD-SX90CR CCD cameras with 25 mm Tamron lenses were used, at a cost of approximately $1,500. However, the captured images are resized and processed using a low-pass filter prior to the feature extraction step, suggesting that comparable results could be obtained using cameras of lower quality, resolution and, consequently, lower cost.

Moreover, illumination Method 2 uses four blue LEDs, with a total cost of approximately $150. Illumination Method 1 uses three downlight LEDs, with a total cost of approximately $250. If a system that performs quasi-simultaneous capture using both illumination methods was implemented, the total illumination cost would be approximately $400. However, the described two-view acquisition setup was implemented using an open structure with prototypal material. An implementation with a closed structure would result in minor light dispersion and stronger illumination on the palm. As a result, LEDs with lower intensity could be used to reduce the cost. Such an acquisition setup would have low complexity and cost compared to other three-dimensional palmprint recognition methods described in the literature.

6.2.6.3 Interoperability

Several different methods for palmprint recognition are commercially available and described in the literature. However, the majority of reported approaches use ad hoc acquisition devices and do not rely on standard methods for sample acquisition, sample processing, the exchange of palmprint data, or matching of palmprint samples.

Currently, a standard only exists for the exchange of palmprint data [266] in AFIS systems. However, this standard is typically used for forensic or investigative applications and applies to palmprint samples captured either from latent impressions or using optical-based devices.

The interoperability between palmprint recognition systems is currently limited, and experiments using mixed databases comprising samples captured using different acquisition techniques have not been performed.

6.2.6.4 Usability

Usability was evaluated during the collection of dataset *PB*. The efficiency, effectiveness, and user satisfaction related to the acquisition procedure were evaluated using a method similar to that described in [342]. As stated in the ISO 9241-11 [165], usability is defined as *"the extent to which a product can be used by specified users to achieve specified goals with effectiveness, efficiency and satisfaction in a specified context of use"*. Based on this definition, the three main aspects of usability can be defined as follows:

- *Effectiveness* measures the accuracy and completeness with which the users achieve the specified goals. The completion rate and the number of errors influence this aspect.
- *Efficiency* measures the resources used in relation to the accuracy and completeness and is usually measured in terms of time.
- *User satisfaction* is subjective and describes the way the technology is perceived by the users and meets their expectations. It is influenced by factors such as the ease of use and the usefulness of the technology.

A measure of the effectiveness can be defined by considering the quality of the captured images. The higher the quality of the images that are acquired, the more likely it is that accurate recognition will be achieved. Because a standard tool for the measurement of touchless palmprint samples is not available, the normalized match score was used as a quality measure. The normalized match score defines the ability to properly match a sample to other samples from the same individual and is computed as follows:

$$o(x_i) = \frac{s_m(x_{ii}) + (\mu(s_m(x_{ij})) - s_m(x_{ii}))}{\sigma(s_m(x_{ij}))} \quad , \tag{6.4}$$

where x_i is the considered sample, $s_m(x_{ii})$ is the match score obtained by comparing the sample x_i with x_i itself, and $\mu(s_m(x_{ij}))$ and $\sigma(s_m(x_{ij}))$ are the mean and standard deviation, respectively, of the match scores obtained by comparing the sample x_i with the other samples pertaining to the same individual.

The class of each sample x_i was defined as:

$$q(x_i) = \begin{cases} \text{"sufficient"} & \text{if } o(x_i) > t_{EER} \\ \text{"poor"} & \text{otherwise} \end{cases} \quad , \tag{6.5}$$

where the value t_{EER} was chosen as the lowest normalized match score for which, by discarding the images with "poor" quality, the system obtained EER = 0 %.

Table 6.9 reports the percentage of the images belonging to the two quality classes for each evaluated dataset and the corresponding t_{EER} value. The results demonstrate that by using a small value of t_{EER}, it is possible to obtain EER = 0 % and discard only a relatively small number of samples of "poor" quality.

The efficiency was evaluated on the basis of qualitative measurements of the time needed for every biometric acquisition, as described in [342]. As described in Sect. 5.3.2, a user interface was designed to improve the ease of use of the system by showing a live feed from the cameras with a superimposed circle (Fig. 5.23). When the palm of the user is placed over the circle, the acquisition is performed.

Table 6.9 Effectiveness of the acquisition systems based on Methods 2 and 3, evaluated by considering the percentage of images of "sufficient" quality

Dataset	t_{EER}	Percentage of images with "sufficient" quality	Percentage of images with "poor" quality
PB—Method 2	0.10	66.25 %	33.75 %
PB—Method 3	0.11	60.78 %	39.22 %

The results demonstrate that by using a small value of t_{EER} it is possible to obtain EER $= 0\%$ and discard only a relatively small number of samples of "poor" quality

A minimum amount of instruction was given to the users. They were only required to extend the open hand in a relaxed position inside the acquisition volume and place the palm over the circle superimposed on the live feed.

The guided acquisition procedure proved to be intuitive and easy to use. In the majority of cases, it was sufficient to instruct people on how to perform the acquisition and where to place their hand for correct placement. However, the acquisition device is still in a prototype phase, and some supervision was required. If the device was enclosed in a structure, the acquisition procedure would be almost completely intuitive, and completely unsupervised acquisitions would be possible.

As mentioned in Sect. 6.2.1, the time considered includes the training time needed to describe to the volunteers how the acquisitions are performed, the time needed for the proper placement of the hand inside the acquisition volume, and the time needed to capture the image. The entire acquisition procedure for each sample took approximately 5 s, including the time required for positioning the hand, the time for the shutter duration to adapt, and the time required to ensure that the hand is still (approximately 2 s). The actual capture of the image was performed almost instantly, with shutter times ranging from 0.02 to 0.03 s.

User satisfaction was evaluated by asking each volunteer a series of questions about the performed acquisitions in the form of a survey. Two questions were asked to evaluate their satisfaction regarding the usability of the system:

- *Q1*: Is the acquisition procedure comfortable?
- *Q2*: What do you think about the time needed for every acquisition?

Five answers were possible for both Q1 and Q2:

- *A1*: very poor,
- *A2*: poor,
- *A3*: sufficient,
- *A4*: good,
- *A5*: excellent.

The two questions Q1 and Q2 were asked in regards to acquisition Methods 2 and 3. Table 6.10 reports the mean values of the responses of the users to the survey. Histograms of the obtained answers are shown in Fig. 6.26.

Table 6.10 Comparison of the usability of acquisition Methods 2 and 3

	Question	Mean vote	
		Method 2	Method 3
Q1	Is the acquisition procedure comfortable?	4.09	4.28
Q2	What do you think about the time needed for every acquisition?	4.16	4.22

The results indicate that the volunteers whose samples were collected for the dataset considered both methods to have good acquisition comfort
Note: The possible responses were: (1) very poor; (1) poor; (3) sufficient; (4) good; (5) excellent

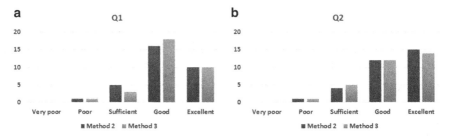

Fig. 6.26 Comparison of the usability of acquisition Methods 2 and 3: (**a**) answers to the question Q1 "Is the acquisition procedure comfortable?"; (**b**) answers to the question Q2 "What do you think about the time needed for every acquisition?". The results indicate that the volunteers whose samples were collected for the dataset considered both methods to have good acquisition comfort

The mean values for the responses to question Q1 were 4.09 and 4.28 regarding the acquisitions performed using Methods 2 and 3, respectively. These results indicate that the volunteers whose samples were collected for the dataset considered both methods to have good acquisition comfort. Slightly better results were obtained for acquisition Method 3, most likely due to the lower illumination intensity, which translated to a less invasive acquisition.

The mean values reported for question Q2 regarding the acquisitions performed using Methods 2 and 3 were 4.16 and 4.22, respectively. These results indicate that the users had a good opinion about the required acquisition time.

In conclusion, the evaluation of usability indicated good results for the described palmprint acquisition method for both Methods 2 and 3.

6.2.6.5   Social Acceptance

Evaluation of the social acceptance of the proposed system was performed during the collection of the dataset *PB* by asking the volunteers a set of questions in the form of a survey, similar to surveys reported elsewhere in the literature [111]. Specifically, four questions were asked:

- *Q3*: Are you worried about hygiene issues?
- *Q4*: Are you worried about possible security leaks due to latent palmprints?

Table 6.11 Comparison of the usability of acquisition Methods 2 and 3

	Question	Mean vote
Q3	Are you worried about hygiene issues?	4.38
Q4	Are you worried about possible security breaches due to latent palmprints?	4.23
Q5	Do you think that biometric data could be improperly used for police investigations?	3.87
Q6	Do you feel that the system invades your privacy?	3.92

The data demonstrate that the users had a good attitude toward the considered biometric system
Note: The possible responses were: (1) very worried; (2) worried; (3) normal; (4) not worried; (5) high trust

- Q5: Do you think that biometric data could be improperly used for police investigations?
- Q6: Do you feel that the system invades your privacy?

Five answers were possible for each question:

- A1: very worried,
- A2: worried,
- A3: normal,
- A4: not worried,
- A5: high trust.

Table 6.11 reports the mean values of the responses of the users to the survey, and histograms of the obtained answers are shown in Fig. 6.27. The results indicate that the users had a good attitude toward the considered biometric system, particularly concerning aspects related to hygiene (Q3), latent impressions (Q4), and privacy (Q6). However, some people expressed less confidence about improper use of biometric data (Q5).

Finally, two more general questions were asked:

- Q6: Would you be willing to use the touchless palmprint biometric system daily?
- Q7: Do you prefer touchless systems over touch-based systems?

All volunteers responded that they prefer to use touchless biometric systems over touch-based biometric systems, and almost all volunteers stated that they would be willing to use the proposed touchless system daily.

6.2.6.6 Security

One of the advantages of touchless acquisition techniques over touch-based techniques is the absence of latent impressions left on the sensors, which can pose a security threat. The methods described here do not permit a latent palmprint to be lifted.

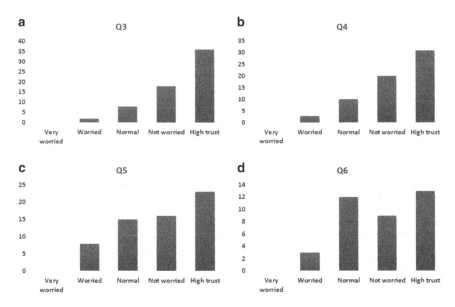

Fig. 6.27 Comparison of the social acceptability of the acquisitions performed using Methods 2 and 3: (**a**) answers to question Q3 "Are you worried about hygiene issues?"; (**b**) answers to question Q4 "Are you worried about possible security breaches due to latent palmprints?" (**c**) answers to question Q5 "Do you consider the system a hygienic solution?"; (**d**) answers to question Q6 "Do you feel that the system invades your privacy?". The results demonstrate that the users had a good attitude toward the considered biometric system

At the present stage, it would be possible to trick the acquisition sensor using a fake palmprint (e.g., a printed scan) because a module for verifying the liveness of the palm has not been incorporated. However, simple palmprint liveness detection algorithms have been implemented using NIR illumination and a CCD camera [400].

6.2.6.7   Privacy

Techniques for protecting the privacy of biometric data are necessary for the described touchless palmprint recognition method and for touch-based methods. Palmprint samples can pose a threat to users' privacy because they can be used to diagnose diseases, genetic disorders, or even schizophrenia [38, 196].

Techniques for privacy protection have not yet been implemented. However, there are several methods in the literature for the creation of encrypted template databases or the generation of cancelable biometrics [196].

6.2.7 Comparisons with Other Methods in the Literature

As mentioned in Sect. 4.1.3, it is possible to divide the methods for palmprint recognition based on the type of acquisition performed. Specifically, touch-based and touchless methods can be distinguished, and each category can be divided into methods based on two-dimensional images and methods based on three-dimensional models.

To test the validity of the proposed method, the described methods were compared to the other methods reported in the literature based on the type of acquisition. Two aspects are considered in the comparison: advantages related to the type of acquisition and the recognition accuracy obtained.

6.2.7.1 Comparison Related to the Type of Acquisition

The advantages of the described methods over the methods in the literature can be summarized based on the different types of acquisitions:

- *Advantages over Touch-Based Two-Dimensional Methods.* Compared to touch-based two-dimensional methods, the described methods are not affected by problems related to contact of the palm with the sensor, including distortion, dirt, sweat, and latent impressions. Moreover, the absence of contact increases the usability and acceptability of the system, particularly because no pegs are used. The use of three-dimensional information improves accuracy and also permits palmprint images to be captured without imposing a fixed position. Compared to methods based on inked acquisitions, optical devices, and flatbed scanners, the described method enables faster acquisition.
- *Advantages over Touch-Based Three-Dimensional Methods.* As stated above, the described methods are not affected by problems related to contact of the palm with the sensor. Moreover, reported methods for performing palmprint recognition using touch-based three-dimensional acquisitions use setups based on structured light illumination, which are complex and expensive. The described methods require a simpler setup based on a two-view acquisition system and LED illumination. Moreover, the described method performs a faster capture of the image.
- *Advantages over Touchless Two-Dimensional Methods.* Compared to the touch-less two-dimensional palmprint recognition methods reported in the literature, the described methods do not require the user to place the back of the hand on a fixed surface. By using a fully touchless acquisition, the described methods avoid problems related to dirt or cultural aspects. The described methods also increase the usability and acceptability of the system. Moreover, in the described acquisition method, the users are not required to place their hand perfectly horizontal, spread their fingers unnaturally, or hold their hand in uncomfortable positions. The acquisition procedure is performed automatically by simply requiring the volunteers to place their hand inside the acquisition volume. A greater acquisition distance is also used.

- *Advantages over Touchless Three-Dimensional Methods.* Previously reported methods for touchless three-dimensional palmprint recognition use expensive acquisition setups based on laser scanners, which require the user to hold the hand still during the computation of the three-dimensional model. The described methods use a lower cost setup comprising a two-view acquisition system and LED illumination. Moreover, the image capture is performed rapidly and automatically.

However, the described method presents some disadvantages, particularly related to the lack of constraints. Lower-quality acquisitions can be obtained due to excessive rotations of the hand or motion blur. Moreover, the resolution of the three-dimensional models reconstructed using the described methods is inferior to that obtained using structured light illumination systems or laser scanners.

6.2.7.2   Comparison According to the Obtained Accuracy

The accuracy of the described methods was compared with the most recent methods published in the literature for palmprint recognition, classified according to the type of acquisition. Specifically, the size of the collected dataset and the obtained EER value were considered. The results are summarized in Table 6.12 and indicate that the accuracy of the described method is comparable or superior to the accuracy of the most recent methods reported in the literature. Moreover, the described method has the aforementioned advantages of fully touchless, less-constrained acquisition, faster acquisition, and lower cost.

6.2.8   Final Considerations

For final considerations on the evaluated biometric aspects, the (a) accuracy, (b) robustness, (c) computational speed, (d) cost, (e) interoperability, (f) usability, (g) social acceptance, (h) security, and (i) privacy are considered and summarized:

- *Accuracy.* The described methods for touchless and less-constrained palmprint recognition enabled good accuracy. By considering multiple comparisons and different illumination methods, it was possible to obtain a recognition accuracy comparable or superior to those of the most recent methods in the literature. Moreover, the obtained FMR and FNMR values indicated that the method could be deployable in high-security scenarios.
- *Robustness.* The described methods proved to be robust to small variations in the roll orientation of the hand during acquisition. Moreover, the method performance was similar in all tested environmental illumination situations.
- *Computational Speed.* Both the acquisition time and processing time were considered to evaluate the computational speed.

Table 6.12 Comparison of the accuracy obtained by the described method (boldface) with the most recent approaches in the literature, classified according to the type of acquisition

Ref.	Type of acquisition	Device used	Size of dataset (palms)	EER (%)
[269]	Touch-based two-dimensional	CCD-based with pegs	250	0.10
[218]		CCD-based with pegs	386	0.02
[292]		CCD-based with pegs	386	0.14
[39]		Optical device	160	<0.01
[302]		Flatbed scanner	80	0.60
[368]		Flatbed scanner	384	0.20
[219]	Touch-based three-dimensional	CCD-based and projector, with pegs	100	0.03
[175]	Touchless two-dimensional	Mobile device	200	0.14
[19]		Ad-hoc device	602	0.16
[344]		Ad-hoc device	602	0.06
[261]		Ad-hoc device	470	0.2
[431]		Ad-hoc device	602	0.41
[186]	Touchless three-dimensional	Laser scanner	354	0.22
[185]		Laser scanner	114	0.28
Described method		**Two-view CCD-based system**	64	0.08

The comparison indicates that the accuracy of the described method is comparable or superior to the accuracy of the most recent methods in the literature

The acquisition time consists of the time needed to position the hand inside the acquisition volume, the time spent in adapting the shutter duration, the time waiting for the hand to be still, and the time for the actual capture of the image. The system described here requires approximately 5 s for a complete acquisition, of which at most 0.06 s is required for the actual capture.

No study in the literature reports the complete acquisition times because this time depends on the type of acquisition device used, the operational conditions, and the familiarity of each user with the specific device. However, the time required by the system described here for image capture is considerably shorter than that required by previously reported methods using touch-based three-dimensional acquisitions, which require capture times of up to 2.5 s.

Regarding the processing times, at the present stage, the described methods have not been optimized, and real-time use is not feasible. However, a parallel C/C++ implementation, for example, based on OpenCV libraries and the CUDA architecture, would dramatically reduce the computational times and likely enable real-time use.

- *Cost.* The considered acquisition setup consists of two CCD cameras and LED illumination and is less expensive than previously reported methods based on touchless three-dimensional acquisition. Moreover, the cost of the cameras could be reduced by using low-cost cameras with lower resolution. A less expensive LED illumination source could also be used by reducing the scale of the system and using an enclosed structure.

- *Interoperability.* Currently, the interoperability between palmprint recognition methods in the literature is very limited, and the different acquisition devices are generally not compatible. The only existing standard is for the exchange of palmprint data in AFIS systems, which consider latent impressions or acquisitions performed using an optical device.
- *Usability.* The described methods were found to be effective based on the ratio of the samples with good quality to the total number of samples. Good efficiency was also achieved using an intuitive, automated acquisition procedure. Moreover, a survey administered to the study participants revealed positive user satisfaction regarding the described technology.
- *Social Acceptance.* A survey administered to the study participants revealed good social acceptance of the described technology, specifically regarding the aspects of hygiene, security leaks, and invasion of privacy. However, some users had concerns regarding improper uses of biometric data.
- *Security.* In contrast to touch-based systems, latent palmprints cannot be lifted from the described palmprint recognition system because it is based on touchless acquisitions. Currently, a liveness detection module is not incorporated in the system, but this task could be accomplished using simple procedures described in the literature
- *Privacy.* Currently, techniques for privacy protection are not included. However, several methods have been reported for the encryption of templates or the generation of cancelable biometrics.

6.3 Summary

In this chapter, the experimental results for the described palmprint recognition methods were introduced and described.

The method based on acquisitions at a fixed distance was able to compute realistic three-dimensional models. Good accuracy recognition was also achieved, and the results were comparable to the most recent reported touch-based methods for palmprint recognition. However, the acquisition procedure imposes some constraints.

The method based on acquisitions at an uncontrolled distance achieved very good accuracy and in many cases was superior to the most recent methods in the literature. In particular, the obtained FMR and FNMR values would permit the use of the method in high-security scenarios. In addition, the acquisition procedure is nearly unconstrained. Good robustness to variations in hand orientation and differences in environmental illumination was also obtained.

This method was also evaluated based on other biometric factors, including computational speed, cost, interoperability, usability, social acceptance, security, and privacy. Notably, the computational speed of the method could be optimized and easily parallelized, while the cost could be reduced using low-cost cameras and LEDs with lower intensity.

Usability and social acceptance were evaluated by considering the quality of the samples, the time needed for the acquisitions, and by asking questions in the form of a survey. Good results were obtained for all of these aspects.

The system has a security advantage because it does not permit latent palmprint impressions to be lifted. However, techniques for security and privacy protection must still be considered.

Chapter 7
Conclusions

This book aimed to introduce touchless and less-constrained biometric systems for palmprint recognition. Innovative methods for touchless and less-constrained palmprint recognition were described.

First, a feasibility study for touchless palmprint recognition based on acquisitions performed at a fixed distance was described. This method achieved good recognition accuracy comparable to the accuracy of the most recently described touch-based methods but without the problems of distortions and dirt that are typical of touch-based acquisitions. However, a fixed hand position was required.

The obtained results enabled the extension of the described algorithms using novel, fully touchless, and less-constrained palmprint acquisitions. The described methods for palmprint recognition achieved accurate recognition using a less-constrained, innovative acquisition setup compared to the previously reported methods. For example, the described methods performed recognition without requiring the hand to be placed on any surface or in a specific position. Moreover, the use of three-dimensional reconstructed models enabled the biometric data to be represented independent of the position, orientation, and distance of the user's hand.

Compared to previous methods for performing touch-based acquisitions, the described methods were not affected by problems associated with contact of the palm with the sensor. The described methods also had greater usability and acceptability because no pegs or surfaces were used to guide the hand. Compared to the methods in the literature that only use two-dimensional samples, the computation of three-dimensional models in the described method realized a metric representation that was invariant with respect to the acquisition position, orientation, and distance. In this manner, less-constrained acquisitions with a relaxed position of the hand could be performed. With respect to other methods in the literature based on a touchless three-dimensional acquisition of the palmprint, the described approach used an innovative setup with a lower cost that can capture the samples considerably more rapidly.

© Springer International Publishing Switzerland 2014
A. Genovese et al., *Touchless Palmprint Recognition Systems*,
Advances in Information Security 60, DOI 10.1007/978-3-319-10365-5_7

All steps used in biometric systems were considered in the design and implementation of the palmprint recognition system, including steps related to acquisition, segmentation and preprocessing, image enhancement, and feature extraction and matching. The described approaches utilize original optical acquisition systems, image processing techniques, three-dimensional reconstruction methods, and pattern recognition algorithms.

Biometric datasets of palms containing a sufficient number of samples to produce significant results were collected to test the described approaches. The obtained results demonstrated good accuracy that was in many cases superior to the accuracy of most recent methods in the literature. For example, by combining different illumination methods, the palmprint recognition methods achieved an EER of 0.08 % for a dataset of 640 samples. Moreover, low FMR values were obtained, indicating that high-security applications of the described technology are possible.

Good results were also obtained regarding robustness, usability and social acceptance. The computational speed, cost, privacy, and security of the obtained methods were also considered.

7.1 Future Developments

The innovative methods for touchless and less-constrained palmprint recognition described in this book are still in the prototype phase, and some aspects of the systems used could be considered for improvement if a final device is to be produced and used in a real-world scenario.

First, simultaneous acquisition using illuminations with different wavelengths could be considered. The obtained results demonstrated that the combination of match scores obtained by comparing samples captured using different illuminations increased the recognition accuracy.

Moreover, the system could be integrated with information related to fingerprints and hand shape to increase the accuracy.

In addition, an enclosed structure would increase the usability of the system by hiding the parts of the hand that do not concern the final user.

A real-time hand detector could be implemented to accurately detect when a hand is present in the acquisition area and perform a faster acquisition as soon as the hand is inside the acquisition volume.

Finally, a quality detection module could be designed and implemented to automatically discard poor-quality samples. A real-time implementation of the quality detection module would give users real-time feedback on the captured sample, which would increase the intuitiveness and usability of the acquisition system.

By integrating these aspects, the described systems and methods could be used in scenarios in which accurate, fast, and unobtrusive recognition is required, such as medium-security applications for access control to restricted areas or logical resources. Moreover, many studies have focused on biometric recognition using low-cost devices such as webcams and smartphones. In this context, the described methods could be realized with low cost and effort using off-the-shelf components, enabling the implementation of a low-cost, touchless, less-constrained palmprint recognition system. However, the use of environmental illumination alone should be investigated.

References

1. DNA - from nature to technology. http://www.ieeeghn.org/wiki/index.php/DNA_-_From_Nature_to_Technology
2. Minolta Vivid 910 Noncontact 3D Digitizer. http://www.konicaminolta.it/fileadmin/CONTENT/Measurement_Instruments/Download/Catalogue_Download/vivid910_e9.pdf
3. NEC Automated Palmprint Identification System. http://nz.nec.com/en_NZ/solutions/public_safety/fingerprint_identification.html
4. OpenCV: Open Source Computer Vision Library. http://opencv.org/
5. Palm reading guide. http://www.md-health.com/Palm-Reading-Guide.html
6. NVIDIA CUDA Compute Unified Device Architecture - Programming Guide. http://docs.nvidia.com/cuda/cuda-c-programming-guide (2007)
7. The first ICB competition on iris recognition (ICIR 2013) (2013). http://iris.idealtest.org/2013/ICIR2013.jsp
8. Abeysundera, H.P., Eskil, M.T.: Palmprint verification using SIFT majority voting. In: E. Gelenbe, R. Lent, G. Sakellari (eds.) Computer and Information Sciences II, pp. 291–297. Springer London (2012)
9. Adler, A.: Biometric system security. In: A.K. Jain, P. Flynn, A.A. Ross (eds.) Handbook of Biometrics, pp. 381–402. Springer US (2008)
10. Ao, M., Yi, D., Lei, Z., Li, S.Z.: Face recognition at a distance: System issues. In: M. Tistarelli, S.Z. Li, R. Chellappa (eds.) Handbook of Remote Biometrics, Advances in Pattern Recognition, pp. 155–167. Springer London (2009)
11. Atick, J.J., Griffin, P.A., Redlich, A.N.: Statistical approach to shape from shading: Reconstruction of three-dimensional face surfaces from single two-dimensional images. Neural Computation 8(6), 1321–1340 (1996)
12. Aykut, M., Ekinci, M.: AAM-based palm segmentation in unrestricted backgrounds and various postures for palmprint recognition. Pattern Recognition Letters 34(9), 955–962 (2013)
13. Azzini, A., Marrara, S., Sassi, R., Scotti, F.: A fuzzy approach to multimodal biometric authentication. In: 11th International Conference on Knowledge-Based Intelligent Information and Engineering Systems (KES), XVII Italian Workshop on Neural Networks, pp. 801–808. Springer Berlin / Heidelberg, Vietri sul Mare, Italy (2007)
14. Azzini, A., Marrara, S., Sassi, R., Scotti, F.: A fuzzy approach to multimodal biometric continuous authentication. Fuzzy Optimization and Decision Making 7(3), 215–302 (2008)
15. Badrinath, G.S., Gupta, P.: An efficient multi-algorithmic fusion system based on palmprint for personnel identification. In: Proceedings of the International Conference on Advanced Computing and Communications (ADCOM), pp. 759–764 (2007)

© Springer International Publishing Switzerland 2014

A. Genovese et al., *Touchless Palmprint Recognition Systems*,

Advances in Information Security 60, DOI 10.1007/978-3-319-10365-5

16. Badrinath, G.S., Gupta, P.: Palmprint verification using SIFT features. In: Proceedings of the First Workshops on Image Processing Theory, Tools and Applications (IPTA), pp. 1–8 (2008)

17. Badrinath, G.S., Gupta, P.: Palmprint based verification system robust to rotation, scale and occlusion. In: Proceedings of the 12th International Conference on Computers and Information Technology (ICCIT), pp. 408–413 (2009)

18. Badrinath, G.S., Gupta, P.: Stockwell transform based palm-print recognition. Applied Soft Computing **11**(7), 4267–4281 (2011)

19. Badrinath, G.S., Gupta, P.: Palmprint based recognition system using phase-difference information. Future Generation Computer Systems **28**(1), 287–305 (2012)

20. Badrinath, G.S., Tiwari, K., Gupta, P.: An efficient palmprint based recognition system using 1D-DCT features. In: D.S. Huang, C. Jiang, V. Bevilacqua, J. Figueroa (eds.) Intelligent Computing Technology, *Lecture Notes in Computer Science*, vol. 7389, pp. 594–601. Springer Berlin Heidelberg (2012)

21. Barni, M., Bianchi, T., Catalano, D., Raimondo, M.D., Donida Labati, R., Failla, P., Fiore, D., Lazzeretti, R., Piuri, V., Scotti, F., Piva, A.: A privacy-compliant fingerprint recognition system based on homomorphic encryption and fingercode templates. In: Proceedings of the 2010 IEEE International Conference on Biometrics: Theory Applications and Systems (BTAS), pp. 1–7. Washington, D.C., USA (2010)

22. Barni, M., Bianchi, T., Catalano, D., Raimondo, M.D., Donida Labati, R., Failla, P., Fiore, D., Lazzeretti, R., Piuri, V., Scotti, F., Piva, A.: Privacy-preserving fingercode authentication. In: Proceedings of the 2010 ACM Workshop on Multimedia and Security, pp. 231–240. New York, NY, USA (2010)

23. Basri, R., Jacobs, D.W.: Lambertian reflectance and linear subspaces. IEEE Transactions on Pattern Analysis and Machine Intelligence **25**(2), 218–233 (2003)

24. Ben Jemaa, S., Frikha, M., Moalla, I., Hammami, M., Ben-Abdallah, H.: Sfax-Miracl hand database for contactless hand biometrics applications. In: A. Elmoataz, D. Mammass, O. Lezoray, F. Nouboud, D. Aboutajdine (eds.) Image and Signal Processing, *Lecture Notes in Computer Science*, vol. 7340, pp. 226–234. Springer Berlin Heidelberg (2012)

25. Besl, P.J., McKay, H.D.: A method for registration of 3-D shapes. IEEE Transactions on Pattern Analysis and Machine Intelligence **14**(2), 239–256 (1992)

26. Bianchi, T., Donida Labati, R., Piuri, V., Piva, A., Scotti, F., Turchi, S.: Implementing fingercode-based identity matching in the encrypted domain. In: Proceedings of the 2010 IEEE Workshop on Biometric Measurements and Systems for Security and Medical Applications (BIOMS), pp. 15–21. Taranto, Italy (2010)

27. Blanz, V., Vetter, T.: Face recognition based on fitting a 3D morphable model. IEEE Transactions on Pattern Analysis and Machine Intelligence **25**(9), 1063–1074 (2003)

28. Bolle, R.M., Ratha, N.K., Pankanti, S.: Confidence interval measurement in performance analysis of biometrics systems using the bootstrap. In: Proceedings of the IEEE Workshop on Empirical Evaluation Methods in Computer Vision (2001)

29. Bolle, R.M., Ratha, N.K., Pankanti, S.: Error analysis of pattern recognition systems - the subsets bootstrap. Computer Vision and Image Understanding **93**(1), 1–33 (2004)

30. Bonissi, A., Donida Labati, R., Perico, L., Sassi, R., Scotti, F., Sparagino, L.: A preliminary study on continuous authentication methods for photoplethysmographic biometrics. In: Proceedings of the 2013 IEEE Workshop on Biometric Measurements and Systems for Security and Medical Applications (BioMS), pp. 28–33 (2013)

31. Bouguet, J.Y.: Camera calibration toolbox for Matlab. http://www.vision.caltech.edu/bouguetj/calib_doc/

32. Bowyer, K.W.: The results of the NICE.II iris biometrics competition. Pattern Recognition Letters **33**(8), 965–969 (2012)

33. Bu, W., Zhao, Q., Wu, X., Tang, Y., Wang, K.: A novel contactless multimodal biometric system based on multiple hand features. In: Proceedings of the 2011 International Conference on Hand-Based Biometrics (ICHB), pp. 1–6 (2011)

34. Business Wire: El Paso police installs Sagem Morpho Palmprint System (2002). http://www.businesswire.com

35. Bustard, J.D., Nixon, M.S.: Toward unconstrained ear recognition from two-dimensional images. IEEE Transactions on Systems, Man and Cybernetics, Part A: Systems and Humans **40**(3), 486–494 (2010)
36. Cai, R., Hu, D.: Image fusion of palmprint and palm vein: Multispectral palm image fusion. In: Proceedings of the 2010 3rd International Congress on Image and Signal Processing (CISP), vol. 6, pp. 2778–2781 (2010)
37. Campisi, P., Maiorana, E., Lo Bosco, M., Neri, A.: User authentication using keystroke dynamics for cellular phones. IET Signal Processing **3**(4), 333–341 (2009)
38. Cannon, M., Byrne, M., Cotter, D., Sham, P., Larkin, C., O'Callaghan, E.: Further evidence for anomalies in the hand-prints of patients with schizophrenia: a study of secondary creases. Schizophrenia Research **13**(2), 179–184 (1994)
39. Cappelli, R., Ferrara, M., Maio, D.: A fast and accurate palmprint recognition system based on minutiae. IEEE Transactions on Systems, Man, and Cybernetics, Part B: Cybernetics **42**(3), 956–962 (2012)
40. Cappelli, R., Ferrara, M., Maltoni, D.: Minutia Cylinder-Code: A new representation and matching technique for fingerprint recognition. IEEE Transactions on Pattern Analysis and Machine Intelligence **32**(12), 2128–2141 (2010)
41. Chellappa, R., Veeraraghavan, A., Ramanathan, N.: Gait biometrics, overview. In: S.Z. Li, A.K. Jain (eds.) Encyclopedia of Biometrics, pp. 628–633. Springer US (2009)
42. Chen, B., Shen, J., Sun, H.: A fast face recognition system on mobile phone. In: Proceedings of the International Conference on Systems and Informatics, pp. 1783–1786 (2012)
43. Chen, J., Moon, Y.S., Wong, M.F., Su, G.: Palmprint authentication using a symbolic representation of image. Image and Vision Computing **28**(3), 343–351 (2010)
44. Chen, W.S., Chiang, Y.S., Chiu, Y.H.: Biometric verification by fusing hand geometry and palmprint. In: Proceedings of the Third International Conference on Intelligent Information Hiding and Multimedia Signal Processing (IIHMSP), vol. 2, pp. 403–406 (2007)
45. Cheng, K., Kumar, A.: Contactless finger knuckle identification using smartphones. In: A. Brömme, C. Busch (eds.) BIOSIG, pp. 1–6. IEEE (2012)
46. Chin, Y.J., Ong, T.S., Goh, M.K.O., Hiew, B.Y.: Integrating palmprint and fingerprint for identity verification. In: Proceedings of the Third International Conference on Network and System Security (NSS), pp. 437–442 (2009)
47. Chiu, L.C., Chang, T.S., Chen, J.Y., Chang, N.Y.C.: Fast SIFT design for real-time visual feature extraction. IEEE Transactions on Image Processing **22**(8), 3158–3167 (2013)
48. Cho, S.Y., Wang, L., Ong, W.J.: Thermal imprint feature analysis for face recognition. In: Proceedings of the IEEE International Symposium on Industrial Electronics (ISIE), pp. 1875–1880 (2009)
49. Choi, A.H., Tran, C.N.: Hand vascular pattern technology. In: A.K. Jain, P. Flynn, A.A. Ross (eds.) Handbook of Biometrics, pp. 253–270. Springer US (2008)
50. Choi, H., Choi, K., Kim, J.: Mosaicing touchless and mirror-reflected fingerprint images. IEEE Transactions on Information Forensics and Security **5**(1), 52–61 (2010)
51. Choi, J.Y., De Neve, W., Ro, Y.M.: Towards an automatic face indexing system for actor-based video services in an IPTV environment. IEEE Transactions on Consumer Electronics **56**(1), 147–155 (2010)
52. Choraś, M., Kozik, R.: Feature extraction method for contactless palmprint biometrics. In: D.S. Huang, M. McGinnity, L. Heutte, X.P. Zhang (eds.) Advanced Intelligent Computing Theories and Applications, *Communications in Computer and Information Science*, vol. 93, pp. 435–442. Springer Berlin Heidelberg (2010)
53. Choras, M., Kozik, R., Zelek, A.: A novel shape-texture approach to palmprint detection and identification. In: Proceedings of the Eighth International Conference on Intelligent Systems Design and Applications (ISDA), vol. 3, pp. 638–643 (2008)
54. Choras, R.S., Choras, M.: Hand shape geometry and palmprint features for the personal identification. In: Proceedings of the Sixth International Conference on Intelligent Systems Design and Applications (ISDA), vol. 2, pp. 1085–1090 (2006)

55. Chou, C.T., Shih, S.W., Chen, W.S., Cheng, V.W., Chen, D.Y.: Non-orthogonal view iris recognition system. IEEE Transactions on Circuits and Systems for Video Technology **20**(3), 417–430 (2010)
56. Chu, R., Liao, S., Han, Y., Sun, Z., Li, S.Z., Tan, T.: Fusion of face and palmprint for personal identification based on ordinal features. In: Proceedings of the IEEE Conference on Computer Vision and Pattern Recognition (CVPR)., pp. 1–2 (2007)
57. Cimato, S., Gamassi, M., Piuri, V., Sana, D., Sassi, R., Scotti, F.: Personal identification and verification using multimodal biometric data. In: Proceedings of the 2006 IEEE International Conference on Computational Intelligence for Homeland Security and Personal Safety (CIHSPS), pp. 41–45. Alexandria, VA, USA (2006)
58. Cimato, S., Gamassi, M., Piuri, V., Sassi, R., Cimato, F., Scotti, F.: A biometric verification system addressing privacy concerns. In: Proceedings of the 2007 International Conference on Computational Intelligence and Security (CIS 2007), pp. 594–598. Harbin, China (2007)
59. Cimato, S., Gamassi, M., Piuri, V., Sassi, R., Scotti, F.: Privacy Issues in Biometric Identification. Touch Briefings. Business Briefings Ltd (2006)
60. Cimato, S., Gamassi, M., Piuri, V., Sassi, R., Scotti, F.: A multi-biometric verification system for the privacy protection of iris templates. International Workshop on Computational Intelligence in Security for Information Systems (2008)
61. Cimato, S., Gamassi, M., Piuri, V., Sassi, R., Scotti, F.: Privacy-aware biometrics: Design and implementation of a multimodal verification system. In: Proceedings of the 2008 Annual Computer Security Applications Conference (ACSAC), pp. 130–139. Anaheim, CA, USA (2008)
62. Cimato, S., Piuri, V., Sassi, R., Scotti, F.: Privacy in biometrics. IEEE Press Series on Computational Intelligence. Wiley-IEEE Press (2009)
63. Cimato, S., Sassi, R., Scotti, F.: Biometrics and privacy. Recent Patents on Computer Science **1**, 98–109 (2008)
64. Cimato, S., Sassi, R., Scotti, F.: Biometric privacy. In: H.C.A. van Tilborg, S. Jajodia (eds.) Encyclopedia of Cryptography and Security (2nd ed.), pp. 101–104. Springer (2011)
65. Connie, T., Jin, A.T.B., Ong, M.G.K., Ling, D.N.C.: An automated palmprint recognition system. Image and Vision Computing **23**(5), 501–515 (2005)
66. Crossmatch: L SCAN©1000PX. http://www.crossmatch.com/l-scan-1000px.php
67. Cui, J.: 2D and 3D palmprint fusion and recognition using PCA plus TPTSR method. Neural Computing and Applications pp. 1–6 (2012)
68. Cui, J.: Multispectral fusion for palmprint recognition. Optik - International Journal for Light and Electron Optics (2012)
69. Cui, J., Xu, Y.: Three dimensional palmprint recognition using linear discriminant analysis method. In: Proceedings of the 2011 Second International Conference on Innovations in Bio-inspired Computing and Applications (IBICA), pp. 107–111 (2011)
70. Dai, J., Feng, J., Zhou, J.: Robust and efficient ridge-based palmprint matching. IEEE Transactions on Pattern Analysis and Machine Intelligence **34**(8), 1618–1632 (2012)
71. Dai, J., Zhou, J.: Multifeature-based high-resolution palmprint recognition. IEEE Transactions on Pattern Analysis and Machine Intelligence **33**(5), 945–957 (2011)
72. Dantcheva, A., Erdogmus, N., Dugelay, J.: On the reliability of eye color as a soft biometric trait. In: Proceedings of the 2011 IEEE Workshop on Applications of Computer Vision (WACV), pp. 227–231 (2011)
73. Dass, S.C., Zhu, Y., Jain, A.K.: Validating a biometric authentication system: Sample size requirements. IEEE Transactions on Pattern Analysis and Machine Intelligence **28**(12), 1902–1319 (2006)
74. Daugman, J.: Iris recognition. In: A.K. Jain, P. Flynn, A.A. Ross (eds.) Handbook of Biometrics, pp. 71–90. Springer US (2008)
75. Demirkus, M., Garg, K., Guler, S.: Automated person categorization for video surveillance using soft biometrics. In: Biometric Technology for Human Identification, vol. VII (2010)

76. Denman, S., Bialkowski, A., Fookes, C., Sridharan, S.: Determining operational measures from multi-camera surveillance systems using soft biometrics. In: Proceedings of the 2011 8th IEEE International Conference on Advanced Video and Signal-Based Surveillance (AVSS), pp. 462–467 (2011)
77. Denman, S., Fookes, C., Bialkowski, A., Sridharan, S.: Soft-biometrics: Unconstrained authentication in a surveillance environment. In: Digital Image Computing: Techniques and Applications (DICTA), pp. 196–203 (2009)
78. Derawi, M.O., Yang, B., Busch, C.: Fingerprint recognition with embedded cameras on mobile phones. In: R. Prasad, K. Farkas, A.U. Schmidt, A. Lioy, G. Russello, F.L. Luccio (eds.) Security and Privacy in Mobile Information and Communication Systems, *Lecture Notes of the Institute for Computer Sciences, Social Informatics and Telecommunications Engineering*, vol. 94, pp. 136–147. Springer Berlin Heidelberg (2012)
79. Dewan, S.K.: Elementary, Watson: Scan a palm, find a clue. The New York Times (2003)
80. Doddington, G.R., Przybocki, M.A., Martin, A.F., Reynolds, D.A.: The NIST speaker recognition evaluation - overview, methodology, systems, results, perspective. Speech Communication **31**(2–3), 225–254 (2000)
81. Dong, W., Sun, Z., Tan, T.: A design of iris recognition system at a distance. In: Proceedings of the Chinese Conference on Pattern Recognition, pp. 1–5 (2009)
82. Dong, W., Sun, Z., Tan, T., Qiu, X.: Self-adaptive iris image acquisition system. In: Proceedings of SPIE (2008)
83. Donida Labati, R.: Contactless fingerprint biometrics: Acquisition, processing, and privacy protection. Ph.D. thesis, Università degli Studi di Milano (2013)
84. Donida Labati, R., Genovese, A., Piuri, V., Scotti, F.: Measurement of the principal singular point in contact and contactless fingerprint images by using computational intelligence techniques. In: Proceedings of the 2010 IEEE International Conference on Computational Intelligence for Measurement Systems and Applications (CIMSA), pp. 18–23 (2010)
85. Donida Labati, R., Genovese, A., Piuri, V., Scotti, F.: Fast 3-D fingertip reconstruction using a single two-view structured light acquisition. In: Proceedings of the 2011 IEEE Workshop on Biometric Measurements and Systems for Security and Medical Applications (BioMS), pp. 1–8 (2011)
86. Donida Labati, R., Genovese, A., Piuri, V., Scotti, F.: Iris segmentation: state of the art and innovative methods, *Intelligent Systems Reference Library*, vol. 37. Springer (2012)
87. Donida Labati, R., Genovese, A., Piuri, V., Scotti, F.: Low-cost volume estimation by two-view acquisitions: A computational intelligence approach. In: Proceedings of the 2012 International Joint Conference on Neural Networks (IJCNN), pp. 1–8 (2012)
88. Donida Labati, R., Genovese, A., Piuri, V., Scotti, F.: Quality measurement of unwrapped three-dimensional fingerprints: A neural networks approach. In: Proceedings of the 2012 International Joint Conference on Neural Networks (IJCNN), pp. 1–8 (2012)
89. Donida Labati, R., Genovese, A., Piuri, V., Scotti, F.: Two-view contactless fingerprint acquisition systems: a case study for clay artworks. In: Proceedings of the 2012 IEEE Workshop on Biometric Measurements and Systems for Security and Medical Applications (BioMS), pp. 1–8. Salerno, Italy (2012)
90. Donida Labati, R., Genovese, A., Piuri, V., Scotti, F.: Virtual environment for 3-D synthetic fingerprints. In: Proceedings of the 2012 IEEE International Conference on Virtual Environments Human-Computer Interfaces and Measurement Systems (VECIMS), pp. 48–53 (2012)
91. Donida Labati, R., Genovese, A., Piuri, V., Scotti, F.: Weight estimation from frame sequences using computational intelligence techniques. In: Proceedings of the 2012 IEEE International Conference on Computational Intelligence for Measurement Systems and Applications (CIMSA), pp. 29–34 (2012)
92. Donida Labati, R., Genovese, A., Piuri, V., Scotti, F.: Accurate 3D fingerprint virtual environment for biometric technology evaluations and experiment design. In: Proceedings of the 2013 IEEE International Conference on Computational Intelligence and Virtual Environments for Measurement Systems and Applications (CIVEMSA), pp. 43–48. Milan, Italy (2013)

93. Donida Labati, R., Genovese, A., Piuri, V., Scotti, F.: Contactless fingerprint recognition: a neural approach for perspective and rotation effects reduction. In: Proceedings of the IEEE Workshop on Computational Intelligence in Biometrics and Identity Management (CIBIM). Singapore, Singapore (2013)

94. Donida Labati, R., Genovese, A., Piuri, V., Scotti, F.: Touchless fingerprint biometrics: a survey on 2D and 3D technologies. Journal of Internet Technology **15**(3) (2014)

95. Donida Labati, R., Piuri, V., Scotti, F.: Agent-based image iris segmentation and multiple views boundary refining. In: Proceedings of the IEEE Third International Conference on Biometrics: Theory, Applications and Systems (BTAS), pp. 1–7 (2009)

96. Donida Labati, R., Piuri, V., Scotti, F.: Neural-based iterative approach for iris detection in iris recognition systems. In: Proceedings of the IEEE Symposium on Computational Intelligence for Security and Defence Applications (CISDA), pp. 1–6. Ottawa, Canada (2009)

97. Donida Labati, R., Piuri, V., Scotti, F.: Neural-based quality measurement of fingerprint images in contactless biometric systems. In: Proceedings of the 2010 International Joint Conference on Neural Networks (IJCNN), pp. 1–8 (2010)

98. Donida Labati, R., Piuri, V., Scotti, F.: A neural-based minutiae pair identification method for touch-less fingerprint images. In: Proceedings of the 2011 IEEE Workshop on Computational Intelligence in Biometrics and Identity Management (CIBIM), pp. 96–102 (2011)

99. Donida Labati, R., Piuri, V., Scotti, F.: Biometric privacy protection: Guidelines and technologies. In: M.S. Obaidat, J.L. Sevillano, J. Filipe (eds.) E-Business and Telecommunications, *Communications in Computer and Information Science*, vol. 314, pp. 3–19. Springer Berlin Heidelberg (2012)

100. Donida Labati, R., Sassi, R., Scotti, F.: ECG biometric recognition: Permanence analysis of QRS signals for 24 hours continuous authentication. In: Proceedings of the IEEE International Workshop on Information Forensics and Security (WIFS). Guangzhou, China (2013)

101. Donida Labati, R., Scotti, F.: Noisy iris segmentation with boundary regularization and reflections removal. Image and Vision Computing, Iris Images Segmentation Special Issue **28**(2), 270–277 (2010)

102. Donida Labati, R., Scotti, F.: Fingerprint. In: H.C.A. van Tilborg, S. Jajodia (eds.) Encyclopedia of Cryptography and Security (2nd ed.), pp. 460–465. Springer (2011)

103. Doublet, J., Lepetit, O., Revenu, M.: Contact less hand recognition using shape and texture features. In: Proceedings of the 2006 8th International Conference on Signal Processing, vol. 3, pp. – (2006)

104. Doublet, J., Lepetit, O., Revenu, M.: Contactless hand recognition based on distribution estimation. In: Proceedings of the Biometrics Symposium, 2007, pp. 1–6 (2007)

105. Doublet, J., Lepetit, O., Revenu, M.: Contactless palmprint authentication using circular Gabor filter and approximated string matching. In: Proceedings of the Ninth IASTED International Conference on Signal and Image Processing, SIP, pp. 511–516. ACTA Press, Anaheim, CA, USA (2007)

106. Doublet, J., Revenu, M., Lepetit, O.: Robust grayscale distribution estimation for contactless palmprint recognition. In: Proceedings of the First IEEE International Conference on Biometrics: Theory, Applications, and Systems (BTAS), pp. 1–6 (2007)

107. Doublet, J., Revenu, M., Lepetit, O.: Robust grayscale distribution estimation for contactless palmprint recognition. In: Proceedings of the First IEEE International Conference on Biometrics: Theory, Applications, and Systems (BTAS), pp. 1–6 (2007)

108. Drira, H., Ben Amor, B., Srivastava, A., Daoudi, M., Slama, R.: 3D face recognition under expressions, occlusions, and pose variations. IEEE Transactions on Pattern Analysis and Machine Intelligence **35**(9), 2270–2283 (2013)

109. Duta, N., Jain, A.K., Mardia, K.V.: Matching of palmprints. Pattern recognition letters **23**, 477–485 (2002)

110. Ekinci, M., Aykut, M.: Gabor-based kernel PCA for palmprint recognition. Electronics Letters **43**(20), 1077–1079 (2007)

111. El-Abed, M., Giot, R., Hemery, B., Rosenberger, C.: A study of users' acceptance and satisfaction of biometric systems. In: Proceedings of the IEEE International Carnahan Conference on Security Technology, pp. 170–178 (2010)

112. Fahmy, M.M.M.: Palmprint recognition based on Mel frequency Cepstral coefficients feature extraction. Ain Shams Engineering Journal 1(1), 39–47 (2010)

113. Fancourt, C.L., Bogoni, L., Hanna, K.J., Guo, Y., Wildes, R.P., Takahashi, N., Jain, U.: Iris recognition at a distance. In: Proceedings of Audio and Video Based Person Authentication, pp. 1–13 (2005)

114. Fang, L., Leung, M.K.H., Shikhare, T., Chan, V., Choon, K.F.: Palmprint classification. In: Proceedings of the IEEE International Conference on Systems, Man and Cybernetics (SMC), vol. 4, pp. 2965–2969 (2006)

115. Faundez-Zanuy, M.: On the vulnerability of biometric security systems. IEEE Aerospace and Electronic Systems Magazine 19(6), 3–8 (2004)

116. FBI: A practical guide for palm print capture - document overview. https://www.fbibiospecs.org/docs/PalmGuidance%20v1.0.pdf

117. FBI: The Science of Fingerprints. Classification and Uses. U.S. Department of Justice, FBI. Superintendent of Documents, U.S. Government Printing Office, Washington, D.C. (2006)

118. Feng, Y., Li, J., Huang, L., Li, C.: Real-time ROI acquisition for unsupervised and touch-less palmprint. World Academy of science, Engineering and Technology 78, 823–827 (2011)

119. Ferrer, M.A., Vargas, F., Morales, A.: BiSpectral contactless hand based biometric system. In: Proceedings of the 2011 2nd National Conference on Telecommunications (CONATEL), pp. 1–6 (2011)

120. Fierrez, J., Ortega-Garcia, J.: On-line signature verification. In: M. Savvides, J. Heo, S.W. Park (eds.) Handbook of Biometrics, pp. 189–210. Springer US (2008)

121. Flynn, P.: Voice biometrics. In: A.K. Jain, P. Flynn, A.A. Ross (eds.) Handbook of Biometrics, pp. 529–548. Springer US (2008)

122. Franzgrote, M., Borg, C., Tobias Ries, B.J., Bussemaker, S., Jiang, X., Fieleser, M., Zhang, D.: Palmprint verification on mobile phones using accelerated competitive code. In: Proceedings of the 2011 International Conference on Hand-Based Biometrics (ICHB), pp. 1–6 (2011)

123. Fratric, I., Ribaric, S.: Colour-based palmprint verification - an experiment. In: Proceedings of the 14th IEEE Mediterranean Electrotechnical Conference (MELECON), pp. 890–895 (2008)

124. Fuertes, J.J., Travieso, C.M., Ferrer, M.A., Alonso, J.B.: Intra-modal biometric system using hand-geometry and palmprint texture. In: Proceedings of the 2010 IEEE International Carnahan Conference on Security Technology (ICCST), pp. 318–322 (2010)

125. Fujitsu, I.: PalmSecure-SL (2012). http://pr.fujitsu.com/en/news/2003/03/31.html

126. Gamassi, M., Lazzaroni, M., Misino, M., Piuri, V., Sana, D., Scotti, F.: Accuracy and performance of biometric systems. In: Proceedings of the 2004 IEEE Instrumentation and Measurement Technology Conference (IMTC), pp. 510–515. Como, Italy (2004)

127. Gamassi, M., Lazzaroni, M., Misino, M., Piuri, V., Sana, D., Scotti, F.: Quality assessment of biometric systems: a comprehensive perspective based on accuracy and performance measurement. IEEE Transactions on Instrumentation and Measurement 54(4), 1489–1496 (2005)

128. Gamassi, M., Piuri, V., Sana, D., Scotti, F., Scotti, O.: Scalable distributed biometric systems - advanced techniques for security and safety. IEEE Instrumentation Measurement Magazine 9(2), 21–28 (2006)

129. Gamassi, M., Piuri, V., Sana, D., Scotti, O., Scotti, F.: A multi-modal multi-paradigm agent-based approach to design scalable distributed biometric systems. In: Proceedings of the 2005 IEEE International Conference on Computational Intelligence for Homeland Security and Personal Safety (CIHSPS), pp. 65–70. Orlando, FL, USA (2005)

130. Gamassi, M., Piuri, V., Scotti, F.: Fingerprint local analysis for high-performance minutiae extraction. In: Proceedings of the 2005 IEEE International Conference on Image Processing (ICIP), vol. 3, pp. 265–268. Genoa, Italy (2005)

131. González-Rodríguez, J., Toledano, D.T., Ortega-García, J.: Voice biometrics. In: A.K. Jain, P. Flynn, A.A. Ross (eds.) Handbook of Biometrics, pp. 151–170. Springer US (2008)

132. Guerchouche, R., Coldefy, F.: Camera calibration methods evaluation procedure for images rectification and 3D reconstruction. Orange Labs, France Telecom R & D (2008)

133. Gui, J., Jia, W., Zhu, L., Wang, S.L., Huang, D.S.: Locality preserving discriminant projections for face and palmprint recognition. Neurocomputing **73**(13–15), 2696–2707 (2010)

134. Guo, Z., Zhang, D., Zhang, L., Liu, W.: Feature band selection for online multispectral palmprint recognition. IEEE Transactions on Information Forensics and Security **7**(3), 1094–1099 (2012)

135. Guo, Z., Zhang, D., Zhang, L., Zuo, W.: Palmprint verification using binary orientation co-occurrence vector. Pattern Recognition Letters pp. 1219–1227 (2009)

136. Guo, Z., Zhang, D., Zhang, L., Zuo, W., Lu, G.: Empirical study of light source selection for palmprint recognition. Pattern Recognition Letters **32**(2), 120–126 (2011)

137. Guo, Z., Zuo, W., Zhang, L., Zhang, D.: A unified distance measurement for orientation coding in palmprint verification. Neurocomputing **73**(4–6), 944–950 (2010)

138. Gupta, A., Sachdeva, M., Garg, U.: OPMAOP: Opposite Pair Matching Approach in Offline Palmprint. In: Proceedings of the IEEE International Advance Computing Conference (IACC), pp. 519–524 (2009)

139. Han, D., Guo, Z., Zhang, D.: Multispectral palmprint recognition using wavelet-based image fusion. In: Proceedings of the 9th International Conference on Signal Processing (ICSP), pp. 2074–2077 (2008)

140. Han, F., Hu, J., Alkhathami, M., Xi, K.: Compatibility of photographed images with touch-based fingerprint verification software. In: Proceedings of the IEEE Conference on Industrial Electronics and Applications, pp. 1034–1039 (2011)

141. Han, Y., Sun, Z., Wang, F., Tan, T.: Palmprint recognition under unconstrained scenes. In: Y. Yagi, S. Kang, I. Kweon, H. Zha (eds.) Computer Vision - ACCV 2007, *Lecture Notes in Computer Science*, vol. 4844, pp. 1–11. Springer Berlin Heidelberg (2007)

142. Han, Y., Tan, T., Sun, Z., Hao, Y.: Embedded palmprint recognition system on mobile devices. In: S.W. Lee, S.Z. Li (eds.) Advances in Biometrics, *Lecture Notes in Computer Science*, vol. 4642, pp. 1184–1193. Springer Berlin Heidelberg (2007)

143. Hao, Y., Sun, Z., Tan, T., Ren, C.: Multispectral palm image fusion for accurate contact-free palmprint recognition. In: Proceedings of the 15th IEEE International Conference on Image Processing (ICIP), pp. 281–284 (2008)

144. Hartley, R.I., Zisserman, A.: Multiple View Geometry in Computer Vision, second edn. Cambridge University Press (2004)

145. Heikkila, J., Silvén, O.: A four-step camera calibration procedure with implicit image correction. Proceedings of the IEEE Computer Society Conference on Computer Vision and Pattern Recognition (CVPR'97) pp. 1106–1112 (1997)

146. Hennings-Yeomans, P.H., Kumar, B.V.K.V., Savvides, M.: Palmprint classification using multiple advanced correlation filters and palm-specific segmentation. IEEE Transactions on Information Forensics and Security **2**(3), 613–622 (2007)

147. Hicks, T., Coquoz, R.: Forensic DNA evidence. In: S.Z. Li, A.K. Jain (eds.) Encyclopedia of Biometrics, pp. 573–579. Springer US (2009)

148. Hiew, B.Y., Andrew, B.J., Pang, Y.H.: Digital camera based fingerprint recognition. In: Proceedings of the IEEE International Conference on Telecommunications and Malaysia International Conference on Communications, pp. 676–681 (2007)

149. Hiew, B.Y., Teoh, A.B.J., Ngo, D.C.L.: Automatic digital camera based fingerprint image preprocessing. In: Proceedings of the International Conference on Computer Graphics, Imaging and Visualisation, pp. 182–189 (2006)

150. Hiew, B.Y., Teoh, A.B.J., Ngo, D.C.L.: Preprocessing of fingerprint images captured with a digital camera. In: Proceedings of the 9th International Conference on Control, Automation, Robotics and Vision (ICARCV), pp. 1–6 (2006)

151. Hiew, B.Y., Teoh, A.B.J., Pang, Y.H.: Digital camera based fingerprint recognition. In: Proceedings of the IEEE International Conference on Telecommunications and Malaysia International Conference on Communications (ICT-MICC), pp. 676–681 (2007)

152. Huang, D.S., Jia, W., Zhang, D.: Palmprint verification based on principal lines. Pattern Recognition **41**(4), 1316–1328 (2008)
153. Huang, W., Lin, X., Dai, X.: A novel approach for palmprint ridges features extraction. In: Proceedings of the 2nd International Congress on Image and Signal Processing (CISP), pp. 1–5 (2009)
154. Hurley, D.J., Arbab-Zavar, B., Nixon, M.S.: The ear as a biometric. In: A.K. Jain, P. Flynn, A.A. Ross (eds.) Handbook of Biometrics, pp. 131–150. Springer US (2008)
155. Impedovo, D., Pirlo, G.: Automatic signature verification: The state of the art. IEEE Transactions on Systems, Man, and Cybernetics, Part C: Applications and Reviews **38**(5), 609–635 (2008)
156. Imtiaz, H., Fattah, S.A.: A DCT-based feature extraction algorithm for palm-print recognition. In: Proceedings of the 2010 IEEE International Conference on Communication Control and Computing Technologies (ICCCCT), pp. 657–660 (2010)
157. Imtiaz, H., Fattah, S.A.: A histogram-based dominant wavelet domain feature selection algorithm for palm-print recognition. Computers & Electrical Engineering **39**(4), 1114–1128 (2013)
158. Imtiaz, H., Fattah, S.A.: A wavelet-based dominant feature extraction algorithm for palm-print recognition. Digital Signal Processing **23**(1), 244–258 (2013)
159. Indian Institute of Technology Delhi: IIT Delhi Touchless Palmprint Database (Version 1.0). http://www4.comp.polyu.edu.hk/%7ecsajaykr/IITD/Database_Palm.htm
160. Institute of Automation, Chinese Academy of Sciences: CASIA Multispectral Palmprint database. http://www.idealtest.org/dbDetailForUser.do?id=6
161. Institute of Automation, Chinese Academy of Sciences: CASIA palmprint image database. http://biometrics.idealtest.org/dbDetailForUser.do?id=5
162. International Biometric Group: Bioprivacy initiative (2003). http://www.bioprivacy.org/
163. International Biometric Group: Biometrics market and industry report, BMIR 2009–2014 (2009). http://www.ibgweb.com
164. International Organization for Standards: ISO/IEC JTC1 SC37 Standing Document 2, version 8, Harmonized Biometric Vocabulary (1997)
165. International Organization for Standards: ISO 9241-11 Ergonomic requirements for office work with visual display terminals (VDTs) - Part 11: guidance on usability (1998)
166. Ito, K., Aoki, T., Nakajima, H., Kobayashi, K., Higuchi, T.: A phase-based palmprint recognition algorithm and its experimental evaluation. In: Proceedings of the International Symposium on Intelligent Signal Processing and Communications (ISPACS), pp. 215–218 (2006)
167. Jain, A.K., Bolle, R.M., Pankanti, S.: Biometrics: Personal Identification in Networked Society. The Kluwer international series in engineering and computer science. Kluwer Academic Publishers (1999)
168. Jain, A.K., Dass, S.C., Nandakumar, K.: Soft biometric traits for personal recognition systems. In: Proceedings of the International Conference on Biometric Authentication, Hong Kong, pp. 731–738 (2004)
169. Jain, A.K., Demirkus, M.: On latent palmprint matching. Tech. Rep. MSU-CSE-08-8, Department of Computer Science, Michigan State University, East Lansing, Michigan (2008)
170. Jain, A.K., Feng, J.: Latent palmprint matching. IEEE Transactions on Pattern Analysis and Machine Intelligence **31**(6), 1032–1047 (2009)
171. Jain, A.K., Flynn, P.J., Ross, A.A.: Handbook of Biometrics. Springer Science + Business Media, LLC (2008)
172. Jain, A.K., Nandakumar, K., Nagar, A.: Biometric template security. EURASIP Journal on Advances in Signal Processing **2008**, 1–17 (2008)
173. Jain, A.K., Ross, A., Prabhakar, S.: An introduction to biometric recognition. IEEE Transactions on Circuits and Systems for Video Technology **14**(1), 4–20 (2004)
174. Jain, A.K., Ross, A.A., Pankanti, S.: A prototype hand geometry-based verification system. In: Proceedings of the 2nd Int'l Conference on Audio- and Video-based Biometric Person Authentication, Washington D.C. (1999)

175. Jia, W., Hu, R.X., Gui, J., Zhao, Y., Ren, X.M.: Palmprint recognition across different devices. Sensors **12**(6), 7938–7964 (2012)

176. Jia, W., Huang, D.S., Zhang, D.: Palmprint verification based on robust line orientation code. Pattern Recognition **41**(5), 1504–1513 (2008)

177. Jia, W., Ling, B., Chau, K.W., Heutte, L.: Palmprint identification using restricted fusion. Applied Mathematics and Computation **205**(2), 927–934 (2008)

178. Jia, W., Zhu, Y.H., Liu, L.F., Huang, D.S.: Fast palmprint retrieval using principal lines. In: Proceedings of the IEEE International Conference on Systems, Man and Cybernetics (SMC), pp. 4118–4123 (2009)

179. Jing, X., Li, S., Zhang, D., Lan, C., Yang, J.: Optimal subset-division based discrimination and its kernelization for face and palmprint recognition. Pattern Recognition **45**(10), 3590–3602 (2012)

180. Jing, X.Y., Zhang, D.: A face and palmprint recognition approach based on discriminant DCT feature extraction. IEEE Transactions on Systems, Man, and Cybernetics, Part B: Cybernetics **34**(6), 2405–2415 (2004)

181. Jovanovic, B.D., Levy, P.S.: A look at the rule of three. The American Statistician **51**(2), 137–139 (1997)

182. Kamgar-Parsi, B., Lawson, W., Kamgar-Parsi, B.: Toward development of a face recognition system for watchlist surveillance. IEEE Transactions on Pattern Analysis and Machine Intelligence **33**(10), 1925–1937 (2011)

183. Kanchana, S., Balakrishnan, G.: Quadtree decomposition for palm print feature representation in palmprint recognition system. In: Proceedings of the 2012 IEEE International Conference on Advanced Communication Control and Computing Technologies (ICACCCT), pp. 291–294 (2012)

184. Kanhangad, V., Kumar, A., Zhang, D.: Combining 2D and 3D hand geometry features for biometric verification. In: Proceedings of the IEEE Computer Society Conference on Computer Vision and Pattern Recognition Workshops (CVPR), pp. 39–44 (2009)

185. Kanhangad, V., Kumar, A., Zhang, D.: Contactless and pose invariant biometric identification using hand surface. IEEE Transactions on Image Processing **20**(5), 1415–1424 (2011)

186. Kanhangad, V., Kumar, A., Zhang, D.: A unified framework for contactless hand verification. IEEE Transactions on Information Forensics and Security **6**(3), 1014–1027 (2011)

187. Kekre, H.B., Bharadi, V.A.: Fingerprint & palmprint segmentation by automatic thresholding of Gabor magnitude. In: Proceedings of the 2009 2nd International Conference on Emerging Trends in Engineering and Technology (ICETET), pp. 235–241 (2009)

188. Kekre, H.B., Sarode, T., Vig, R., Pranay, A., Aashita, I., Saurabh, B.: Palmprint identification using Kronecker product of DCT and Walsh transforms for multi-spectral images. In: Proceedings of the 2011 International Conference on Hand-Based Biometrics (ICHB), pp. 1–7 (2011)

189. Khan, Z., Mian, A., Hu, Y.: Contour Code: Robust and efficient multispectral palmprint encoding for human recognition. In: Proceedings of the 2011 IEEE International Conference on Computer Vision (ICCV), pp. 1935–1942 (2011)

190. Kim, H.S., Bae, B.: Finger pattern identification for authentication purpose. In: Proceedings of the IEEE International Symposium on Industrial Electronics (ISIE), pp. 1674–1678 (2009)

191. Kisku, D.R., Gupta, P., Sing, J.K., Hwang, C.J.: Multispectral palm image fusion for person authentication using ant colony optimization. In: Proceedings of the 2010 International Workshop on Emerging Techniques and Challenges for Hand-Based Biometrics (ETCHB), pp. 1–7 (2010)

192. Koller, D., Walchshäusl, L., Eggers, G., Neudel, F., Kursawe, U., Kühmstedt, P., Heinze, M., Ramm, R., Bräuer-Burchardt, C., Notni, G., Kafka, R., Neubert, R., Seibert, H., Neves, M.C., Nouak, A.: 3D capturing of fingerprints - on the way to a contactless certified sensor. In: BIOSIG, pp. 33–44 (2011)

193. Komarinski, P.: Automated Fingerprint Identification Systems (AFIS). Elsevier Science (2005)

194. Kong, A., Zhang, D., Kamel, M.: Palmprint identification using feature-level fusion. Pattern Recognition **39**(3), 478–487 (2006)
195. Kong, A., Zhang, D., Kamel, M.: Three measures for secure palmprint identification. Pattern Recognition **41**(4), 1329–1337 (2008)
196. Kong, A., Zhang, D., Kamel, M.: A survey of palmprint recognition. Pattern Recognition **42**(7), 1408–1418 (2009)
197. Kong, A.W.K., Zhang, D.: Competitive coding scheme for palmprint verification. In: Proceedings of the 17th International Conference on Pattern Recognition (ICPR), vol. 1, pp. 520–523 (2004)
198. Kong, A.W.K., Zhang, D., Lu, G.: A study of identical twins' palmprints for personal verification. Pattern Recognition **39**(11), 2149–2156 (2006)
199. Kostadinov, D., Bogdanova, S.: Logistic regression classifier for palmprint verification. In: Proceedings of the 2012 19th International Conference on Systems, Signals and Image Processing (IWSSIP), pp. 413–416 (2012)
200. Kovesi, P.D.: MATLAB and Octave functions for computer vision and image processing. Centre for Exploration Targeting, School of Earth and Environment, The University of Western Australia. http://www.csse.uwa.edu.au/~pk/research/matlabfns/
201. Kozik, R., Zelek, A., Choras, M.: Palmprint recognition enhanced by the shape features. In: Proceedings of the 7th Computer Information Systems and Industrial Management Applications (CISIM), pp. 214–215 (2008)
202. Kumar, A.: Incorporating cohort information for reliable palmprint authentication. In: Proceedings of the Sixth Indian Conference on Computer Vision, Graphics Image Processing (ICVGIP), pp. 583–590 (2008)
203. Kumar, A., Hanmandlu, M., Madasu, V.K., Vasikarla, S.: A palm print authentication system using quantized phase feature representation. In: Proceedings of the 2011 IEEE Applied Imagery Pattern Recognition Workshop (AIPR), pp. 1–8 (2011)
204. Kumar, A., Ravikanth, C.: Personal authentication using finger knuckle surface. IEEE Transactions on Information Forensics and Security **4**(1), 98–110 (2009)
205. Kumar, A., Wong, D.C.M., Shen, H.C., Jain, A.K.: Personal verification using palmprint and hand geometry biometric. In: J. Kittler, M.S. Nixon (eds.) Audio- and Video-Based Biometric Person Authentication, *Lecture Notes in Computer Science*, vol. 2688, pp. 668–678. Springer Berlin Heidelberg (2003)
206. Kumar, A., Zhang, D.: Combining fingerprint, palmprint and hand-shape for user authentication. In: Proceedings of the 18th International Conference on Pattern Recognition (ICPR), vol. 4, pp. 549–552 (2006)
207. Laadjel, M., Bouridane, A., Kurugollu, F., Nibouche, O., Yan, W.: Partial palmprint matching using invariant local minutiae descriptors. In: Y.Q. Shi (ed.) Transactions on Data Hiding and Multimedia Security V, *Lecture Notes in Computer Science*, vol. 6010, pp. 1–17. Springer Berlin Heidelberg (2010)
208. Laadjel, M., Kurugollu, F., Bouridane, A., Boussakta, S.: Degraded partial palmprint recognition for forensic investigations. In: Proceedings of the 2009 16th IEEE International Conference on Image Processing (ICIP), pp. 1513–1516 (2009)
209. Lee, C., Lee, S., Kim, J.: A study of touchless fingerprint recognition system. In: D.Y. Yeung, J.T. Kwok, A. Fred, F. Roli, D. Ridder (eds.) Structural, Syntactic, and Statistical Pattern Recognition, *Lecture Notes in Computer Science*, vol. 4109, pp. 358–365. Springer Berlin Heidelberg (2006)
210. Lee, C., Lee, S., Kim, J., Kim, S.J.: Preprocessing of a fingerprint image captured with a mobile camera. In: D. Zhang, A.K. Jain (eds.) Advances in Biometrics, *Lecture Notes in Computer Science*, vol. 3832, pp. 348–355. Springer Berlin / Heidelberg (2005)
211. Leyvand, T., Meekhof, C., Wei, Y.C., Sun, J., Guo, B.: Kinect identity: Technology and experience. Computer **44**(4), 94–96 (2011)
212. Li, F., Leung, M.K.H., Chian, C.S.: Making palm print matching mobile. CoRR **abs/0912.0578** (2009)

213. Li, J., Shi, G.: A novel palmprint feature processing method based on skeleton image. In: Proceedings of the IEEE International Conference on Signal Image Technology and Internet Based Systems (SITIS), pp. 221–228 (2008)

214. Li, J., Shi, G., Zheng, Y., Liu, Y.: The research on offline palmprint identification. In: Proceedings of the 2009 WRI World Congress on Computer Science and Information Engineering, vol. 1, pp. 587–590 (2009)

215. Li, R., Huang, B., Li, R., Li, W.: Test sample size determination for biometric systems based on confidence elasticity. In: Proceedings of the International Joint Conference on Neural Networks (IJCNN), pp. 1–7 (2012)

216. Li, R., Tang, D., Li, W., Zhang, D.: Second-level partition for estimating FAR confidence intervals in biometric systems. In: X. Jiang, N. Petkov (eds.) Computer Analysis of Images and Patterns, *Lecture Notes in Computer Science*, vol. 5702, pp. 58–65. Springer Berlin Heidelberg (2009)

217. Li, S.Z., Jain, A.K. (eds.): Handbook of Face Recognition, 2nd Edition. Springer (2011)

218. Li, W., Zhang, B., Zhang, L., Yan, J.: Principal line-based alignment refinement for palmprint recognition. IEEE Transactions on Systems, Man, and Cybernetics, Part C: Applications and Reviews **42**(6), 1491–1499 (2012)

219. Li, W., Zhang, D., Lu, G., Luo, N.: A novel 3-D palmprint acquisition system. IEEE Transactions on Systems, Man and Cybernetics, Part A: Systems and Humans **42**(2), 443–452 (2012)

220. Li, W., Zhang, D., Xu, Z.: Palmprint identification by Fourier transform. International Journal of Pattern Recognition and Artificial Intelligence **16**(04), 417–432 (2002)

221. Li, W., Zhang, D., Zhang, D.: Three dimensional palmprint recognition. In: Proceedings of the IEEE International Conference on Systems, Man and Cybernetics (SMC), pp. 4847–4852 (2009)

222. Li, W., Zhang, D., Zhang, D., Lu, G., Yan, J.: Efficient joint 2D and 3D palmprint matching with alignment refinement. In: Proceedings of the 2010 IEEE Conference on Computer Vision and Pattern Recognition (CVPR), pp. 795–801 (2010)

223. Li, W., Zhang, D., Zhang, D., Lu, G., Yan, J.: 3-D palmprint recognition with joint line and orientation features. IEEE Transactions on Systems, Man, and Cybernetics, Part C: Applications and Reviews **41**(2), 274–279 (2011)

224. Li-cong, Z., Ding, X.M., Yan-qiang, Z., Qiang, L., Cheng-qi, W.: Embedded online palmprint verification system based on Ethernet. In: Proceedings of the 2nd International Congress on Image and Signal Processing (CISP), pp. 1–5 (2009)

225. Ling, H., Soatto, S., Ramanathan, N., Jacobs, D.W.: Face verification across age progression using discriminative methods. IEEE Transactions on Information Forensics and Security **5**(1), 82–91 (2010)

226. Liu, E., Jain, A.K., Tian, J.: A coarse to fine minutiae-based latent palmprint matching. IEEE Transactions on Pattern Analysis and Machine Intelligence (2013)

227. Liu, M., Li, L.: Cross-correlation based binary image registration for 3D palmprint recognition. In: Proceedings of the 2012 IEEE 11th International Conference on Signal Processing (ICSP), vol. 3, pp. 1597–1600 (2012)

228. Louis, T.A.: Confidence intervals for a binomial parameter after observing no successes. The American Statistician **35**(3), 154–154 (1981)

229. Lowe, D.G.: Distinctive image features from scale-invariant keypoints. International Journal of Computer Vision **60**(2), 91–110 (2004)

230. Lu, C.W., Fan, I., Han, C.C., Chang, J.C., Fan, K.C., Liao, H.Y.M.: Palmprint verification using gradient maps and support vector machines. In: Proceedings of the 2012 Asia-Pacific Signal Information Processing Association Annual Summit and Conference (APSIPA ASC), pp. 1–4 (2012)

231. Lu, G., Zhang, D., Kong, W.K., Wong, M.: A palmprint authentication system. In: A.K. Jain, P. Flynn, A.A. Ross (eds.) Handbook of Biometrics, pp. 171–187. Springer US (2008)

232. Lu, J., Tan, Y.P.: Improved discriminant locality preserving projections for face and palmprint recognition. Neurocomputing **74**(18), 3760–3767 (2011)

233. Lu, J., Zhao, Y., Hu, J.: Enhanced Gabor-based region covariance matrices for palmprint recognition. Electronics Letters **45**(17), 880–881 (2009)
234. Luo, N., Guo, Z., Wu, G., Song, C.: Joint palmprint and palmvein verification by dual competitive coding. In: Proceedings of the 2011 3rd International Conference on Advanced Computer Control (ICACC), pp. 538–542 (2011)
235. Ma, S., Wu, G., Zhang, N., Li, H., Luo, N., Chen, Q.: Embedded three-dimensional surface measurement system for palmprint. In: Proceedings of the 2011 International Conference on Hand-Based Biometrics (ICHB), pp. 1–5 (2011)
236. Madasu, H., Gupta, H.M., Mittal, N., Vasikarla, S.: An authentication system based on palmprint. In: Proceedings of the Sixth International Conference on Information Technology: New Generations (ITNG), pp. 399–404 (2009)
237. Malassiotis, S., Aifanti, N., Strintzis, M.G.: Personal authentication using 3-D finger geometry. IEEE Transactions on Information Forensics and Security **1**(1), 12–21 (2006)
238. Maltoni, D., Maio, D., Jain, A.K.: Handbook of Fingerprint Recognition. Springer Professional Computing. Springer London, Limited (2009)
239. Mansfield, A.J., Wayman, J.L.: Best Practices in Testing and Reporting Performance of Biometric Devices: Version 2.01. NPL report. Centre for Mathematics and Scientific Computing, National Physical Laboratory (2002)
240. Mansfield, T., Kelly, G., Chandler, D., Kane, J.: Biometric Product Testing Final Report V1.0. Contract **92** (2001)
241. Mansoor, A.B., Masood, H., Mumtaz, M., Khan, S.A.: A feature level multimodal approach for palmprint identification using directional subband energies. Journal of Network and Computer Applications **34**(1), 159–171 (2011)
242. Masood, H., Asim, M., Mumtaz, M., Mansoor, A.B.: Combined contourlet and non-subsampled contourlet transforms based approach for personal identification using palmprint. In: Digital Image Computing: Techniques and Applications (DICTA), pp. 408–415 (2009)
243. Masood, H., Mumtaz, M., Butt, M.A.A., Mansoor, A.B., Khan, S.A.: Wavelet based palmprint authentication system. In: Proceedings of the International Symposium on Biometrics and Security Technologies (ISBAST), pp. 1–7 (2008)
244. Matey, J.R., Kennell, L.R.: Iris recognition - beyond one meter. In: M. Tistarelli, S.Z. Li, R. Chellappa (eds.) Handbook of Remote Biometrics, Advances in Pattern Recognition, pp. 23–59. Springer London (2009)
245. Matey, J.R., Naroditsky, O., Hanna, K., Kolczynski, R., LoIacono, D.J., Mangru, S., Tinker, M., Zappia, T.M., Zhao, W.Y.: Iris on the move: Acquisition of images for iris recognition in less constrained environments. Proceedings of the IEEE **94**(11), 1936–1947 (2006)
246. Matuska, S., Hudec, R., Benco, M.: The comparison of CPU time consumption for image processing algorithm in Matlab and OpenCV. In: Proceedings of the ELEKTRO 2012, pp. 75–78 (2012)
247. Meraoumia, A., Chitroub, S., Bouridane, A.: 2D and 3D palmprint information and Hidden Markov Model for improved identification performance. In: Proceedings of the 2011 11th International Conference on Intelligent Systems Design and Applications (ISDA), pp. 648–653 (2011)
248. Meraoumia, A., Chitroub, S., Bouridane, A.: Fusion of multispectral palmprint images for automatic person identification. In: Proceedings of the 2011 Saudi International Electronics, Communications and Photonics Conference (SIECPC), pp. 1–6 (2011)
249. Methani, C., Namboodiri, A.M.: Pose invariant palmprint recognition. In: M. Tistarelli, M.S. Nixon (eds.) Advances in Biometrics, *Lecture Notes in Computer Science*, vol. 5558, pp. 577–586. Springer Berlin Heidelberg (2009)
250. Methani, C., Namboodiri, A.M.: Video based palmprint recognition. In: Proceedings of the 2010 20th International Conference on Pattern Recognition (ICPR), pp. 1352–1355 (2010)
251. Michael, G.K.O., Connie, T., Hoe, L.S., Jin, A.T.B.: Locating geometrical descriptors for hand biometrics in a contactless environment. In: Proceedings of the 2010 International Symposium in Information Technology (ITSim), vol. 1, pp. 1–6 (2010)

252. Michael, G.K.O., Connie, T., Jin, A.T.B.: Design and implementation of a contactless palm print and palm vein sensor. In: Proceedings of the 2010 11th International Conference on Control Automation Robotics Vision (ICARCV), pp. 1268–1273 (2010)

253. Michael, G.K.O., Connie, T., Jin, A.T.B.: An innovative contactless palm print and knuckle print recognition system. Pattern Recognition Letters 31(12), 1708–1719 (2010)

254. Michael, G.K.O., Connie, T., Jin, A.T.B.: Robust palm print and knuckle print recognition system using a contactless approach. In: Proceedings of the 2010 the 5th IEEE Conference on Industrial Electronics and Applications (ICIEA), pp. 323–329 (2010)

255. Michael, G.K.O., Connie, T., Teoh, A.B.J.: Touch-less palm print biometrics: Novel design and implementation. Image and Vision Computing 26(12), 1551–1560 (2008)

256. Michael, G.K.O., Connie, T., Teoh, A.B.J.: A contactless biometric system using palm print and palm vein features. In: D.G. Chetty (ed.) Advanced Biometric Technologies (2011)

257. Michal, C., Kozik, R.: Contactless palmprint and knuckle biometrics for mobile devices. Pattern Analysis & Applications 15(1), 73–85 (2012)

258. Morales, A., Ferrer, M.A., Alonso, J.B., Travieso, C.M.: Comparing infrared and visible illumination for contactless hand based biometric scheme. In: Proceedings of the 42nd Annual IEEE International Carnahan Conference on Security Technology (ICCST), pp. 191–197 (2008)

259. Morales, A., Ferrer, M.A., Daz, F., Alonso, J.B., Travieso, C.M.: Contact-free hand biometric system for real environments. In: Proceedings of the 16th European Signal Processing Conference, Laussane, Switzerland (2008)

260. Morales, A., Ferrer, M.A., Kumar, A.: Improved palmprint authentication using contactless imaging. In: Proceedings of the 2010 Fourth IEEE International Conference on Biometrics: Theory Applications and Systems (BTAS), pp. 1–6 (2010)

261. Morales, A., Ferrer, M.A., Kumar, A.: Towards contactless palmprint authentication. IET Computer Vision 5(6), 407–416 (2011)

262. Morales, A., Ferrer, M.A., Travieso, C.M., Alonso, J.B.: Multisampling approach applied to contactless hand biometrics. In: Proceedings of the 2012 IEEE International Carnahan Conference on Security Technology (ICCST), pp. 224–229 (2012)

263. Morales, A., Kumar, A., Ferrer, M.A.: Incorporating color information for reliable palmprint authentication. In: Proceedings of the 2011 18th IEEE International Conference on Image Processing (ICIP), pp. 3193–3196 (2011)

264. Mu, M., Ruan, Q., Guo, S.: Shift and gray scale invariant features for palmprint identification using complex directional wavelet and local binary pattern. Neurocomputing 74(17), 3351–3360 (2011)

265. Mu, M., Ruan, Q., Ming, Y.: Shape parameters of Gaussian as descriptor for palmprint recognition based on dual-tree complex wavelet transform. In: Proceedings of the 2010 IEEE 10th International Conference on Signal Processing (ICSP), pp. 1406–1409 (2010)

266. National Science and Technology Council (NSTC): Palmprint recognition. http://www.biometrics.gov/documents/palmprintrec.pdf

267. Negi, A., Panigrahi, B., Prasad, M.V.N., Das, M.: A palmprint classification scheme using heart line feature extraction. In: Proceedings of the 9th International Conference on Information Technology (ICIT), pp. 180–181 (2006)

268. Nguyen, K., Fookes, C., Sridharan, S., Denman, S.: Quality-driven super-resolution for less constrained iris recognition at a distance and on the move. IEEE Transactions on Information Forensics and Security 6(4), 1248–1258 (2011)

269. Nibouche, O., Jiang, J.: Palmprint matching using feature points and SVD factorisation. Digital Signal Processing 23(4), 1154–1162 (2013)

270. Nibouche, O., Jiang, J., Trundle, P.: Analysis of performance of palmprint matching with enforced sparsity. Digital Signal Processing 22(2), 348–355 (2012)

271. Niinuma, K., Park, U., Jain, A.K.: Soft biometric traits for continuous user authentication. IEEE Transactions on Information Forensics and Security 5(4), 771–780 (2010)

272. Odinaka, I., Lai, P.H., Kaplan, A.D., O'Sullivan, J., Sirevaag, E.J., Rohrbaugh, J.W.: ECG biometric recognition: A comparative analysis. IEEE Transactions on Information Forensics and Security **7**(6), 1812–1824 (2012)

273. Paar, G., Perucha, M.d., Bauer, A., Nauschnegg, B.: Photogrammetric fingerprint unwrapping. Journal of Applied Geodesy **2**, 13–20 (2008)

274. Palanikumar, S., Sasikumar, M., Rajeesh, J.: Palmprint enhancement using GA-AIVHE method. In: Proceedings of the 2010 IEEE International Conference on Communication Control and Computing Technologies (ICCCT), pp. 637–642 (2010)

275. Pan, X., Ruan, Q., Wang, Y.: Palmprint recognition using fusion of local and global features. In: Proceedings of the International Symposium on Intelligent Signal Processing and Communication Systems (ISPACS), pp. 642–645 (2007)

276. Pan, X., Ruan, Q., Wang, Y.: Palmprint recognition using contourlets-based local fractal dimensions. In: Proceedings of the 9th International Conference on Signal Processing (ICSP), pp. 2108–2111 (2008)

277. Pan, X., Ruan, Q.Q.: A modified preprocessing method for palmprint recognition. In: Proceedings of the 2006 8th International Conference on Signal Processing, vol. 2 (2006)

278. Pan, X., Ruan, Q.Q.: Palmprint recognition using Gabor feature-based $(2D)^2PCA$. Neurocomputing **71**(13–15), 3032–3036 (2008)

279. Pan, X., Ruan, Q.Q.: Palmprint recognition with improved two-dimensional locality preserving projections. Image and Vision Computing **26**(9), 1261–1268 (2008)

280. Pan, X., Ruan, Q.Q., Wang, Y.X.: An improved 2DLPP method on Gabor features for palmprint recognition. In: Proceedings of the IEEE International Conference on Image Processing (ICIP), vol. 2, pp. 413–416 (2007)

281. Pang, X., Song, Z., Xie, W.: Extraction of valley-ridge lines from the point cloud-based 3D fingerprint model. IEEE Computer Graphics and Applications (2012)

282. Park, U., Tong, Y., Jain, A.K.: Age-invariant face recognition. IEEE Transactions on Pattern Analysis and Machine Intelligence **32**(5), 947–954 (2010)

283. Parziale, G., Chen, Y.: Advanced technologies for touchless fingerprint recognition. Handbook of Remote Biometrics pp. 83–109 (2009)

284. Parziale, G., Diaz-Santana, E., Hauke, R.: The surround imager: A multi-camera touchless device to acquire 3D rolled-equivalent fingerprints. In: Proceedings of the International Conference of Biometrics (ICB), pp. 244–250 (2006)

285. Pentland, A., Choudhury, T.: Face recognition for smart environments. Computer **33**(2), 50–55 (2000)

286. Pillai, A., Mil'shtein, S.: Can contactless fingerprints be compared to existing database? In: Proceedings of the 2012 IEEE Conference on Technologies for Homeland Security (HST), pp. 390–394 (2012)

287. Piuri, V., Scotti, F.: Fingerprint biometrics via low-cost sensors and webcams. In: Proceedings of the 2008 IEEE International Conference on Biometrics: Theory, Applications and Systems (BTAS), pp. 1–6. Washington, D.C., USA (2008)

288. Plataniotis, K.N., Hatzinakos, D., Lee, J.K.M.: ECG biometric recognition without fiducial detection. In: Proceedings of the Biometrics Symposium: Special Session on Research at the Biometric Consortium Conference, pp. 1–6 (2006)

289. Poh, N., Bengio, S.: Estimating the confidence interval of expected performance curve in biometric authentication using joint bootstrap. In: Proceedings of the IEEE International Conference on Acoustics, Speech and Signal Processing, vol. 2, pp. 137–140 (2007)

290. Poh, N., Martin, A., Bengio, S.: Performance generalization in biometric authentication using joint user-specific and sample bootstraps. IEEE Transactions on Pattern Analysis and Machine Intelligence **29**(3), 492–498 (2007)

291. Poinsot, A., Yang, F., Paindavoine, M.: Small sample biometric recognition based on palmprint and face fusion. In: Proceedings of the Fourth International Multi-Conference on Computing in the Global Information Technology (ICCGI), pp. 118–122 (2009)

292. Prasad, S.M., Govindan, V., Sathidevi, P.S.: Image quality augmented intramodal palmprint authentication. IET Image Processing **6**(6), 668–676 (2012)

293. Proença, H.: Iris recognition: On the segmentation of degraded images acquired in the visible wavelength. IEEE Transaction on Pattern Analysis and Machine Intelligence **32**(8), 1502–1516 (2010)

294. Proença, H., Du, E.Y., Scharcanski, J.: Introduction to the special issue on unconstrained biometrics: advances and trends. Signal, Image and Video Processing **5**(4), 399–400 (2011)

295. Pulli, K., Baksheev, A., Kornyakov, K., Eruhimov, V.: Real-time computer vision with OpenCV. Communications of the ACM **55**(6), 61–69 (2012)

296. Punsawad, Y., Wongsawat, Y.: Palmprint image enhancement using phase congruency. In: Proceedings of the IEEE International Conference on Robotics and Biomimetics (ROBIO), pp. 1643–1646 (2009)

297. Qin, A.K., Suganthan, P.N., Tay, C.H., Pa, H.S.: Personal identification system based on multiple palmprint features. In: Proceedings of the 9th International Conference on Control, Automation, Robotics and Vision (ICARCV), pp. 1–6 (2006)

298. Raghavendra, R., Dorizzi, B., Rao, A., Kumar, G.H.: Designing efficient fusion schemes for multimodal biometric systems using face and palmprint. Pattern Recognition **44**(5), 1076–1088 (2011)

299. Ran, Y., Rosenbush, G., Zheng, Q.: Computational approaches for real-time extraction of soft biometrics. In: Proceedings of the 19th International Conference on Pattern Recognition, pp. 1–4 (2008)

300. Raposo, R., Hoyle, E., Peixinho, A., Proenca, H.: UBEAR: A dataset of ear images captured on-the-move in uncontrolled conditions. In: Proceedings of the IEEE Workshop on Computational Intelligence in Biometrics and Identity Management, pp. 84–90 (2011)

301. Ribaric, S., Fratric, I., Kis, K.: A biometric verification system based on the fusion of palmprint and face features. In: Proceedings of the 4th International Symposium on Image and Signal Processing and Analysis (ISPA), pp. 12–17 (2005)

302. Ribaric, S., Marcetic, M.: Personal recognition based on the Gabor features of colour palmprint images. In: Proceedings of the 2012 Proceedings of the 35th International Convention MIPRO, pp. 967–972 (2012)

303. RNCOS: Biometric market forecast to 2014 (2012)

304. Ross, A., Abaza, A.: Human ear recognition. Computer **44**(11), 79–81 (2011)

305. Ross, A.A., Nandakumar, K., Jain, A.K.: Handbook of Multibiometrics (International Series on Biometrics). Springer-Verlag New York, Inc., Secaucus, NJ, USA (2006)

306. Rotinwa-Akinbile, M.O., Aibinu, A.M., Salami, M.J.E.: A novel palmprint segmentation technique. In: Proceedings of the 2011 First International Conference on Informatics and Computational Intelligence (ICI), pp. 235–239 (2011)

307. Rotinwa-Akinbile, M.O., Aibinu, A.M., Salami, M.J.E.: Palmprint recognition using principal lines characterization. In: Proceedings of the 2011 First International Conference on Informatics and Computational Intelligence (ICI), pp. 278–282 (2011)

308. Ryan, R.: The importance of biometric standards. Biometric Technology Today **2009**(7), 7–10 (2009)

309. Sadowitz, M., Latifi, S., Walker, D.: An overview of iris and retina scans and their fusion in a biometric system. In: Proceedings of the International Conference on Image Processing, Computer Vision and Pattern Recognition (IPCV), pp. 119–123 (2008)

310. Sakdanupab, M., Covavisaruch, N.: An efficient approach for automatic palmprint classification. In: Proceedings of the IEEE International Conference on Signal Image Technology and Internet Based Systems (SITIS), pp. 229–234 (2008)

311. Sanchez-Reillo, R., Sanchez-Avila, C., Gonzalez-Marcos, A.: Biometric identification through hand geometry measurements. IEEE Transactions on Pattern Analysis and Machine Intelligence **22**(10), 1168–1171 (2000)

312. Sang, H., Liu, F.: Defocused palmprint recognition using 2DPCA. In: Proceedings of the International Conference on Artificial Intelligence and Computational Intelligence (AICI), vol. 1, pp. 611–615 (2009)

313. Santos Sierra, A., Sánchez-Àvila, C., Mendaza Ormaza, A., Guerra Casanova, J.: An approach to hand biometrics in mobile devices. Signal, Image and Video Processing 5(4), 469–475 (2011)
314. Sarkar, S., Liu, Z.: Gait recognition. In: A.K. Jain, P. Flynn, A.A. Ross (eds.) Handbook of Biometrics, pp. 109–130. Springer US (2008)
315. Savvides, M., Heo, J., Park, S.W.: Face recognition. In: A.K. Jain, P. Flynn, A.A. Ross (eds.) Handbook of Biometrics, pp. 43–70. Springer US (2008)
316. Scheenstra, A., Ruifrok, A., Veltkamp, R.C.: A survey of 3D face recognition methods. In: Lecture Notes in Computer Science, pp. 891–899. SpringerVerlag (2005)
317. Schuckers, S.A.C., Schmid, N.A., Abhyankar, A., Dorairaj, V., Boyce, C.K., Hornak, L.A.: On techniques for angle compensation in nonideal iris recognition. IEEE Transactions on Systems, Man, and Cybernetics, Part B: Cybernetics 37(5), 1176–1190 (2007)
318. Scotti, F.: Computational intelligence techniques for reflections identification in iris biometric images. In: Proceedings of the IEEE International Conference on Computational Intelligence for Measurement Systems and Applications (CIMSA), pp. 84–88 (2007)
319. Scotti, F., Piuri, V.: Adaptive reflection detection and location in iris biometric images by using computational intelligence techniques. IEEE Transactions of Instrumentation and Measurement 59(7), 1825–1833 (2010)
320. Seely, R.D., Goffredo, M., Carter, J.N., Nixon, M.S.: View invariant gait recognition. In: M. Tistarelli, S.Z. Li, R. Chellappa (eds.) Handbook of Remote Biometrics, Advances in Pattern Recognition, pp. 61–81. Springer London (2009)
321. Shafaei, S., Inanc, T., Hassebrook, L.G.: A new approach to unwrap a 3-D fingerprint to a 2-D rolled equivalent fingerprint. In: Proceedings of the IEEE 3rd International Conference on Biometrics: Theory, Applications, and Systems, pp. 1–5 (2009)
322. Shah, S., Ross, A.: Iris segmentation using geodesic active contours. IEEE Transaction on Information Forensics Security 4(4), 824–836 (2009)
323. Shang, P., Li, T.: Multifractal characteristics of palmprint and its extracted algorithm. Applied Mathematical Modelling 33(12), 4378–4387 (2009)
324. Shanmugapriya, D., Padmavathi, G.: A survey of biometric keystroke dynamics: Approaches, security and challenges. CoRR abs/0910.0817 (2009)
325. Shashikala, K.P., Raja, K.B.: Palmprint identification using transform domain and spatial domain techniques. In: Proceedings of the 2012 International Conference on Computing Sciences (ICCS), pp. 105–109 (2012)
326. Shekhar, S., Kumar, B.S., Ramesh, S.: Robust approach for palm (ROI) extraction in palmprint recognition system. In: Proceedings of the 2012 IEEE International Conference on Engineering Education: Innovative Practices and Future Trends (AICERA), pp. 1–6 (2012)
327. Shu, W., Zhang, D.: Automated personal identification by palmprint. Optical Engineering 37(8), 2359–2362 (1998)
328. Si, Y., Mei, J., Gao, H.: Novel approaches to improve robustness, accuracy and rapidity of iris recognition systems. IEEE Transactions on Industrial Informatics 8(1), 110–117 (2012)
329. Sidlauskas, D.P., Tamer, S.: Hand geometry recognition. In: A.K. Jain, P. Flynn, A.A. Ross (eds.) Handbook of Biometrics, pp. 91–107. Springer US (2008)
330. Singh, S., Ramalho, M., Correia, P.L., Soares, L.D.: PP-RIDER: A rotation-invariant degraded partial palmprint recognition technique. In: 2012 Proceedings of the 20th European Signal Processing Conference (EUSIPCO), pp. 1499–1503 (2012)
331. Snedecor, G.W., Cochran, W.G.: Statistical Methods, Seventh Edition. Iowa State University (1980)
332. Song, Y., Lee, C., Kim, J.: A new scheme for touchless fingerprint recognition system. In: Proceedings of 2004 International Symposium on Intelligent Signal Processing and Communication Systems (ISPACS), pp. 524–527 (2004)
333. Su, C.L.: Palm-print recognition by matrix discriminator. Expert Systems and Applications 36(7), 10,259–10,265 (2009)

334. Sun, D., Qiu, Z., Qiang, L.: Palmprint identification using Gabor wavelet probabilistic neural networks. In: Proceedings of the 2006 8th International Conference on Signal Processing, vol. 4, pp. – (2006)

335. Sun, Q., Tang, Y., Hu, P., Peng, J.: Kinect-based automatic 3D high-resolution face modeling. In: 2012 International Conference on Image Analysis and Signal Processing (IASP), pp. 1–4 (2012)

336. Sun, Z., Dong, W., Tan, T.: Technology roadmap for smart iris recognition. In: Proceedings of the International Conference on Computer Graphics & Vision, pp. 12–19 (2008)

337. Tan, Z., Yang, J., Shang, Z., Shi, G., Chang, S.: Minutiae-based offline palmprint identification system. In: Proceedings of the WRI Global Congress on Intelligent Systems (GCIS), vol. 4, pp. 466–471 (2009)

338. The Hong Kong Polytechnic University: PolyU 2D + 3D palmprint database. http://www4.comp.polyu.edu.hk/~biometrics/2D_3D_Palmprint.htm

339. The Hong Kong Polytechnic University: PolyU hyperspectral palmprint database. http://www4.comp.polyu.edu.hk/~biometrics/HyperspectralPalmprint/HSP.htm

340. The Hong Kong Polytechnic University: PolyU multispectral palmprint database. http://www4.comp.polyu.edu.hk/~biometrics/MultispectralPalmprint/MSP.htm

341. The Hong Kong Polytechnic University: PolyU palmprint database. http://www4.comp.polyu.edu.hk/~biometrics/polyudb.htm

342. Theofanos, M., Stanton, B., Sheppard, C., Micheals, R., Zhang, N., Wydler, W., Nadel, L., Rubin, R.: Usability Testing of Height and Angles of Ten-Print Fingerprint Capture. Tech. rep., NISTIR (2008)

343. Tistarelli, M., Li, S.Z., Chellappa, R.: Handbook of Remote Biometrics: for Surveillance and Security, 1st edn. Springer Publishing Company, Incorporated (2009)

344. Tiwari, K., Arya, D.K., Badrinath, G.S., Gupta, P.: Designing palmprint based recognition system using local structure tensor and force field transformation for human identification. Neurocomputing **116**(0), 222–230 (2013)

345. Tsalakanidou, F., Malassiotis, S., Strintzis, M.G.: A 3D face and hand biometric system for robust user-friendly authentication. Pattern Recognition Letters **28**(16), 2238–2249 (2007)

346. Turk, M., Pentland, A.: Eigenfaces for recognition. Journal of Cognitive Neuroscience **3**(1), 71–86 (1991)

347. Universidad de Las Palmas de Gran Canaria: GPDS 100 Contactless hands 2Band database. http://www.gpds.ulpgc.es/download/

348. Valarmathy, S., Kumar, M.A., Sudha, M.: Improvement in palmprint recognition rate using fusion of multispectral palmprint images. In: Proceedings of the 2012 International Conference on Computing, Communication and Applications (ICCCA), pp. 1–5 (2012)

349. Vedaldi, A., Fulkerson, B.: VLFeat: An open and portable library of computer vision algorithms (2008). http://www.vlfeat.org/

350. Velardo, C., Dugelay, J.: Weight estimation from visual body appearance. In: Proceedings of the 2010 Fourth IEEE International Conference on Biometrics: Theory Applications and Systems (BTAS), pp. 1–6 (2010)

351. Wan, M., Lai, Z., Shao, J., Jin, Z.: Two-dimensional local graph embedding discriminant analysis (2DLGEDA) with its application to face and palm biometrics. Neurocomputing **73**(1–3), 197–203 (2009)

352. Wang, J., Li, D., Li, M., Lin, Y.: Research on the extraction to the region of interest area in palmprint. In: Proceedings of the 2012 24th Chinese Control and Decision Conference (CCDC), pp. 3714–3718 (2012)

353. Wang, J.G., Yau, W.Y., Suwandy, A.: Feature-level fusion of palmprint and palm vein for person identification based on a "Junction Point" representation. In: Proceedings of the 15th IEEE International Conference on Image Processing (ICIP), pp. 253–256 (2008)

354. Wang, J.G., Yau, W.Y., Suwandy, A., Sung, E.: Fusion of palmprint and palm vein images for person recognition based on "Laplacianpalm" feature. In: Proceedings of the IEEE Conference on Computer Vision and Pattern Recognition (CVPR), pp. 1–8 (2007)

355. Wang, L., El-Maksoud, R.H.A., Sasian, J.M., Kuhn, W.P., Gee, K., Valencia, V.S.: A novel contactless aliveness-testing (CAT) fingerprint sensor. In: R.J. Koshel, G.G. Gregory (eds.) Novel Optical Systems Design and Optimization XII, vol. 7429. SPIE (2009)

356. Wang, M., Ruan, Q.: Palmprint recognition based on two-dimensional methods. In: Proceedings of the 2006 8th International Conference on Signal Processing, vol. 4 (2006)

357. Wang, R., Ramos, D., Firrez, J.: Improving radial triangulation-based forensic palmprint recognition according to point pattern comparison by relaxation. In: A.K. Jain, A.A. Ross, S. Prabhakar, J. Kim (eds.) ICB, pp. 427–432. IEEE (2012)

358. Wang, X., Lei, L., Wang, M.: Palmprint verification based on 2D - Gabor wavelet and pulse-coupled neural network. Knowledge-Based Systems **27**(0), 451–455 (2012)

359. Wang, X., Liang, J., Wang, M.: On-line fast palmprint identification based on adaptive lifting wavelet scheme. Knowledge-Based Systems **42**, 68–73 (2013)

360. Wang, Y., Hassebrook, L.G., Lau, D.L.: Noncontact, depth-detailed 3D fingerprinting. SPIE Newsroom (2009)

361. Wang, Y., Hassebrook, L.G., Lau, D.L.: Data acquisition and processing of 3-D fingerprints. IEEE Transactions on Information Forensics and Security **5**(4), 750–760 (2010)

362. Wang, Y., Lau, D.L., Hassebrook, L.G.: Fit-sphere unwrapping and performance analysis of 3d fingerprints. Applied Optics **49**(4), 592–600 (2010)

363. Wang, Y., Ruan, Q.: An improved unsharp masking method for palmprint image enhancement. In: Proceedings of the First International Conference on Innovative Computing, Information and Control (ICICIC), vol. 2, pp. 669–672 (2006)

364. Wang, Y., Ruan, Q.: Kernel fisher discriminant analysis for palmprint recognition. In: Proceedings of the 18th International Conference on Pattern Recognition (ICPR), vol. 4, pp. 457–460 (2006)

365. Wang, Y., Ruan, Q.: Palm-line extraction using steerable filters. In: Proceedings of the 2006 8th International Conference on Signal Processing, vol. 3, pp. – (2006)

366. Wang, Y., Ruan, Q., Pan, X.: An improved square-based palmprint segmentation method. In: Proceedings of the International Symposium on Intelligent Signal Processing and Communication Systems (ISPACS), pp. 316–319 (2007)

367. Wang, Y., Ruan, Q., Pan, X.: Palmprint recognition method using dual-tree complex wavelet transform and local binary pattern histogram. In: Proceedings of the International Symposium on Intelligent Signal Processing and Communication Systems (ISPACS), pp. 646–649 (2007)

368. Wang, Y.X., Sun, G.H.: Palmprint recognition using palm-line direction field texture feature. In: Proceedings of the 2012 International Conference on Machine Learning and Cybernetics (ICMLC), vol. 3, pp. 1130–1134 (2012)

369. Wayman, J.L., Jain, A.K., Maltoni, D., Maio, D.: Biometric Systems: Technology, Design and Performance Evaluation. Springer-Verlag London Limited (2005)

370. Wei, Z., Han, Y., Sun, Z., Tan, T.: Palmprint image synthesis: A preliminary study. In: Proceedings of the 15th IEEE International Conference on Image Processing (ICIP), pp. 285–288 (2008)

371. Wheeler, F.W., Weiss, R.L., Tu, P.H.: Face recognition at a distance system for surveillance applications. In: Proceedings of the Fourth IEEE International Conference on Biometrics: Theory Applications and Systems (BTAS), pp. 1–8 (2010)

372. Wong, K.Y.E., Chekima, A., Dargham, J.A., Sainarayanan, G.: Palmprint identification using Sobel operator. In: Proceedings of the 10th International Conference on Control, Automation, Robotics and Vision (ICARCV), pp. 1338–1341 (2008)

373. Wong, K.Y.E., Sainarayanan, G., Chekima, A.: Palmprint identification using wavelet energy. In: Proceedings of the International Conference on Intelligent and Advanced Systems (ICIAS), pp. 714–719 (2007)

374. Wong, M., Zhang, D., Kong, W.K., Lu, G.: Real-time palmprint acquisition system design. IEE Proceedings - Vision, Image and Signal Processing **152**(5), 527–534 (2005)

375. Woodard, D.L., Flynn, P.J.: 3D finger biometrics. In: D. Maltoni, A.K. Jain (eds.) Biometric Authentication, *Lecture Notes in Computer Science*, vol. 3087, pp. 238–247. Springer Berlin Heidelberg (2004)

376. Wu, J., Qiu, Z.: A hierarchical palmprint identification method using hand geometry and grayscale distribution features. In: Proceedings of the 18th International Conference on Pattern Recognition (ICPR), vol. 4, pp. 409–412 (2006)

377. Wu, X., Wang, K., Zhang, D.: HMMs based palmprint identification. In: D. Zhang, A.K. Jain (eds.) Biometric Authentication, *Lecture Notes in Computer Science*, vol. 3072, pp. 775–781. Springer Berlin Heidelberg (2004)

378. Wu, Y.P., Tian, J.W., Xu, D., Zhang, X.J.: Palmprint recognition based on RB K-means and hierarchical SVM. In: Proceedings of the 2007 International Conference on Machine Learning and Cybernetics, vol. 6, pp. 3641–3647 (2007)

379. Xiao-yong, W., Dan, X., Ngo, C.W.: Multibiometrics based on palmprint and handgeometry. In: Proceedings of the Fourth Annual ACIS International Conference on Computer and Information Science, pp. 495–500 (2005)

380. Xin, C., Wu, X., Qiushi, Z., Youbao, T.: A contactless hand shape identification system. In: Proceedings of the 2011 3rd International Conference on Advanced Computer Control (ICACC), pp. 561–565 (2011)

381. Xiong, W., Toh, K.A., Yau, W.Y., Jiang, X.: Model-guided deformable hand shape recognition without positioning aids. Pattern Recognition **38**(10), 1651–1664 (2005)

382. Xu, X., Guo, Z.: Multispectral palmprint recognition using quaternion principal component analysis. In: Proceedings of the 2010 International Workshop on Emerging Techniques and Challenges for Hand-Based Biometrics (ETCHB), pp. 1–5 (2010)

383. Xu, Y., Fan, Z., Qiu, M., Zhang, D., Yang, J.Y.: A sparse representation method of bimodal biometrics and palmprint recognition experiments. Neurocomputing **103**, 164–171 (2013)

384. Yan, Y., Zhang, Y.J.: Discriminant projection embedding for face and palmprint recognition. Neurocomputing **71**(16–18), 3534–3543 (2008)

385. li Yang, W., li Wang, L.: Research of palmprint identification method using Zernike moment and neural network. In: Proceedings of the 2010 Sixth International Conference on Natural Computation (ICNC), vol. 3, pp. 1310–1313 (2010)

386. Yang, W., Wang, S., Jie, L., Shao, G.: A new palmprint identification technique based on a two-stage neural network classifier. In: Proceedings of the Fourth International Conference on Natural Computation (ICNC), vol. 5, pp. 18–23 (2008)

387. Yang, X., Feng, J., Zhou, J.: Palmprint indexing based on ridge features. In: Proceedings of the 2011 International Joint Conference on Biometrics, IJCB, pp. 1–8. IEEE Computer Society, Washington, DC, USA (2011)

388. Yashodha, G., Bremananlh, R.: Rotation invariant palmprint recognition: An overview and implementation. In: Proceedings of the 2012 International Conference on Machine Vision and Image Processing (MVIP), pp. 145–148 (2012)

389. Yih, E.W.K., Sainarayanan, G., Chekima, A., Narendra, G.: Palmprint identification using sequential modified Haar wavelet energy. In: Proceedings of the International Conference on Signal Processing, Communications and Networking (ICSCN), pp. 411–416 (2008)

390. You, J., Kong, W.K., Zhang, D., Cheung, K.H.: On hierarchical palmprint coding with multiple features for personal identification in large databases. IEEE Transactions on Circuits and Systems for Video Technology **14**(2), 234–243 (2004)

391. Yu, P., Xu, D.: Palmprint recognition using generalized discriminant analysis. In: Proceedings of the International Conference on Audio, Language and Image Processing (ICALIP), pp. 1517–1521 (2008)

392. Yu, P., Xu, D., Zhou, H.: Feature level fusion using palmprint and finger geometry based on Canonical Correlation Analysis. In: Proceedings of the 2010 3rd International Conference on Advanced Computer Theory and Engineering (ICACTE), vol. 5, pp. V5–260–V5–264 (2010)

393. Yu, P., Yu, P., Xu, D.: Comparison of PCA, LDA and GDA for palmprint verification. In: Proceedings of the 2010 International Conference on Information Networking and Automation (ICINA), vol. 1, pp. V1–148–V1–152 (2010)

394. Yu, P.F., Xu, D.: Palmprint recognition based on modified DCT features and RBF neural network. In: Proceedings of the 2008 International Conference on Machine Learning and Cybernetics, vol. 5, pp. 2982–2986 (2008)

395. Yue, F., Zuo, W., Zhang, D., Li, B.: Fast palmprint identification with multiple templates per subject. Pattern Recognition Letters **32**(8), 1108–1118 (2011)
396. Yue, F., Zuo, W., Zhang, D., Wang, K.: Orientation selection using modified FCM for competitive code-based palmprint recognition. Pattern Recognition **42**(11), 2841–2849 (2009)
397. Zhang, B., Li, W., Qing, P., Zhang, D.: Palm-print classification by global features. IEEE Transactions on Systems, Man, and Cybernetics: Systems **43**(2), 370–378 (2013)
398. Zhang, D.: Online palmprint classification. In: Palmprint Authentication, *International Series on Biometrics*, vol. 3, pp. 155–167. Springer US (2004)
399. Zhang, D., Guo, Z., Lu, G., Zhang, D., Zuo, W.: An online system of multispectral palmprint verification. IEEE Transactions on Instrumentation and Measurement **59**(2), 480–490 (2010)
400. Zhang, D., Guo, Z., Lu, G., Zhang, L., Liu, Y., Zuo, W.: Online joint palmprint and palmvein verification. Expert Systems with Applications **38**(3), 2621–2631 (2011)
401. Zhang, D., Kanhangad, V., Luo, N., Kumar, A.: Robust palmprint verification using 2D and 3D features. Pattern Recognition **43**(1), 358–368 (2010)
402. Zhang, D., Kong, W.K., You, J., Wong, M.: Online palmprint identification. IEEE Transactions on Pattern Analysis and Machine Intelligence **25**(9), 1041–1050 (2003)
403. Zhang, D., Lu, G.: 3D Biometrics. Springer Science + Business Media, New York (2013)
404. Zhang, D., Lu, G., Li, W., Zhang, D., Luo, N.: Palmprint recognition using 3-D information. IEEE Transactions on Systems, Man, and Cybernetics, Part C: Applications and Reviews **39**(5), 505–519 (2009)
405. Zhang, D., Shu, W.: Two novel characteristics in palmprint verification: datum point invariance and line feature matching. Pattern Recognition **32**(4), 691–702 (1999)
406. Zhang, D., Zuo, W., Yue, F.: A comparative study of palmprint recognition algorithms. ACM Computing Surveys (CSUR) **44**(1), 2:1–2:37 (2012)
407. Zhang, D.D.: Palmprint Authentication. International Series on Biometrics. Springer (2004)
408. Zhang, H., Hu, D.: Palmprint verification system using Moiré pattern. In: Proceedings of the 2009 IEEE International Conference on Robotics and Biomimetics (ROBIO), pp. 1224–1229 (2009)
409. Zhang, J., Cheng, Y., Chen, C.: Low resolution gait recognition with high frequency super resolution. In: T.B. Ho, Z.H. Zhou (eds.) PRICAI 2008: Trends in Artificial Intelligence, *Lecture Notes in Computer Science*, vol. 5351, pp. 533–543. Springer Berlin / Heidelberg (2008)
410. Zhang, L., Li, H.: Encoding local image patterns using Riesz transforms: With applications to palmprint and finger-knuckle-print recognition. Image and Vision Computing **30**(12), 1043–1051 (2012)
411. Zhang, L., Li, H., Niu, J.: Fragile bits in palmprint recognition. IEEE Signal Processing Letters **19**(10), 663–666 (2012)
412. Zhang, Q., Zhu, X.: Study of the thinning algorithm for thenar palmprint. In: Proceedings of the 2010 First ACIS International Symposium on Cryptography and Network Security, Data Mining and Knowledge Discovery, E-Commerce Its Applications and Embedded Systems (CDEE), pp. 179–182 (2010)
413. Zhang, S., Gu, X.: Palmprint recognition method based on score level fusion. Optik - International Journal for Light and Electron Optics (2012)
414. Zhang, X., Gao, Y.: Face recognition across pose: A review. Pattern Recognition **42**(11), 2876–2896 (2009)
415. Zhang, Z.: A flexible new technique for camera calibration. IEEE Transactions on Pattern Analysis and Machine Intelligence **22**(11), 1330–1334 (2000)
416. Zhao, Q., Jain, A.K., Abramovich, G.: 3D to 2D fingerprints: Unrolling and distortion correction. In: Proceedings of the 2011 International Joint Conference on Biometrics (IJCB), pp. 1–8 (2011)
417. Zheng, Y., Liu, Y., Shi, G., Li, J., Wang, Q.: Segmentation of offline palmprint. In: Proceedings of the Third International IEEE Conference on Signal-Image Technologies and Internet-Based System (SITIS), pp. 804–811 (2007)

418. Zheng, Y., Shi, G., Wang, Q., Zhang, L.: Palmprint image quality measures in minutiae-based recognition. In: Proceedings of the 14th International Workshop on Systems, Signals and Image Processing, 2007 and 6th EURASIP Conference focused on Speech and Image Processing, Multimedia Communications and Services, pp. 140–143 (2007)

419. Zheng, Y., Shi, G., Wang, Q., Zhang, L.: Location of special areas on palmprint. In: Proceedings of the Congress on Image and Signal Processing (CISP), vol. 2, pp. 786–791 (2008)

420. Zheng, Y., Shi, G., Zhang, L., Wang, Q., Zhao, Y.: Research on offline palmprint image enhancement. In: Proceedings of the IEEE International Conference on Image Processing (ICIP), vol. 1, pp. 541–544 (2007)

421. Zhou, J., Sun, D., Qiu, Z., Xiong, K., Liu, D., Zhang, Y.: Palmprint recognition by fusion of multi-color components. In: Proceedings of the International Conference on Cyber-Enabled Distributed Computing and Knowledge Discovery (CyberC), pp. 273–278 (2009)

422. Zhou, S., Krueger, V., Chellappa, R.: Probabilistic recognition of human faces from video. Computer Vision and Image Understanding 91(1–2), 214–245 (2003)

423. Zhou, S.K., Chellappa, R., Zhao, W.: Unconstrained Face Recognition. International Series on Biometrics. Springer US, Boston, MA (2006)

424. Zhou, Y., Guo, T., Wu, M., Zhao, T.: Latent palmprint image segmentation based on dissimilarity tolerance. In: Proceedings of the 2010 International Conference on Multimedia Communications (Mediacom), pp. 83–86 (2010)

425. Zhou, Y., Kumar, A.: Contactless palm vein identification using multiple representations. In: Proceedings of the 2010 Fourth IEEE International Conference on Biometrics: Theory Applications and Systems (BTAS), pp. 1–6 (2010)

426. Zhou, Y., Kumar, A.: Human identification using palm-vein images. IEEE Transactions on Information Forensics and Security 6(4), 1259–1274 (2011)

427. Zhou, Y., Zeng, Y., Lizhen, Hu, W.: Application and development of palm print research. Technology and Health Care 10(5), 383–390 (2002)

428. qing Zhu, L.: 2D finger shape recognition based on local zero-order moment features. In: Proceedings of the 2nd International Congress on Image and Signal Processing (CISP), pp. 1–4 (2009)

429. Zhu, X., Liu, D.: Analysis of divisibility in thenar palmprint with texture features. In: 2010 First ACIS International Symposium on Cryptography and Network Security, Data Mining and Knowledge Discovery, E-Commerce Its Applications and Embedded Systems (CDEE), pp. 183–186 (2010)

430. Zhu, X., Zhang, Q., Liu, D., Lv, W.: An edge extraction algorithm of thenar palmprint image based on wavelet multi-scale. In: Proceedings of the 2010 Third International Symposium on Information Processing (ISIP), pp. 555–558 (2010)

431. Zuo, W., Yue, F., Zhang, D.: On accurate orientation extraction and appropriate distance measure for low-resolution palmprint recognition. Pattern Recognition 44(4), 964–972 (2011)

432. Zuo, W., Zhang, H., Zhang, D., Wang, K.: Post-processed LDA for face and palmprint recognition: What is the rationale. Signal Processing 90(8), 2344–2352 (2010)

Printed in the United States
By Bookmasters